Texts in Computing

Volume 5

Bridges from Classical
to
Nonmonotonic Logic

Volume 1
Programming Languages and Operational Semantics
Maribel Fernández

Volume 2
An Introduction to Lambda Calculi for Computer Scientists
Chris Hankin

Volume 3
Logical Reasoning: A First Course
Rob Nederpelt and Fairouz Kamareddine

Volume 4
The Haskell Road to Logic, Maths and Programming
Kees Doets and Jan van Eijck

Volume 5
Bridges from Classical to Nonmonotonic Logic
David Makinson

Texts in Computing Series Editor
Ian Mackie, King's College London

Bridges from Classical to Nonmonotonic Logic

David Makinson

King's College London

ISBN 1-904987-00-1
King's College Publications
Scientific Director: Dov Gabbay
Managing Director: Jane Spurr
Department of Computer Science
Strand, London WC2R 2LS, UK
kcp@dcs.kcl.ac.uk

Cover design by Richard Fraser, www.avalonarts.co.uk
Printed by Lightning Source, Milton Keynes, UK

Contents

Preface

Who Are We Writing For?

This book is directed to all those who have heard of nonmonotonic reasoning and would like to get a better idea of what it is all about. What are its driving ideas? In what ways does it differ from classical logic? How does it relate to probability? More generally, how does it behave and how can it be used? We will try to answer these questions as clearly as possible, without undue technicality on the one hand, nor vagueness or hand waving on the other.

It is written for the student in a classroom, the instructor teaching a course, but also for the solitary reader. The lone reader faces a particularly difficult task, for there is nobody to turn to when the going gets tough. In sympathy, we try to help as far as possible: explaining all points fully, saying some things in more than one way to get the point across, providing recapitulations at the end of each chapter, giving exercises and selected solutions. These will be useful to all readers, but especially for those working alone.

What Does the Reader Need to Know Already?

Tackling a subject such as this does require a minimal background, and in honesty we must make it clear from the beginning what is needed. To those without any grounding in classical logic at all, who may out of curiosity have picked up the volume, we say: put it down, and go to square one. Get the rudiments of classical propositional logic (alias truth-functional logic) under your belt, and then come back. Otherwise you will be like someone trying to learn about algebra before knowing any arithmetic, counterpoint without sol-fa, or style without the elements of grammar.

For that purpose, students of computer science, mathematics, philosophy or linguistics should take the introductory course in logic offered by their department, and read whatever textbook the instructor recommends. If working alone with an interest in computation or mathematics, try chapters 6-8 of James Hein *Discrete Structures, Logic, and Computability* (Boston: Jones and Bartlett, second edition 2002). Those whose background is in the humanities should try L.T.F. Gamut *Logic, Language and Meaning: Volume I. Introduction to Logic* (Chicago University Press, 1991). And for those lucky enough to find it, there is the author's out-of-print *Topics in Modern Logic* (London: Methuen 1973; chapters 1 and 3).

In the Introduction of this book we do review some features of classical propositional logic, but with a special purpose. We bring out certain aspects that tend to be passed over in most presentations, but are essential for unfolding our theme. In particular, we explain some very general concepts that reveal themselves not only in classical consequence but also in other contexts. Among these are the general notion of a closure operation or relation, the property of compactness, and the idea of a Horn rule.

The reader should also be familiar with a few simple mathematical tools. These are of two kinds. First: some 'working set theory' — basic operations on sets, such as finite intersection, union and relative complement, indexed families of sets, infinite intersection and union; ordered pairs, Cartesian products, the treatment of relations and functions as sets of ordered pairs, and the notion of a well-ordering. Second: mathematical induction as a method of proof, in both its simple and course-of-values forms over countable sets. This is needed in order to establish routine properties of the inductively defined sets that will be encountered, beginning with the set of formulae of propositional logic.

These tools are often taught along with elementary logic, and also as part of first courses in computing and discrete mathematics. For the reader who lacks them, there is no alternative to going back to an elementary course or to reading the first few chapters of an introductory book. A good old standby is Seymour Lipschutz *Set Theory and Related Topics* (New York: McGraw-Hill Education, second edition 1998), especially the first five chapters. Alternatively, chapters 1-4 of the book of Hein mentioned above. For those who would like to do it in elegance and style, the first twelve chapters of Paul Halmos' *Naïve Set Theory* (New York: van Nostrand, 1960) are unbeatable.

The proofs of some results in this book, for example Theorem 2.7, appeal to maximality principles such as Zorn's Lemma. Familiarity with these principles, as set out say in chapter 9 of Lipschutz or chapters 14–17 of Halmos, is needed for full understanding of those proofs, and is in any case a premium investment. However, even without them the student may get a partial understanding: read the theorem for the finite case only, and recall that for a finite set, if some subset of it has a property then it is always included in at least one maximal subset with the same property.

In the author's opinion, all these things should be taught in high school, and in some privileged places they are. They are fun to learn, and indispensable in the electronic world. But sadly, there are also students who are allowed to go through an entire undergraduate education without ever being exposed to them.

So, for those who do not have the necessary minimal background we say goodbye — and hope to see you again later. For those who are ready, we say: welcome and read on!

Main Themes

From the outside, nonmonotonic logic is often seen as a rather mysterious affair. Even from the inside, it can appear to lack unity, with multiple systems proposed by as many authors going in different directions. The few available textbooks tend to perpetuate this impression.

Our main purpose is to take some of the mystery out of the subject and show that it is not as unfamiliar as may at first sight seem. In fact, it is easily accessible to anybody with the minimal background that we have described in classical propositional logic and basic mathematical tools — provided certain misunderstandings and a tenacious habit, both signalled in the first chapter, are put aside.

As we shall show, there are logics that act as natural bridges between classical consequence and the principal kinds of nonmonotonic logic to be found in the literature. These logics, which we call *paraclassical*, are very simple to define and easy to study. They provide three main ways of getting more out of your premises than is allowed by strict deduction, that is, by good old classical consequence. In other words, they are principled ways of creeping, crawling or jumping to conclusions. Like classical logic, they are perfectly monotonic, but they already display some of the distinctive features of the nonmonotonic systems that they prefigure, as well as providing easy conceptual passage to them. They give us, in effect, three main paths from the classical homeland to nonmonotonic shores.

The book examines the three one by one. We begin with the simplest among them, whose moving idea is to use *additional background assumptions* along with current premises. Then we consider ways of getting the same result by *excluding certain classical valuations*. And finally we examine a third means to the same end, by *adding rules* alongside the premises.

In each case we obtain a monotonic bridge system that may be rendered nonmonotonic in a natural and meaningful way. In fact, each of the bridge systems leads to quite a range of nonmonotonic ones, and this is where the diverse systems of the literature show themselves. But they are no longer a disorderly crowd. They fall into place as variants, natural and indeed to be expected, of three basic ideas.

The book then turns to the subtle question of the relation between logic and probability — more specifically, between classical logic, probabilistic inference, and nonmonotonic reasoning. On the one hand, there are several different ways of characterizing classical consequence in probabilistic terms. On the other hand, we can also use probability to define consequence operations, both monotonic and nonmonotonic. They turn out to be quite different in certain important respects from the qualitative operations of earlier chapters; but as we show there are also ways of bringing them closer together.

There are obvious resemblances between some of the ways of generating nonmonotonic inference relations and constructions that have been used for other purposes — for example, the logics of belief revision and update, as well as counterfactual conditionals and conditional directives. The last chapter of the book discusses the links between these different kinds of 'belief management' and their residual differences. It also presents sample representation theorems for some of the principal systems of nonmonotonic logic. We do not attempt anything like a complete coverage of all the different representations that may be found in the literature; there are too many, and still growing. Two strategic examples are selected, one with a complete proof and the other with its central construction merely sketched.

Topics Not Dealt With

We owe it to the reader — and especially to the instructor who may be thinking of using the book — to say clearly what topics, associated with nonmonotonic reasoning, are *not* covered.

All inference relations studied are defined over a purely propositional language using only Boolean connectives. They could be extended to first-order classical logic, but most of the interesting questions appear to arise already at the propositional level. In this subject, to work in a first-order language is to increase overheads for little added value in understanding.

We will not be examining logics in which classical connectives are reinterpreted in a non-Boolean manner. Systems of logic programming with negation using various forms of 'negation as failure' are sometimes presented in this way although, as we will suggest in Chapter 4, they are more transparently seen as rules about propositions in a fragment of the classical language. The study of logic programming has now become a world of its own, with an emphasis on questions of computational complexity, which are not at the centre of our concern. For a recent review of logic programming using the 'answer set semantics' see Gelfond and Leone (2002); for an overview of various approaches to logic programming with negation see Brewka, Dix and Konolige (1997) chapters 6–7; and for an encyclopaedic account see the book of Baral (2003).

Nor will we be examining languages that add non-classical connectives to the usual classical ones. In particular, we will not be considering autoepistemic logics. These are formed by adding to the Boolean connectives a special kind of modal operator whose 'introspective' reading engenders nonmonotonic behaviour. Despite their correspondence with certain maverick default-rule logics under translations due to Konolige and others, they are quite different from the mainstream ones, for reasons that we will explain in Chapter 4. The reader interested in studying autoepistemic logic is referred to chapter 4.2 of Brewka, Dix and Konolige (1997) or, in more detail, the overview of Konolige (1994).

There are also two approaches to nonmonotonic reasoning in which logical connectives have little role to play. They are the theory of defeasible inheritance nets, and the abstract theory of argument defeat. In both cases the focus is on the notion of one path (in a net) or argument (in a discussion) defeating or undercutting another, and on ascertaining the final effect of complex patterns of iterated defeat. Here too, the issues at stake are rather special, and not discussed in this volume. For defeasible inheritance nets, the reader is referred to the overview of Horty (1994). For argument defeat, consult the recent survey of Prakken and Vreeswijk (2001) and the paper of García and Simari (to appear).

Thus this book does not pretend to be anything near a comprehensive treatment of all the investigations that have gone under the name of nonmonotonic logic. But it does present some very central ideas, structuring them in a coherent perspective, and seeks to explain them as clearly as possible.

Strategy of Presentation

When the author first began planning this text, he followed engrained habits and sought for maximal generality. 'We have available a multitude of different formal approaches to nonmonotonic reasoning', he thought. 'So in order to put some order into the affair, we need to find the most general schema possible, under which they all fall. We can then present the different accounts as so many special cases of the general schema'.

However, it quickly became clear that this strategy is hopeless. It does work quite well when focussing on the *kinds of consequence relation that are generated*, for these may be classified according to the sets of regularity conditions that they satisfy. One may thus begin with a minimal set of conditions, defining a very broad class of consequence relations, and gradually add to the conditions, defining narrower classes. Indeed, this was the strategy followed in the author's paper 'General theory of cumulative inference' (Makinson, 1989) and survey 'General Patterns in Nonmonotonic Reasoning' (Makinson, 1994). But if, as in this book, one is primarily interested in the principal *modes of generation* of consequence relations, the strategy makes little sense. The modes differ abruptly from each other; and when one abstracts upon them in an attempt to obtain a 'most general mode', one comes up with formulations that are opaque to intuition, clumsy to work with, and mathematically close to empty.

For this reason, a totally different principle guides the organization of this book. It is the principle of *theme and variations*. For each of the three main ways of 'going nonmonotonic' — namely, by adding background assumptions, restricting the set of valuations, and adding background rules — we begin by providing a paradigm formulation, and then sketch some of the many specializations, variations, and generalizations. A few variations already appear at the level of the monotonic bridge systems, and they multiply at the nonmonotonic level. They are most easily understood as an open family of relatives of a central exemplar, rather than as particular cases of an all-embracing definition.

For the mathematician this may go rather against the grain, but in the present enterprise it is the only reasonable way to proceed. And after all, even mathematicians are accustomed to this procedure in certain cases. For example, when giving an overview of different approaches to axiomatizing set theory, nobody at the present state of play would try to give a most abstract definition of what in general constitutes a set theory, and then fit in the Zermelo–Fraenkel version, Quine's New Foundations, and so on as special cases. The standard procedure is to delineate a few broad lines of approach in conceptual terms, present exemplars of each, and finally sketch some of their many variations. That is the way in which we proceed in this book.

Review and Explore Sections

Each chapter ends with a 'Review and explore' section. It contains three packages to help the reader review the material covered and to go further into the literature. First, a *recapitulation* of the essential message of the chapter. Second, a *checklist* of the key concepts, both formal and informal, that were introduced there. The concepts are not explained all over again, but are simply listed for checking off at review time. The reader can relocate the formal definitions and informal explanations by looking for the corresponding italicised terms in the main text. Third, a short selection of texts for *further reading*. Some of these cover essentially the same ground as the section itself, albeit from a different angle, in more detail or with particular attention to aspects that we have not dwelt on. Some go further. In general, these will be 'bite size' — short papers or chapters. Occasionally, a more extended text is mentioned.

What is the Best Way to Read this Book?

Do it pencil in hand; scribble in the margins. Take nothing on faith; check out the assertions; find errors (and communicate them to the author: makinson@dcs.kcl.ac.uk); pose questions.

Notoriously, the best test of whether one has understood a definition is to be able to identify positive and negative examples. Nor has one understood a theorem very well if unable to apply it to straightforward cases and recognize some of its more immediate consequences. Without this one may have the illusion of understanding, but not the real thing.

For this reason, the book includes *exercises*. Many of them ask readers to verify claims made in the flow of the text. To help the brave loner maintain the discipline of working out the exercises, and also to take some of the load off instructors, selected exercises, marked by asterisks, are given answers at the end of the text.

As well as exercises, there are some *problems*. They are more demanding. In general they require more than checking positive and negative instances of a definition or straight applications with a couple of steps of argument. Their solutions may need perceptive guessing plus the ability to prove or disprove the guesses. Both the art of making good guesses and the ability to check them out are acquired skills, and grow with practice.

Finally, *projects* are longer-term tasks. Whether to attempt any of them depends on the interests and time of the reader, and the goals of the instructor. In general, they involve consulting items from the literature and working on them. When suggesting a project we will usually indicate a specific text as entry-point.

Those strapped for time and wanting to cover essentials only, could skim or even omit section 2.3, which presents specializations and generalizations of the basic pattern of that chapter, and likewise sections 3.3, 4.3 — provided they promise the author to come back some day later! They could also omit the rather technical section 5.4. Below that, they risk not getting the general picture.

For the Instructor

The author's experience is that in a graduate class, teaching can take place at average of one section per hour, without counting section 1.1 and the brief 'review and explore' sections. This adds up to about 20 hours of instruction time for the entire book, or about 15 hours for a minimal version like the one mentioned above.

Of course, this will vary with the level and background of the students. In particular, those whose background in classical logic did not include much exposure to the notion of a consequence relation/operation or concepts such as compactness may need considerably more than one hour for the revision in section 1.2. With them in mind, there are particularly many exercises in that section. On the other hand, the sections entitled 'specializations and generalizations' provide instructors with a starting point for more detailed treatments of their favourite special topics, with open schedules.

Conventions

Theorems are numbered by their Chapter, followed by a digit. For example, the first explicitly displayed theorem in the book occurs in section 1.3 and is numbered Theorem 1.1. However, only major results are displayed and numbered in this way. Many lesser facts are simply stated in the flow of the text, and the attentive reader should mark them as they are found. The same applies to definitions. Only a few key ones are given special display; the others are within the text, with their central terms italicized.

Generally speaking, the notation used is fairly standard. One exception: we use plain brackets rather than angular ones for ordered pairs — thus (x, y) instead of $\langle x, y \rangle$. In Chapter 4 we also simplify the usual way of writing default rules. Symbols special to nonmonotonic logic are recalled in a glossary (appendix B).

In this preface, we have given references in full. Likewise in the suggestions for further reading at the end of each section. But in the main text, they are called by author name and date, e.g. Gabbay (1985), and are answered with full details in the reference list at the end of the book.

Acknowledgements

As the basic ideas underlying this book were developed, they were articulated in workshop and conference presentations, journal publications, and the classroom.

The author would like to thank the organisers of the following meetings and occasions, large and small, for the opportunity to air ideas that went into this book. They include: Workshop on Cognitive Economics, Porquerolles, September 2001; KR-02 Special Session on Belief Change, Toulouse, 19–21 April 2002; ASL European Summer Meeting Special Session on Nonmonotonic Logic, Münster, 4–8 June 2002; Prague International Colloquium on Formal Epistemology, 10–13 September 2002; King's College London Department of Computer Science Colloquium, 9 October 2002; Manchester University Mathematics Department Colloquium, 18 November 2002; University of Leipzig Department of Computer Science, 14 May 2003; Dresden University Department of Computer Science, 19 May 2003; University of Buenos Aires Department of Computer Science, 17 July 2003; University of Bahía Blanca Department of Computer Science, 07 August 2003; Augustus de Morgan Conference on Agents and Knowledge Representation (King's College, 03 November 2003); University of New South Wales Department of Computer Science Colloquium, 02 April 2004.

The general vision of nonmonotonic logic developed here was outlined, in a form suitable for professional logicians, in Makinson (2003a). A thumbnail sketch, adapted for an audience of economists interested in logic, was given in Makinson (2003b). A stripped-down version of the present text, without such things as exercises, answers and 'review and explore' sections, will appear as the overview Makinson (to appear).

Much of the text was written while the author taught an MSc course on Nonmonotonic Reasoning in the Department of Computer Science, King's College London in the spring semesters of 2003 and 2004. Thanks to all the students and auditors for their questions, which helped make the presentation more transparent; particularly to Audun Stolpe and Robert Schubert for their perceptive queries, Xavier Parent and Simon Speed for finding bugs in exercises and providing some model answers; and David Gabelaia for comments and important observations.

Many other people made helpful comments on particular points during the gestation process. They include Gerd Brewka, Björn Bjurling, Marc Denecker, Michael Freund, Donald Gillies, Dov Gabbay, Jörg Hansen, Daniel Lehmann, João Marcos, Wlodek Rabinowicz, Hans Rott, Karl Schlechta, and an anonymous referee for the *Logic Journal of the IGPL.*

The book is dedicated to the memory of my former co-author Carlos Alchourrón, who died in January 1996. Despite his fascination with the logic of belief revision he distrusted its neighbour nonmonotonic logic, and I could never convince him otherwise. While writing this book, I realized that it is a continuation of our conversations.

Chapter 1

Introduction

1.1 We Are All Nonmonotonic

In the stories of Sherlock Holmes, his companion Watson often speaks of the master's amazing powers of deduction. Yet those who have some acquaintance with deductive logic, whether in the form it took at the end of the nineteenth century when Conan Doyle was writing, or as it is understood today, realize that the game is not the same. None of the conclusions drawn by Sherlock Holmes follow deductively, in the strict sense of the term, from the evidence. They involve presumption and conjecture, and the ever-present possibility of going wrong. According to Watson, Sherlock Holmes usually got it right. But in real life, the incidence of failure is very much greater than pleasant fiction allows.

Nevertheless, for all its fallibility, it is reasoning. Appeal is made not only to the observations explicitly mentioned but also, implicitly, to a reservoir of background knowledge, a supply of rules of thumb, a range of heuristic guides. Most important, conclusions may be withdrawn as more information comes to hand, and new ones may be advanced in their place. This does not necessarily mean that there was an error in the earlier reasoning. The previous inferences may still be recognized as the most reasonable ones to have been made with the information available.

This is the essence of nonmonotonic reasoning. It is performed not only by Sherlock Holmes, but also by medical practitioners, garage mechanics, computer systems engineers, and all those who are required to give a diagnosis of a problem in order to pass to action. Robots negotiating their way through obstacles have to make inferences of this kind, and to do it quickly 'in real time' so as to continue their work without pause.

1

Archaeologists sifting through the debris of a site may see their early conclusions about the date, function and origin of an artefact change as more evidence comes to hand.

In some circumstances, we may decline to make such inferences, believing that the evidence is not yet sufficient to draw any conclusions at all. This can be an eminently rational attitude, for it is preferable to deluding oneself by exaggerating the certainty of the conclusions that one might draw. But there are also contexts where urgent action is needed on the basis of conclusions whose uncertainty is all too apparent – for example, in some medical situations the patient may die if action is not taken swiftly. There may be no time to conduct further tests to enlarge the information base, and a diagnosis is needed immediately in order to decide what action to take. In these cases, we must reach conclusions in full recognition of their fallibility, even fragility. If we wait for deductive certainty before ever drawing a conclusion, we can be waiting forever.

This kind of reasoning often involves handling simultaneously large quantitites of material. It may be done well, or poorly. Winston Churchill once declared: 'True genius resides in the capacity for evaluation of uncertain, hazardous, and conflicting information.' In general, it is carried out intuitively, with little reflection or understanding of the mechanisms involved. But it cries out for formal analysis.

In formal terms, we are said to be *reasoning nonmonotonically* when we allow that a conclusion that is well drawn from given information may need to be withdrawn when we come into possession of further information, even when none of the old premises are abandoned. In brief, a consequence relation is *nonmonotonic* iff it can happen that a proposition x is a consequence of a set A of propositions, but not a consequence of some superset $A \cup B$ of A.

At this point the reader may interject 'Of course, that's the way in which all inference has to be; it can't be otherwise. There is nothing new about all this. Surely standard systems of logic must already be prepared to deal with it'.

Indeed, although the word is recent, there is nothing new about the idea of nonmonotonicity. Epistemologists have recognized the phenomenon for hundreds of years; for example, both Locke and Hume insisted upon it in the seventeenth and eighteenth centuries. It has for long been familiar to writers on jurisprudence, as well as authors on the philosophy of the empirical sciences. But still today, mainstream systems of logic do not take uncertainty and nonmonotonicity into account. They focus on purely deductive inference, where the conclusion follows of necessity, without possible exception or doubt, from the premises. They are monotonic: when a proposition is a consequence of a set of premisses, then it remains a consequence of any larger set formed by adding new premisses, so long as none of the old ones are discarded.

This is fine when working in some contexts, notably that of pure mathematics. Indeed, logic as we know it today was developed in order to obtain a deeper understanding of deduction in mathematics. The resulting system is known as classical logic, and is made up of two main parts: propositional (alias truth-functional) logic, and predicate (alias first-order, also quantificational) logic. Its quite extraordinary success in the analysis of mathematical reasoning has tended to hide its limitations in areas outside its intended domain.

This is not to say that there is anything wrong with deductive logic. Nor is it necessarily to be regretted that historically things developed in the way that they did, for a clear understanding of classically valid inference is needed before one can begin to make sense of any other kind of reasoning. Although our subject is nonmonotonic reasoning, we will constantly make use of classical logic. Indeed, we do this in two ways. As our enterprise is mathematical in nature, our own reasoning will be carried out in accord with the principles of classical deduction; and the nonmonotonic systems studied will be defined in ways that use classical consequence as a central component.

1.2 Recalling Classical Consequence

As already mentioned, we assume some familiarity with classical propositional consequence. But we refresh the memory by recalling the definition, and some of its most salient characteristics that are not always covered in introductory texts. They will be indispensable for everything that follows.

Classical logic uses a formal language whose *formulae* are made up from an infinite list of elementary letters by means of a suitable selection of truth-functional connectives. For example, we may use the two-place connectives $\wedge, \vee$ and the one-place connective $\neg$, understood in terms of their usual truth-tables for conjunction, disjunction, and negation. These three connectives are together functionally complete, in the sense that all truth-functional connectives can be expressed with them. Formulae made up in this way will be called *Boolean*, and we write the set of all of them as L. Material implication $\rightarrow$ and equivalence $\leftrightarrow$, also understood in terms of their usual truth-tables, are introduced as abbreviations in the usual way.

An *assignment* is a function on the set of all elementary letters into the two-element set $\{1,0\}$. Each assignment may be extended in a unique way to a *Boolean valuation* (more briefly *valuation* when the context is clear), which is a function v on the set of all formulae into the two-element set $\{1,0\}$ that agrees with the assignment on elementary letters and behaves in accord with the standard truth-tables for compound formulae made up using $\wedge, \vee, \neg$. When A is a *set* of formulae, we write $v(A) = 1$ as shorthand for: $v(a) = 1$ for all $a \in A$. To keep notation down, we will usually use the same letter v for both an assignment and the valuation that it determines.

Let A be any set of formulae, and let x be an individual formula. One says that x is a *classical consequence* of A iff there is no valuation v such that $v(A) = 1$ whilst $v(x) = 0$. The standard notation is $A \vdash x$, and the sign $\vdash$ is called 'gate' or 'turnstile'. When dealing with individual formulae on the left, the notation is simplified a little by dropping parentheses, writing $a \vdash x$ in place of $\{a\} \vdash x$.

Thus classical consequence is a *relation* between formulae, or more generally between *sets* of formulae on the left and individual ones on the right. It may also be seen as an *operation* acting on sets A of formulae to give larger sets $Cn(A)$. In effect, the operation gathers together all the formulae that are consequences of given premises. The two representations of classical consequence are trivially interchangeable. Given a relation $\vdash$, we may define the operation Cn by setting $Cn(A) = \{x : A \vdash x\}$. Conversely we may define $\vdash$ from Cn by the rule: $A \vdash x$ iff $x \in Cn(A)$. Again we simplify notation by eliminating parentheses for singleton premises, writing $x \in Cn(a)$ for $x \in Cn(\{a\})$.

Both of the representations are useful. Sometimes one is more convenient than another. For example, it is often easier to visualize things in terms of the relation, but more concise to formulate and prove them using the operation. The same will be true when we come to non-classical consequence. For this reason, we will constantly be hopping from one notation to the other, and the reader should get into the habit of doing the same.

Consequence is intimately related with consistency. We say that a set A of formulae is classically *consistent* (or *satisfiable*) iff there is some Boolean valuation v with $v(A) = 1$, i.e. $v(a) = 1$ for all $a \in A$. Otherwise we say that it is *inconsistent* (or *unsatisfiable*). Clearly classical consequence and consistency are inter-definable: $A \vdash x$ iff $A \cup \{\neg x\}$ is inconsistent; in the other direction, A is consistent iff $A \nvdash f$ where f is an arbitrary contradiction, e.g. $p \wedge \neg p$.

The relation of classical consequence has a number of useful properties. To begin with, it is a *closure relation*, in the sense that it satisfies the following three conditions for all formulae a, x and all sets A, B of formulae:

Expressed in the language of Cn, this means that classical consequence

Reflexivity alias *Inclusion*	$A \vdash a$ whenever $a \in A$
Cumulative Transitivity (CT), alias *Cut*	Whenever $A \vdash b$ for all $b \in B$ and $A \cup B \vdash x$ then $A \vdash x$
Monotony	Whenever $A \vdash x$ and $A \subseteq B$ then $B \vdash x$

is a *closure operation* in the sense that it satisfies the following conditions for all sets A, B of formulae.

Inclusion alias *Reflexivity*	$A \subseteq Cn(A)$
Cumulative Transitivity (CT), alias *Cut*	$A \subseteq B \subseteq Cn(A)$ implies $Cn(B) \subseteq Cn(A)$
Monotony	Whenever $A \subseteq B$ then $Cn(A) \subseteq Cn(B)$

The first condition has two names. It is usually called *reflexivity* in its application to a relation, and *inclusion* when applied to an operation. But it is exactly the same rule in the two cases, under the translation from one notation to the other.

The second condition has various names in the literature, most commonly *cumulative transitivity*, abbreviated CT, or *cut*. Care should be taken with the latter term however. In work on Gentzen systems for classical logic, for example, it is used not only for this particular rule but also for a number of variants.

Some readers may be a little surprised to see cumulative transitivity for the relation $\vdash$ where they are accustomed to seeing plain *transitivity*, either in its singleton version (whenever $a \vdash b$ and $b \vdash x$ then $a \vdash x$) or in its general version (whenever $A \vdash b$ for all $b \in B$ and $B \vdash x$ then $A \vdash x$). In fact, when we are given both reflexivity and monotony, then cumulative transitivity is equivalent to the general version of plain transitivity. But we will be focussing on relations that are *not* monotonic, and as first noticed by Gabbay (1985), in this context it turns out best to work with cumulative transitivity rather than its plain companion.

Other readers, already familiar with closure operations in logic or abstract algebra, may be surprised to see cumulative transitivity where they are accustomed to seeing *idempotence*, i.e. the condition that $Cn(A) = Cn(Cn(A))$. Once again, the two are equivalent, not as individual conditions, but given the other two conditions defining the notion of a closure operation. But here too, when considering relations that fail monotony it turns out best to focus on CT rather than idempotence.

The third condition, monotony, is the main character of our play, to be conspicuous by its absence after being murdered in the first act. As a special case, it implies *singleton monotony*: whenever $a \vdash x$ then $\{a, b\} \vdash x$. Classical consequence also satisfies a closely related property, known as *singleton conjunctive monotony*, alias the rule of *strengthening the premiss*, alias $\wedge$+(left): whenever $a \vdash x$ then $a \wedge b \vdash x$. These two are not quite the same, as the latter concerns the connective of conjunction; but they are equivalent for any system in which the conjunction of two propositions behaves, as a premiss, just like the set of its two conjuncts.

The three conditions defining the notion of a closure relation are examples of what are known as *Horn rule*, so called after Alfred Horn who drew attention to their importance. Roughly speaking, a Horn rule for a relation tells us that if such-and-such and so-and-so (any number of times) are all elements of the relation, then so too is something else. None of the suppositions of a Horn rule may be negative — none of them can require that something is *not* an element of the relation. Nor is the conclusion allowed to be disjunctive — it cannot say that given the suppositions, *either* this *or* that is in the relation. Horn rules have very useful properties, most notably that whenever a Horn rule is satisfied by every relation in a family, then the relation formed by taking the intersection of the entire family also satisfies the rule.

The three conditions for consequence as a relation, taken together, are equivalent to their counterparts as an operation, under either of the two definitions. Indeed, they are equivalent taken separately, with the nuance that to pass from CT as here formulated for Cn to CT formulated for $\vdash$ requires a little help from reflexivity.

Finally, we recall that classical consequence is *compact*, in the sense that whenever $A \vdash x$ then there is a finite subset $A' \subseteq A$ with $A' \vdash x$. In the language of operations, whenever $x \in Cn(A)$ then there is a finite $A' \subseteq A$ with $x \in Cn(A')$.

Intimately related to compactness is the following *maximalizability property*, which we will use as a tool many times: whenever $A \nvdash x$ then there is a set $A^+ \supseteq A$ of formulae such that *maximally* $A^+ \nvdash x$. This means that $A^+ \nvdash x$ but for every set $A^{++} \supset A^+$ of formulae we have $A^{++} \vdash x$. The property can be stated more generally, in terms of consistency: whenever A is consistent with B, then there is a set $A^+ \supseteq A$ of formulae such that *maximally* A^+ is consistent with B. In other words, A^+ is consistent with B and there is no set $A^{++} \supset A^+$ of formulae consistent with B.

This property may be inferred from compactness (or obtained *en route* within certain proofs of compactness), or proven separately. Given the length of its name, we will loosely refer to it as 'compactness' as well.

All of these properties of classical consequence are *abstract*, in the sense that they make no reference to any of the connectives $\wedge, \vee, \neg$. Evidently, classical consequence also has a number of properties concerning each of these connectives, arising from their respective truth-tables — for example the two properties that $a \wedge b \vdash a \vdash a \vee b$. Many of these will be familiar to the reader already, and we will not enumerate them. But we recall one that plays a very important role in what follows.

This is the property of *disjunction in the premisses*, alias OR, alias $\vee$+(left). It says that whenever $A \cup \{a\} \vdash x$ and $A \cup \{b\} \vdash x$ then $A \cup \{a \vee b\} \vdash x$. This too is a Horn rule. In the language of operations, it says $Cn(A \cup \{a\}) \cap Cn(A \cup \{b\}) \subseteq Cn(A \cup \{a \vee b\})$.

We end with a historical note. The notion of a closure operation goes back to work of Kuratowski in topology in the 1920s. However, as defined in logic it is more general than in topology; it does not require that $Cn(A \cup B) = Cn(A) \cup Cn(B)$ — which is false for classical and most other kinds of consequence. The notion was defined in essentially its present form by Tarski (1930), and gradually permeated work in abstract algebra, e.g. Cohn (1965), and logic, e.g. Brown and Suszko (1973), Wójcicki (1988).

Exercises

This section contains more exercises than others, to make sure that the student is on firm ground before take-off. Those whose memory of classical logic is rusty may need to reopen their primers before answering some of the questions.

1. *Truth-functional connectives*

    (a) Write out the truth tables for classical conjunction, disjunction and negation.

    (b) Give a precise inductive definition of the set of propositional formulae constructed by the connectives $\wedge, \vee, \neg$.

    (c) Write out the truth tables for material implication $\rightarrow$, material co-implication $\leftrightarrow$, and exclusive disjunction $+$.

    (d) Define $\rightarrow, \leftrightarrow, +$ in terms of $\wedge, \vee, \neg$.

    (e) Define $\vee$ from $\wedge, \neg$, and conversely $\wedge$ from $\vee, \neg$.

2. *Definition of classical consequence*

(a)* Writing $\emptyset$ for the empty set of formulae, what according to our definition of classical consequence, does it mean to say that $\emptyset \vdash x$?

(b) When A is a finite non-empty set of formulae, let $\wedge A$ be the conjunction (in any order, any bracketing) of the elements of A. Verify that $A \vdash x$ iff $\wedge A \vdash x$. Verify also that $\wedge A \vdash x$ iff $\emptyset \vdash \wedge A \to x$.

(c) Verify the claims made in the text that $A \vdash x$ iff $A \cup \{\neg x\}$ is inconsistent, and that A is consistent iff $A \nvdash f$ where f is an arbitrary contradiction.

(d) Let A be any set of formulae and let x be any individual formula, both built using at most the connectives $\wedge, \vee$. Show that whenever $A \vdash x$ then there is at least one elementary letter that occurs in both x and some element of A. In what way does this statement need to be qualified when the connective $\neg$ is allowed?

(e) Call a set F of truth-functional formulae (built using $\wedge, \vee, \neg$) *well-behaved* iff for all formulae $a, b : a \wedge b \in F$ iff $a \in F$ and $b \in F$, $a \vee b \in F$ iff $a \in F$ or $b \in F$, and $\neg a \in F$ iff $a \notin F$. Show that for every valuation $v : L \to \{1,0\}$, the set $\{a \in L : v(a) = 1\}$ is well-behaved. Show also conversely that whenever F is well-behaved then there is a valuation $v : L \to \{1,0\}$ with $F = \{a \in L : v(a) = 1\}$. Using this as a lemma, show that $A \vdash x$ iff x is contained in every well-behaved set X of formulae that includes A.

3. *Conditions defining closure operations*

(a)* Establish each of the three closure properties of reflexivity, cumulative transitivity, and monotony for classical consequence, in either their relational or their operational formulations.

(b)* Check the equivalence of the closure properties for Cn with those for $\vdash$, via the definition of $Cn(A)$ as $\{x : A \vdash x\}$. Pinpoint where assistance from reflexivity is needed to get from CT for the operation Cn to CT for the relation $\vdash$.

(c) Reformulate CT for the operation Cn so that it becomes equivalent to CT for the relation $\vdash$ without assistance from reflexivity.

(d) Reformulate CT for the relation $|$- so that it becomes equivalent to CT for the operation Cn without assistance from reflexivity.

4. *Idempotence and transitivity*

   (a) Express plain transitivity as a property of the operation Cn. Express idempotence (rather awkwardly) as a property of the relation $\vdash$.

   (b)* In the text it was claimed that when we are given both reflexivity and monotony, then cumulative transitivity is equivalent to the general version of plain transitivity. Show it.

   (c)* Likewise, in the text it was claimed that in the definition of a closure operation, we can replace cumulative transitivity by idempotence if we are given inclusion and monotony. Show it.

   (d) Show that if compactness is assumed, then singleton transitivity is sufficient to imply the general version of transitivity.

5. *Rules for disjunction*

   (a)* Show that classical consequence satisfies the rule of disjunction in the premisses (OR).

   (b)* Consider the following rule: whenever $A \cup \{a \vee b\} \vdash x$ then either $A \cup \{a\} \vdash x$ or $A \cup \{b\} \vdash x$. Is it a Horn rule? Does it hold for classical consequence?

6*. *Rules for conjunction* Consider the following rule, known as *conjunction in the conclusion*, alias AND, alias $\wedge+$ (right): whenever $A \vdash x$ and $A \vdash y$ then $A \vdash x \wedge y$. Is it a Horn rule? Does it hold for classical consequence?

7. *Topological Condition* Show, as remarked in the text, that the topological condition $Cn(A \cup B) = Cn(A) \cup Cn(B)$ fails for classical consequence.

Problems

The first three problems concern compactness for classical logic. They are suitable for students who have already been exposed to at least one proof of compactness, to refresh memory of it and try their hand at another.

1. Prove that classical consequence is compact, using the following strategy. Suppose that there is no finite subset $A' \subseteq A$ such that $A' \vdash x$. Use Zorn's Lemma (or a step-by-step argument using a fixed enumeration of all the formulae of the language) to show that there is a maximal set $A^+ \supseteq A$ of formulae with the same property. Show that A^+ is well behaved with respect to $\wedge, \vee, \neg$ in the sense of exercise 2e; and finally apply the result of that exercise.

2. Prove that classical consequence is compact, using the following quite
   different strategy.   First, some preliminaries.   Fix an enumeration
   of all the elementary letters of the language.   By an *n-assignment*
   we mean any function on the first n of these letters into the set
   $\{1,0\}$. Observe that every n-assignment determines a unique Boolean
   valuation on the set of all formulae built out of the letters on which
   the assignment is defined. To simplify notation, use the same letter
   v for both. Now suppose that there is no finite subset $A' \subseteq A$ such
   that $A' \vdash x$. Call an n-assignment v *special* iff for every m there
   is an $(n + m)$-assignment v' that satisfies every formula $a \in A$ built
   using at most the first $(n + m)$ letters, but does not satisfy x. Show
   from the hypothesis that there is a special 0-assignment. Show that
   for every n, if there is a special n-assignment then there is a special
   $(n+1)$-assignment. Use these two facts to define a 'master assignment'
   on the set of all proposition letters, that satisfies A but not x. Use
   the master assignment to conclude.

3. If you are familiar with the idea of an axiomatization of the relation of
   classical consequence, and with the notion of the strong completeness
   of the axiomatic system with respect to classical consequence, show
   how compactness may be obtained as a corollary of the strong
   completeness theorem.

*The next two problems explore the very general notions of closure
operations and closed sets. They give us a way of generating, and a way of
representing, closure operations. They are suitable for students accustomed
to working with sets.*

4*. Let X be an arbitrary set. To fix ideas you can think of X as the
    set of all propositional formulae, but the ideas are completely general.
    Let F be any family of subsets of X. Define the operation Cl:
    $2^X \rightarrow 2^X$ by the equality $Cl(A) = \cap\{B \in F : A \subseteq B\}$. Show that Cl
    is a closure operation.

5. Conversely, let Cl be any closure operation over an arbitrary set X.
   Call a set A of formulae *closed* under Cl iff $A = Cl(A)$. Show
   that the closure of any set $A \subseteq X$ of formulae coincides with the
   intersection of all closed sets that include it. That is, show that
   $Cl(A) = \cap\{B \subseteq X : A \subseteq B \text{ and } B = Cl(B)\}$.

*The last two problems explore the relation between the notion of a closure
relation and a rather abstract concept of deduction. They are suitable for
students accustomed to working with sets and arguing by induction.*

7. Let $R \subseteq 2^X \times X$ be any relation between subsets of X and elements of X. We say that R *allows chaining* iff for every $A \subseteq X$ the following holds: $(A, x) \in R$ whenever there is a finite sequence $(x_1, \ldots, x_n)$ of elements of X such that $x_n = x$ and for all $i \leq n$, either $x_i \in A$ or there is a subset $A' \subseteq \{x_1, \ldots, x_{i-1}\}$ with $(A', x_i) \in R$. Show that if R is a closure relation then it allows *chaining*.

8. Again, let $R \subseteq 2^X \times X$ be any relation between subsets of X and elements of X. We say that R *allows tree development* iff for every $A \subseteq X$ the following holds: $(A, x) \in R$ whenever there is a finite tree of elements of X whose root is x and whose leaves are all elements of A, such that for all non-leaf nodes y in the tree, $(Y, y) \in R$ where Y is the set of parents (looking leafwards) of y in the tree. Show that if R is a closure relation then it allows tree development.

1.3   Some Misunderstandings and a Habit to Suspend

For a person coming to nonmonotonic reasoning for the first time, it can be rather difficult to get a clear grip on what is going on. This is partly due to certain misunderstandings, which are very natural but distort understanding from the beginning. In this section we clear them away so that the reader can proceed without hidden impediments.

Weaker or Stronger?

The first thing that one hears about nonmonotonic logic is, evidently, that it is not monotonic. In other words, it fails the principle that whenever x follows from a set A of propositions then it also follows from every set B with $B \supseteq A$. By contrast, classical logic satisfies this principle, as we have seen in the preceding section.

Given this failure, it is natural to imagine that nonmonotonic logic is weaker than classical logic. And indeed, in one sense it is. Typically, the set of Horn rules satisfied by a nonmonotonic consequence relation is a proper subset of those holding for classical consequence. For example, with preferential consequence relations (to be explained in Chapter 3) the rules of reflexivity and cumulative transitivity always hold while monotony may not. And since classical consequence is itself a limiting case of preferential consequence, any Horn rule that is satisfied by all preferential consequence relations is satisfied by classical consequence.

But in another and more basic sense, the nonmonotonic logics that we will be studying are *stronger* than their classical counterpart. Recall that classical consequence is a relation, i.e. under the usual understanding of relations in set-theoretical terms, it is a set of ordered pairs. Specifically, $\vdash$ is a set of ordered pairs (A, x), where A is a set of Boolean formulae and x is an individual Boolean formula. It is at this level that the most basic comparison of strength arises.

Suppose we take a nonmonotonic consequence relation $\vdash\!\!\!\sim$ (usually pronounced 'snake'). It too is a set of ordered pairs (A, x). Under the principal modes of generation that we will be studying, it is a *superset* of the classical consequence relation, over the same set of Boolean formulae. In other words, we have $\vdash\, \subseteq\, \vdash\!\!\!\sim\, \subseteq 2^L \times L$, where $\subseteq$ is set inclusion.

Likewise, suppose that we take a nonmonotonic consequence operation, usually referred to by the letter C. Then we have $Cn \leq C$. Here $\leq$ is not quite set inclusion between the two operations, but set inclusion between their values. That is, $Cn \leq C$ means: $Cn(A) \subseteq C(A)$ for all sets A of formulae.

In this sense, nonmonotonic consequence relations are typically stronger than classical consequence, and when they are so we will call them *supraclassical* relations.

To be fair, there is a lot of looseness in talk of 'weaker' and 'stronger' relations. A person might retort to the preceding paragraph that it spells out precisely a sense in which we should say that nonmonotonic consequence relations $\vdash\!\!\!\sim$ are weaker than classical $\vdash$. In common language, we say that the relation of sisterhood is stronger than that of sibling. It is the sub-relation that is described as stronger, and the super-relation that is described as weaker. Since $\vdash$ is a subrelation of $\vdash\!\!\!\sim$ we should say that classical consequence is the stronger!

In fact, we seem to tolerate two contradictory ways of speaking. One is rooted in informal discourse and the other is anchored in more technical language. We do tend to say that the relation of being a sister is stronger than that of being a sibling: in this case the sub-relation is ordinarily seen as stronger. On the other hand, without exception, logicians describe classical consequence as stronger than, say, intuitionistic or relevantist consequence. In this case it is the super-relation that is described as stronger.

In the end, it does not matter which way we speak, so long as we understand and agree on what we mean and do not allow the coexistence of two conflicting ways of speaking to engender confusion. Our terminology for consequence relations will be constant. The super-relation will be called stronger, and the sub-relation weaker. Moreover, any loss of Horn rules will be described a loss of regularity, rather than as a loss of strength.

Classical or Non-Classical?

In so far as monotony fails, the logic of nonmonotonic consequence relations certainly differs from classical logic. But it would be quite misleading to refer to it as a kind of 'non-classical logic' as that term is usually employed, for example in reference to intuitionistic logic.

For in contrast to the intuitionistic case, our relations do not reject as incorrect any elements of classical consequence. As already remarked, each of them includes classical consequence. Nor do we suggest that there is anything incorrect about the Horn property of monotony. It is perfectly appropriate for purely deductive reasoning, but can fail for other kinds of reasoning.

As already emphasized, there is nothing wrong with classical logic. Moreover, we need to understand and use it when trying to understand other kinds of reasoning. In effect, we will show how the 'good old relation of classical consequence' may be deployed in certain ways to define stronger relations that are of practical value, but happen to fail monotony. Rather than talk of non-classical logics, it is more illuminating to speak of more sophisticated ways of employing classical logic, which generate non-monotonic behaviour.

One Logic or Many?

There is a third common misunderstanding of what nonmonotonic logic is all about. From the classical context, we are familiar with the idea that there is just one core logic, apart from notational differences and features like the choice of primitive connectives. That core is classical logic, and it is also the logic that we use when reasoning ourselves in the metalanguage.

Even intuitionists and relevantists, who do not accept all of classical logic, feel the same way — but each about their own system, which is a subsystem of the classical one. They have some difficulties, one might add maliciously, in reconciling this view with their own practice in the metalanguage, where they usually use classical logic; but that is another matter.

Given the unicity of classical inference, it is natural for the student, puzzled by seeing several different kinds of nonmonotonic consequence, to ask: what is *real* nonmonotonic inference? Which is the *correct* nonmonotonic consequence relation? What is the one that we use in practice, even if we can study others?

The answer is that *there isn't one*. There is no unique nonmonotonic consequence relation, but indefinitely many of them. There are all the relations that can be generated from certain kinds of structure, whose ingredients are allowed to vary within the boundaries of suitable constraints (which we will be exploring). Likewise, there are all the relations satisfying certain syntactic conditions, (which we will also study). Moreover, if one tries to get away from non-uniqueness by intersecting all the many such relations, one ends up with just classical logic again.

Leaving aside technical details, the essential message is as follows. Don't expect to find *the* nonmonotonic consequence relation that will always, in all contexts, be the right one to use. Rather, expect to find several *families* of such relations, interesting *syntactic conditions* that they sometimes satisfy but sometimes fail, and principal *ways of generating* them mathematically from underlying structures.

A Habit to Suspend

In the following pages, we will be showing that there are systems that act as natural bridges between classical consequence and nonmonotonic logics. These bridge systems are also supraclassical, but they are perfectly monotonic, indeed they are closure operations.

'But if these bridge systems are supraclassical', one may ask, 'how are they possible? Surely classical consequence is *already* maximal, in the sense that there is no stronger closure operation in the same underlying language, other than the trivial one under which every proposition of the language implies every other one. So how can the 'bridge logics' be closure operations and at the same time supraclassical?'

Indeed, this maximality observation has been part of the folklore of logic since the early twentieth century. But the formulation above omits a vital element, which is not always made as explicit as it should be. That is the condition of being *closed under substitution*, which we now explain.

By *substitution* we mean what is often called, at greater length, *uniform substitution of arbitrary formulae for the elementary letters in a formula*. For example, when a is the formula $p \wedge (q \vee \neg r)$, where p, q, r are three distinct elementary letters, we may consider the substitution σ that replaces all occurrences of p by r, say; all occurrences of q by $\neg p$; and (simultaneously, not subsequently) all occurrences of r by $\neg(p \wedge s)$. That will give us $\sigma(a) = r \wedge (\neg p \vee \neg\neg(p \wedge s))$. Simplifications, such as the elimination of the double negation, are not part of the substitution, but possible later actions.

Substitution, in this sense, is a function, not an inference. For those accustomed to algebraic terminology, a substitution is an endomorphism on the absolutely free algebra of formulae into itself. In general, we do not have $a \vdash \sigma(a)$; one need only consider the counterexample where a is an elementary letter p and σ takes p to another elementary letter q. On the other hand it is true that when a Boolean formula a is a classical tautology, then so too is $\sigma(a)$ for any substitution σ. For example $p \vee \neg p$ is a tautology, and so to is $\sigma(p \vee \neg p) = \sigma(p) \vee \neg\sigma(p)$ for every substitution σ. In other words, writing T for the set of classical tautologies, and writing $\sigma(T)$ for $\{\sigma(a) : a \in T\}$, we have $\sigma(T) \subseteq T$ for every substitution σ. In this sense we say that the set of tautologies is *closed under substitution*. So too is the relation of classical consequence. In other words, whenever $A \vdash x$ then $\sigma(A) \vdash \sigma(x)$. In the language of operations, whenever $x \in Cn(A)$ then $\sigma(x) \in Cn(\sigma(A))$; more concisely $\sigma(Cn(A)) \subseteq Cn(\sigma(A))$.

In passing, we note that uniform substitution should not be confused with another operation, which is also sometimes called by the same name. This is the replacement of one or more occurrences of any formula (not just an elementary letter) by another formula to which it is classically equivalent (not by an arbitrary formula). Evidently, the output of such a manipulation is classically equivalent to its input. To avoid confusion, this kind of operation is better given another name, e.g. replacement of equivalents.

The maximality of classical logic may now be expressed as follows.

Theorem 1.1 *There is no supraclassical closure relation in the same language as classical $\vdash$ that is closed under substitution, except for $\vdash$ itself and the total relation.*

Here, the total relation is the one that relates every possible premiss (or set of premisses) to every possible conclusion; as an operation it sends any set of formulae to the set of all formulae. The proof of the observation is straightforward, and we recall it here.

Proof. Let $\vdash^+$ be any closure relation over Boolean formulae that is closed under substitution and also properly supraclassical, i.e. $\vdash \subset \vdash^+$. We want to show that $B \vdash^+ y$ for arbitrary B, y.

By the second hypothesis, there are A, x with $A \vdash^+ x$ but $A \nvdash x$. From the latter, there is a classical valuation v with $v(A) = 1, v(x) = 0$. Take the substitution σ that substitutes tautologies for elementary letters that are true under v, and contradictions for letters that are false under v. We see, by an easy induction on depth of formulae, that $\sigma(A)$ is a set of tautologies while $\sigma(x)$ is a contradiction. Since by the first hypothesis $\vdash^+$ is closed under substitution, $A \vdash^+ x$ implies $\sigma(A) \vdash^+ \sigma(x)$.

But since $\sigma(A)$ is a set of tautologies we have by classical logic that for arbitrary $B, B \vdash \sigma(a)$ for all $\sigma(a) \in \sigma(A)$. Likewise, since $\sigma(x)$ is a contradiction we have $\sigma(x) \vdash y$ for arbitrary formula y. Thus since $\vdash \subseteq \vdash^+$ we have $B \vdash^+ \sigma(a)$ for all $\sigma(a) \in \sigma(A)$, and also $\sigma(x) \vdash^+ y$. Putting these together with $\sigma(A) \vdash^+ \sigma(x)$, we can apply cumulative transitivity and monotony of $\vdash^+$ twice to get $B \vdash^+ y$, completing the proof. ∎

The moral of this story is that the supraclassical closure relations that we will be offering as bridges between classical consequence and nonmonotonic consequence relations *are not closed under substitution*. Nor, for that matter, are the nonmonotonic relations that issue from them. This runs against deeply ingrained habit. Students of logic are brought up with the idea that any decent consequence relation should be purely formal or structural, and hence satisfy substitution. To understand nonmonotonic logic, it is a habit to suspend.

Exercises

1. *Substitutions*

   In the text, we described substitution in terms of replacing elementary letters simultaneously by arbitrary formulae.   A more rigorous definition, enabling us to prove facts by induction on the depth of formulae, is as follows. A *substitution* for a propositional language is defined to be a function on the set L of all formulae of that language into itself that is well-behaved (in algebraic jargon, homomorphic) with respect to the connectives of that language. In the case of the language with which we are working, the primitive connectives are $\neg, \wedge, \vee$. Thus for that language, a substitution is a function $\sigma : L \to L$ such that for all formulae a, b we have: $\sigma(\neg a) = \neg\sigma(a), \sigma(a \wedge b) = \sigma(a) \wedge \sigma(b), \sigma(a \vee b) = \sigma(a) \vee \sigma(b)$.

   (a)* Suppose that the primitive connectives are just $\neg, \to$. What would be the appropriate definition of a substitution?

   (b) The *composition* $\sigma\tau$ of substitutions σ, τ is defined by putting $\sigma\tau(a) = \sigma(\tau(a))$ for all formulae a. Verify by induction on the depth of formulae that it is also a substitution.

   (c) A substitution σ is called *injective* iff whenever $a \neq b$ then $\sigma(a) \neq \sigma(b)$. Give an example of a substitution in our Boolean language that is not injective.

   (d) A substitution σ is said to be *onto* L (alias *surjective*) iff for every $x \in L$ there is an $a \in L$ with $x = \sigma(a)$. Give an example of a substitution that is injective but not surjective.

   (e)* Recalling the definition of a valuation in section 1.2, show that the composition $v\sigma$ of a substitution σ followed by a valuation v is well-defined and is itself a valuation.

   (f) Show by induction on depth of formulae that each substitution is uniquely determined by its values on elementary letters.

2. *Images and closures of sets of formulae under substitutions*
   Let A be any set of Boolean formulae and let σ be a substitution function. By the *image* $\sigma(A)$ of A under σ we mean the set $\{\sigma(a) : a \in A\}$. By the *closure* $\sigma[A]$ of A under σ we mean the least set that includes A and contains $\sigma(a)$ whenever it contains a.

   (a)* Verify that always $\sigma(A) \subseteq \sigma[A]$ and give a simple example where $A \not\subseteq \sigma(A)$.

   (b) Verify that the operation taking A to $\sigma[A]$ is a closure operation in the sense defined in section 1.2, but the operation taking A to $\sigma(A)$ is not.

   (d) Show that, although $\sigma(A)$ and $\sigma[A]$ are not the same, nevertheless for any set A of formulae and any substitution function σ, $\sigma(A) \subseteq A$ iff $\sigma[A] = A$.

3. *Classical consequence*
   Show that, as claimed in the text, the relation of classical consequence is closed under substitution.

Problems

1. Let A be a set of formulae, and consider the rule of *detachment* (also known as *modus ponens*), allowing passage from any pair of formulae $a, a \to x$ to x. This rule can be seen as a three-place relation. Formulate the notion of a set A of formulae being closed under detachment.

2. More generally, formulate the notions of image and closure of a set under a relation of arbitrary arity.

Project

This project is suitable for students familiar with some Hilbert-style axiomatization of the set of all tautologies of classical propositional logic.

1. Let A be any set of formulae, and let consider the least set that includes A and is closed under both substitution and detachment. Show that this coincides with the closure, under detachment, of the closure of A under substitution. On the other hand, give an example to show that it is not necessarily the same as the closure, under substitution, of the closure of A under detachment. What does this tell you about the role of axiom schemes and the rule of substitution in axiomatizations of the set of tautologies?

2. Generalize the positive part of (1) to cover not only the rule of detachment but also any derivation rule of an appropriate kind.

1.4   Three Ways of Getting More Conclusions out of your Premisses

In this overview we will describe three different ways of getting more than is authorized by classical consequence out of a set of premisses. Roughly speaking, the first method uses additional background *assumptions*. The second restricts the set of *valuations* that are considered possible. And the third uses additional background *rules*.

Each of these procedures gives rise to a corresponding kind of monotonic consequence operation. They are not entirely equivalent to each other. But they all give us closure operations in the sense defined in section 1.2, and they are all supraclassical. We will call consequence relations with these two properties *paraclassical*. In other words, a *paraclassical consequence relation* is defined to be any supraclassical closure relation.

The three kinds of paraclassical consequence serve as conceptual bridges to corresponding families of nonmonotonic consequence which are formed essentially by allowing key elements of the respective constructions to vary in a principled way with the premisses under consideration.

To change the metaphor, imagine a solar system. The sun of classical consequence illuminates the firmament from its centre. Three kinds of paraclassical consequence circle around it like planets: *pivotal-assumption*, *pivotal-valuation*, and *pivotal-rule* consequence. Their key ingredients are, respectively, a set of additional background assumptions, a reduced set of valuations, and an additional set of rules. By allowing these to vary in a principled manner with the premisses of any given inference, we will obtain three satellite kinds of nonmonotonic consequence operation: *default-assumption*, *default-valuation*, and *default rule* consequence.

All these concepts are developed over a purely propositional language using only Boolean connectives, without adding further connectives to the usual truth-functional ones.

Exercises

These exercises examine further the concepts of section 1.2. For definitions, see that section.

1. *Supraclassical consequence relations*

(a)* Show that any supraclassical relation $\mathrel{|\!\sim}$ that satisfies plain transitivity satisfies singleton conjunctive monotony.

(b)* Show that any supraclassical relation $\mathrel{|\!\sim}$ that satisfies cumulative transitivity satisfies conjunction in the conclusion.

2. *An existential variant of classical consequence*
Define a relation $\mathrel{|\!\sim}$ of *logical friendliness* between sets A of formulae and individual formulae x as follows: $A \mathrel{|\!\sim} x$ iff for every partial valuation v to just the elementary letters occurring in elements of A, if $v(A) = 1$ then there is a partial valuation w to just the elementary letters in x, which agrees with v over the common letters, such that $w(x) = 1$. Equivalently, iff every partial valuation v to just the elementary letters occurring in elements of A with $v(A) = 1$ can be extended to a partial valuation v^+ to all the elementary letters in $A \cup \{x\}$ agreeing with v over those in A, such that $v^+(x) = 1$. This relation is studied systematically in Makinson (in preparation). Show each of the following for $\mathrel{|\!\sim}$:

(a) It is supraclassical, but distinct from classical consequence and from the total relation.

(b) It is not closed under substitution.

(c) It satisfies the following singleton version of CT: if $A \mathrel{|\!\sim} x$ and $A \cup \{x\} \mathrel{|\!\sim} y$ then $A \mathrel{|\!\sim} y$.

(d) It fails each of the rules AND, plain transitivity, and singleton conjunctive monotony.

(e) It fails the full version of CT.

1.5 Review and Explore

Recapitulation

Nonmonotonic reasoning is not something strange and esoteric. In fact, almost all of our everyday reasoning is nonmonotonic; purely deductive, monotonic inference takes place only in rather special contexts, notably pure mathematics. Nevertheless, a good understanding of classical consequence is needed before one can begin to make sense of any other kind of reasoning, monotonic or otherwise.

When beginning to study nonmonotonic logic, it is important to avoid certain misunderstandings. In particular, one should not confuse the sense in which nonmonotonic reasoning is weaker than its classical counterpart, with the more fundamental sense in which, typically, it is stronger. Again, whereas in classical logic we are examining a single system, in other words a single consequence relation, in nonmonotonic logic we are studying not one but an infinite range of such relations. Thirdly, it is not helpful to think of the subject as a kind of non-classical logic, as that term is usually understood; it is better seen as a range of ways of using classical logic to obtain nonmonotonic results. Finally, whereas classical logic is closed under substitution for elementary letters, this property fails for the supraclassical consequence relations that we will study, whether monotonic or nonmonotonic. It is therefore important for the reader to get out of the habit of taking substitution for granted.

In this book we describe three different ways of getting more out of a set of premises than is classically allowed. The first uses additional background assumptions; the second restricts the set of valuations that are considered possible; the third uses additional background rules. These give rise to three kinds of monotonic consequence operation, serving as conceptual bridges to corresponding families of nonmonotonic consequence.

Checklist of Concepts and Definitions for Revision

Section 1.2: Boolean formulae, assignments of truth-values, Boolean valuations, classical consequence, inference relations versus inference operations, closure operations, Horn rules, compactness. Some specific Horn rules holding for classical consequence: inclusion, cumulative transitivity, monotony, disjunction in the premises, transitivity, idempotence. *Section 1.3*: Inclusion between consequence relations, supraclassical consequence operations, uniform substitution for elementary letters, image and closure under substitution of a set or relation between formulae, a sense in which classical logic is maximal. *Section 1.4*: Paraclassical consequence operations; the intuitive ideas behind pivotal-assumption, pivotal-valuation, pivotal-rule consequence, default-assumption, default-valuation, default-rule consequence.

Further Reading

- G. Antoniou. *Nonmonotonic Reasoning*. MIT Press, Cambridge, MA, 1997. Chapter 13.1–13.4.

- G. Brewka, J. Dix and K. Konolige. *Nonmonotonic Reasoning — An Overview*. CSLI Publications, Stanford, CA, 1997. Chapter 1.

- M. Ginsberg. AI and nonmonotonic reasoning. In *Handbook of Logic in Artificial Intelligence and Logic Programming. Volume 3:*

Nonmonotonic Reasoning and Uncertain Reasoning, D. M. Gabbay *et al.* eds., pp. 1–33. Clarendon Press, Oxford, 1994.

- W. Hodges. Classical logic I: first-order logic. In *The Blackwell Guide to Philosophical Logic*, L. Goble, ed., pp. 9–32. Blackwell, Oxford, 2001.

- J. Horty. Nonmonotonic Logic. In *The Blackwell Guide to Philosophical Logic*, L. Goble, ed., pp. 336–361. Blackwell, Oxford, 2001.

- D. Makinson. Ways of doing logic: what was different about AGM 1985? *Journal of Logic and Computation*, **13**, 3–13, 2003.

- D. Makinson. Bridges between classical and nonmonotonic logic. *Logic Journal of the IGPL*, **11**, 69–96, 2003. http://www3.oup.co.uk/igpl/Volume_11/Issue_01/.

- R. Wójcicki. *Theory of Logical Calculi: Basic Theory of Consequence Operations*. Kluwer, Dordrecht, 1988. Chapter 1 sections 1.0–1.6.

Chapter 2

Using Additional Background Assumptions

2.1 From Classical Consequence to Pivotal Assumptions

We begin by examining the simplest kind of paraclassical consequence and its transformation into a form of nonmonotonic reasoning, namely inference with additional background assumptions.

In daily life, the assumptions that we make when reasoning are not all equally conspicuous. Generally, there will be a few that we display explicitly, because they are special to the situation under consideration or in some other way deserve particular attention. There will usually be many others that we do not bother even to mention, because we take them to be common knowledge, or in some way trivial. There will be yet others of which we are only half aware. This kind of phenomenon was already known to the ancient Greeks, who used the term *enthymeme* to refer to an argument in which one or more premisses are left implicit. That is the idea that we develop in this section.

We work with the same propositional language as in classical logic, with the set of all its formulae called L. Let $K \subseteq L$ be a fixed set of formulae. Intuitively K will be playing the role of a set of background assumptions or, as they are called in Gärdenfors and Makinson (1994), 'expectations'. Let A be any set of formulae, and let x be an individual formula.

23

Definition 2.1 (Pivotal-Assumption Consequence)

- *We say that x is a consequence of A modulo the assumption set K, and write $A \vdash_K x$ alias $x \in Cn_K(A)$ iff there is no valuation v such that $v(K \cup A) = 1$ while $v(x) = 0$. Equivalently: iff $K \cup A \vdash x$.*

- *We call a relation or operation a pivotal-assumption consequence iff it is identical with $\vdash_K$ (resp. Cn_K) for some set K of formulae.*

Thus there is not a unique pivotal-assumption consequence relation, but many — one for each value of K.

Since classical consequence is monotonic, pivotal-assumption consequence relations and operations are supraclassical in the sense defined earlier. That is, for every K we have $\vdash \subseteq \vdash_K$, in the operational notation $Cn \leq Cn_K$.

They also share a number of abstract properties with classical consequence. In particular, they satisfy inclusion, cumulative transitivity and monotony, and thus are closure operations. Being supraclassical closure operations they are, by definition (section 1.4), paraclassical. They are also compact, and have the property of disjunction in the premisses. These positive features may all be verified by straightforward applications of the definitions. For ease of reference we summarise them in Table 2.1.

Table 2.1: Some Features of Pivotal-Assumption Consequence

Supraclassical		
Reflexive		
Cumulatively Transitive (CT)	Closure Relation	Paraclassical
Monotonic		
Disjunction in the Premisses (OR)		
Compact		

On the other hand, since the $\vdash_K$ are supraclassical closure relations, we would expect from Theorem 1.1 that they are not, in general, closed under substitution.

It is instructive to look at a simple example how this failure happens. Let $K = \{p\}$ where p is an elementary letter. Choose any other elementary letter q, and put $A = \{q\}$ and $x = p \wedge q$. Then $A \vdash_K x$ since $\{p, q\} \vdash p \wedge q$. Now let σ be the substitution that replaces every elementary letter by itself, except for the letter p, which is replaced by some elementary letter r distinct from itself and from q, so that $\sigma(p) = r$ and $\sigma(q) = q$. Then $\sigma(A) \nvdash_K \sigma(x)$ since $K \cup \sigma(A) = K \cup \{\sigma(q)\} = K \cup \{q\} = \{p, q\} \nvdash r \wedge q = \sigma(x)$. Analysing this example, we see what is going on: the substitution is applied to the explicit premisses A and the conclusion x, but not to the background assumption set K, because K is held constant.

On the other hand, it is easy to verify that when the background assumption set K is itself closed under substitution then the corresponding consequence relation $\vdash_K$ is also closed under substitution. But this special case is a degenerate one. For as we have just noticed, $\vdash_K$ is always paraclassical (i.e. a supraclassical closure relation), so Theorem 1.1 tells us that when it is also closed under substitution, it must be either classical consequence itself (which happens when $K = Cn(\emptyset)$) or the total relation (which happens when $K \supset Cn(\emptyset)$). To reach the same point more directly: when K is closed under substitution, then either all of its elements are tautologies or one of its elements has a substitution instance which is a contradiction and is also in K, so that $K \cup A$ is inconsistent and thus $K \cup A \vdash x$ for any A, x.

A striking feature of pivotal-assumption consequence, distinguishing it from the next bridge system that we will be describing, is that the positive properties that we have entered into the table above suffice to characterize it. In other words, we have the following 'representation theorem' for pivotal-assumption consequence operations (and likewise for the corresponding relations).

Theorem 2.2 *Let Cn^+ be any paraclassical consequence operation that is compact and satisfies the condition of disjunction in the premisses. Then there is a set K of formulae such that $Cn^+ = Cn_K$.*

The general concept of a representation theorem, and its connections with the concept of a completeness theorem are discussed later in this section.

This particular representation theorem is formulated in Rott (2001, section 4.4 observation 5), but appears to have been part of the folklore for a long time. Before giving a proof, we draw attention to three important properties needed for it.

- We say that a consequence operation C satisfies *left classical equivalence* (LCE) iff whenever $Cn(A) = Cn(B)$ then $C(A) = C(B)$. Note carefully the pattern: the antecedent concerns classical consequence Cn; the consequent concerns whatever consequence operation C we are interested in; thus the principle as a whole relates the two. This property is often known as 'left logical equivalence' (LLE), but this can be a little confusing unless one keeps in mind that 'logical' here means 'classical'.

- We say that a consequence operation C satisfies *right weakening* (RW) iff whenever $x \in C(A)$ and $y \in Cn(x)$ then $y \in C(A)$. In relational notation: whenever $A \mid\!\sim x \vdash y$ then $A \mid\!\sim y$. Note again the interplay between classical Cn and the operation C under consideration.

- We say that a consequence operation C has the *free premiss* property iff whenever $B \subseteq A$ then $C(A) = C(C(B) \cup A)$. This is not an interactive property, but concerns C alone. It says that whenever $B \subseteq A$ then all the propositions in $C(B)$ may be thrown in as free premisses alongside A without affecting the consequences of A. In the particular case that B is the empty set of formulae, the free premiss property tells us that $C(A) = C(C(\emptyset) \cup A)$. In other words, the identity of $C(A)$ is not affected by adding into A the consequences (under the same consequence operation) of the empty set.

Classical consequence itself has all three of these properties, the first one trivially, the second as a form of transitivity, and the third not difficult to verify. To establish the representation theorem, we need to know that *every* paraclassical consequence operation has these properties.

Lemma 2.3 (for Theorem 2.2) *Let Cn^+ be any paraclassical consequence operation. Then Cn^+ satisfies left classical equivalence, right weakening, and free premisses.*

The verification is straightforward. With it in hand, we can prove the representation theorem as follows.

Proof (of Theorem 2.2). Let Cn^+ be any paraclassical consequence operation that is compact and satisfies the condition of disjunction in the premisses. Put $K = Cn^+(\emptyset)$. We claim that $Cn^+ = Cn_K$. It will suffice to show both $Cn_K \leq Cn^+$ and $Cn^+ \leq Cn_K$.

For the inclusion $Cn_K \leq Cn^+$ we need to show that for any $A, Cn(Cn^+(\emptyset) \cup A) \subseteq Cn^+(A)$. Since by supraclassicality $Cn \leq Cn^+$, we have $Cn(Cn^+(\emptyset) \cup A) \subseteq Cn^+(Cn^+(\emptyset) \cup A) = Cn^+(A)$ by the free premiss property of paraclassical operations.

For the converse inclusion $Cn^+ \leq Cn_K$ we need to show that for any A, $Cn^+(A) \subseteq Cn(Cn^+(\emptyset) \cup A)$. This is where we need compactness and disjunction in the premisses.

Suppose $x \in Cn^+(A)$. Then by the compactness of Cn^+ there is a finite $B \subseteq A$ with $x \in Cn^+(B)$. Let b be the conjunction of all the finitely many elements of B. Using left classical equivalence we have $x \in Cn^+(b)$ and thus by right weakening $\neg b \vee x \in Cn^+(b)$. But also, $\neg b \vee x \in Cn(\neg b) \subseteq Cn^+(\neg b)$, using the supraclassicality of Cn^+. Applying disjunction in the premises, we thus have $\neg b \vee x \in Cn^+(b \vee \neg b) = Cn^+(\emptyset)$ using left classical equivalence again.

Since $\neg b \vee x \in Cn^+(\emptyset)$, monotony tells us that to show that $x \in Cn(Cn^+(\emptyset) \cup A)$ as desired, it will suffice to show that $x \in Cn(\{\neg b \vee x\} \cup A)$. But by the construction of b we have $b \in Cn(A)$ and so using disjunctive syllogism for classical consequence, $x \in Cn(\{\neg b \vee x\} \cup A)$, thereby completing the proof. ∎

We end this section with two general remarks: one on the significance of the compactness condition, and the other on the difference between representation and completeness theorems.

What's so Important about Compactness?

Students are often puzzled by the notion of compactness. What is its significance, and why should we be looking at it? The answer depends very much on whether one is considering finite or infinite systems.

A finite logical system is one in which there are only finitely many mutually non-equivalent formulae, modulo whatever notion of logical equivalence one is working with. Of course, in all but the most trivial of cases, there will be infinitely many *formulae*. Even a single elementary letter generates infinitely many distinct formulae by successive applications of negation — but there are only two mutually non-equivalent formulae in this multitude if we are using classical logic. In another terminology, the set of formulae $\{p, \neg p, \neg\neg p, \neg\neg\neg p, \ldots\}$ has just two equivalence classes (the even ones and the odd ones) under classical equivalence. More generally, if a propositional language has only finitely many elementary letters, then the application of Boolean connectives will give us only finitely many mutually non-equivalent formulae under classical equivalence (and thus so too under any supraclassical one). In this case we will say that *the system is finite*.

When the system is finite, then compactness is of no interest as a separate condition, because it is automatically satisfied. Suppose that $A \mathrel{|\!\sim} x$ for some consequence relation in a finite system. Because the entire system is finite, A will have a finite subset A_0 to which it is equivalent, in the sense that $A_0 \mathrel{|\!\sim} a$ for every $a \in A$ and conversely $A \mathrel{|\!\sim} a$ for every $a \in A_0$. Then, provided the consequence relation $\mathrel{|\!\sim}$ satisfies CT, we have $A_0 \mathrel{|\!\sim} x$.

The interest of compactness arises only when the system is infinite. This happens in classical propositional logic when there are infinitely many elementary letters. It can happen in first-order (alias predicate, alias quantificational) logic even when the 'alphabet' is finite, indeed even when there are only two relation letters. It can also happen in certain non-classical propositional logics when the number of elementary letters is finite – for example, in very weak sub-logics of classical logic that do not enable us to prove enough equivalences, and in extensions of classical logic where the language is enriched with further non-truth-functional connectives, as in suitable modal logics.   But in this book, we are working only with Boolean formulae with no extra connectives; and all our logics will include classical consequence.   For us, therefore, compactness is of concern only when considering infinite premiss sets.

In effect, compactness guarantees that even when a set of formulae is essentially infinite (i.e. not equivalent to any one of its finite subsets), nevertheless it behaves rather like a finite subset, in that any individual 'work-job' that it carries out can be carried out by one of its finite subsets. In particular, whenever it implies an individual formula, then some finite subset does. Compactness thus provides a conceptual link between the finite and the infinite. For this reason, it is valuable for proving many properties of infinite systems, by permitting us to reduce the argument to the finite case. Note, however, that there is a limit to the traffic that this link can carry: different consequences x of A may require appeal to different finite subsets of A, and there may be no finite upper bound on the sizes of the finite subsets that are needed for the task.

Thus a mathematician wishing to cover the infinite case along with the finite will find compactness a valuable tool in logic, just it is in abstract algebra and topology. Philosophical logicians trying to get a better understanding of the transition from finitude to infinity, will also need it in their conceptual toolkit. Computer scientists can get a lot of mileage working only with finite systems and ignoring compactness. But sooner or later they too may need to look at an infinite system, and it is best to have tools ready for the occasion.

Representation versus Completeness Theorems

Those familiar with abstract algebra will be accustomed to the use of the term 'representation theorem' for results like Theorem 2.2. Such theorems are legion there — for example, the representation of Boolean algebras as fields of sets, and of groups in terms of transformations. But those coming from classical logic (and its subsystems like intuitionistic logic) may be puzzled by the term. In logic they are accustomed to 'completeness theorems'. They seem to be doing much the same sort of job, so why the different terminology?

The reason comes largely from the fact, underlined in section 1.3, that whereas classical consequence is a *unique* relation, the nonmonotonic consequences that we are studying are *multiple*: different consequence relations are produced by different choices of the parameters (e.g. the background assumption set K) in the generating apparatus.

On the one hand, the completeness theorem for classical logic tells us that whenever x is a classical consequence of A, where this relation is understood as defined semantically in terms of valuations, then x may be obtained from A by the application of certain rules. In other words, whenever $A \vdash x$ then x is in the least superset of A that is closed under the syntactic rules. The rules entertained must be ones for which the notion of 'the least superset' makes sense. In other words, the intersection of any family of supersets of A satisfying the rules must also satisfy them. Usually they will be Horn rules.

On the other hand, a representation theorem tells us that *every* structure satisfying certain syntactic conditions, is identical with (or in some broader sense equivalent to) *some* structure of a semantically defined kind. For example, the representation theorem for Boolean algebras says that *every* Boolean algebra (defined by, say, equations) is isomorphic to *some* field of sets. Again, in the present context, our representation theorem for pivotal-assumption consequence (Theorem 2.2) tells us that *every* relation satisfying certain syntactic conditions (paraclassicality, compactness, and disjunction in the premises) is identical with *some* semantically defined relation (one of the kind $\vdash_K$).

For representation theorems, the syntactic conditions can take a wider variety of forms than for completeness theorems. As we are not closing any set under the conditions, they need not take the form of Horn rules. We will see some examples of this later with the conditions of rational and disjunctive monotony, which have negative premises.

What happens if we try to get a completeness theorem out of Theorem 2.2, say by intersecting *all* the relations satisfying the specified syntactic conditions, i.e. by looking at the *least* such relation? It is not difficult to show that this is just classical consequence all over again!

In general, when dealing with supraclassical inference relations, this pattern repeats itself: interesting representation theorems may be proven, but attempts to establish completeness theorems, by taking the least relation satisfying given Horn conditions, collapse into triviality.

Exercises

1*. Check the claim made in the text that pivotal-assumption consequence operations satisfy inclusion, cumulative transitivity and monotony, and thus are closure operations.
    Hint: Recall the fact, established in Chapter 1, that classical consequence itself has all these three properties, and show that they are inherited by pivotal-assumption operations.

2. Verify that pivotal-assumption consequence operations also have the property of disjunction in the premisses.
    Hint: As for the first exercise.

3*. Verify that pivotal-assumption consequence operations are also compact.
    Hint: As for the first exercise.

4. Take the example in the text showing that pivotal-assumption consequence operations are not in general closed under substitution, and modify it with a different premiss set, different conclusion, and different substitution, but with the same lesson.

5*. Verify the Lemma for Theorem 2.2.

Problem

Prove the claim made in the text, that the least operation Cn^+ satisfying the conditions of Theorem 2.2 is classical consequence.
Hint: Break it into two parts, showing first that $Cn \leq Cn^+$, and then the converse $Cn^+ \leq Cn$.

2.2 From Pivotal Assumptions to Default Assumptions

What has all this to do with *nonmonotonic* inference? Pivotal-assumption consequence relations $\vdash_K$ are, as we have seen, perfectly monotonic. But nonmonotonicity is created if we now allow the background assumption set K to *vary* with the premiss set A. More precisely, when the part of K that we actually use is allowed to vary, in a principled way, with the current premiss set A. This is done by imposing a consistency constraint, and diminishing the usable part of K when it is violated.

Specifically, we go nonmonotonic when we use only the maximal subsets K' of K that are consistent with A, and accept as output

only what is common to their separate outputs. We call this relation
default-assumption consequence, to bring out its close relation to the
preceding pivotal-assumption consequence.

To give the definition more explicitly, let $K \subseteq L$ be a set of formulae,
which again will play the role of a set of background assumptions. Let A
be any set of formulae, and let x be an individual formula.

We say that a subset K' of K is *consistent with* A (more briefly: is
A-*consistent*) iff there is a classical valuation v with $v(K' \cup A) = 1$.

A subset K' of K is called *maximally consistent with* A (more briefly:
maxiconsistent with A, or *maximally* A-*consistent*) iff it is consistent with
A but is not a proper subset of any $K'' \subseteq K$ that is consistent with A.
We can now formulate the main definition.

Definition 2.4 (Default-Assumption Consequence)

- *We define the relation $\mathop{\mid\sim}_K$ of consequence modulo the default
  assumptions K by putting $A \mathop{\mid\sim}_K x$ iff $K' \cup A \vdash x$ for every subset
  $K' \subseteq K$ that is maxiconsistent with A.*

  *Writing C_K for the corresponding operation, this puts $C_K(A) =
  \cap \{Cn(K' \cup A) : K' \subseteq K$ and K' maxiconsistent with $A\}$.*

- *We call a relation or operation a default-assumption consequence iff
  it is identical with $\mathop{\mid\sim}_K$ (resp. C_K) for some set K of formulae.*

The notation used here is designed to run in parallel with that for
pivotal-assumption consequence. Gates become snakes, i.e. $\vdash_K$ becomes
$\mathop{\mid\sim}_K$ and likewise Cn_K becomes C_K. Note again that there is not a unique
default-assumption consequence relation, but many — one for each value of
K.

Example 2.5 *To illustrate the definition, consider the following example,
which may be called the 'Möbius strip'. Put $K = \{p \rightarrow q, q \rightarrow r, r \rightarrow \neg p\}$,
let the premiss set $A = \{p\}$. Then clearly K is inconsistent with A,
so if we were looking at pivotal-assumption consequence we would have
$Cn_K(A) = L$. But for default-assumption consequence we need to find the
maximal subsets $K' \subseteq K$ that are consistent with A.*

- *A little checking shows that these are the three two-element subsets of
  K, namely $K_1 = \{p \rightarrow q, q \rightarrow r\}, K_2 = \{p \rightarrow q, r \rightarrow \neg p\}, K_3 = \{q \rightarrow
  r, r \rightarrow \neg p\}$. So a formula x is a default-assumption consequence
  of A modulo the background assumptions K, i.e. $x \in C_K(A)$, iff
  $x \in Cn(K_i \cup \{p\})$ for $i = 1, 2, 3$.*

- *A bit more checking shows that $Cn(K_1 \cup \{p\}) = Cn(\{p, q, r\})$, while $Cn(K_2 \cup \{p\}) = Cn(\{p, q, \neg r\})$, and $Cn(K_3 \cup \{p\}) = Cn(\{p, \neg q, \neg r\})$. So $x \in C_K(A)$ iff x is in all three of these sets, i.e. iff x is a classical consequence of the disjunction $(p \wedge q \wedge r) \vee (p \wedge q \wedge \neg r) \vee (p \wedge \neg q \wedge \neg r)$.*

- *A final calculation shows that this disjunction is classically equivalent to $(p \wedge q) \vee (p \wedge \neg r)$, i.e. to $p \wedge (q \vee \neg r)$; so finally $C_K(A)$ is just $Cn(p \wedge (q \vee \neg r))$.*

- *Thus, neither q nor r is in $C_K(A)$. On the other hand, $C_K(A)$ is larger than classical consequence $Cn(A) = Cn(p)$, as it also contains $(q \vee \neg r)$.*

Unlike their pivotal counterparts, default-assumption consequence operations/relations are nonmonotonic. That is, we may have $A \mathrel{\vert\!\sim}_K x$ but not $A \cup B \mathrel{\vert\!\sim}_K x$ where A, B are sets of propositions. Likewise, we may have $a \mathrel{\vert\!\sim}_K x$ without $a \wedge b \mathrel{\vert\!\sim}_K x$ where a, b are individual propositions. Since monotony can fail, default-assumption consequence operations are not in general closure operations.

To illustrate the failure of monotony, let $K = \{p \to q, q \to r\}$ where p, q, r are distinct elementary letters of the language and $\to$ is the truth-functional (alias material) conditional connective. Then $p \mathrel{\vert\!\sim}_K r$ since the premiss p is consistent with the whole of K and clearly $\{p\} \cup K \vdash r$. But $\{p, \neg q\} \not\mathrel{\vert\!\sim}_K r$, for the premiss set $\{p, \neg q\}$ is no longer consistent with the whole of K. There is a unique maximal subset $K' \subseteq K$ that is consistent with $\{p, \neg q\}$, namely the singleton $K' = \{q \to r\}$; and clearly $\{p, \neg q\} \cup K' \nvdash r$ — witness the valuation v with $v(p) = 1$ and $v(q) = v(r) = 0$. In general terms, by passing from premiss p to premisses p, q we *gained a premiss*, but because of the consistency requirement we *lost a background assumption*.

Evidently, the same example with $p \wedge \neg q$ in place of $\{p, \neg q\}$ for the enlarged premiss set illustrates the failure of singleton conjunctive monotony.

On the positive side, however, default-assumption consequence relations are supraclassical, as is immediate from the definition. They also satisfy cumulative transitivity and disjunction in the premisses, although these take a bit more effort to verify.

There is a further important property of default-assumption consequence relations. Although they may fail monotony, they always satisfy a weakened version of it called *cautious monotony* (CM). This is a weakened or restricted form of monotony; it is implied by monotony but not conversely. In a singleton form, cautious monotony says: whenever $A \mathrel{\vert\!\sim}_K x$ and $A \mathrel{\vert\!\sim}_K y$ then $A \cup \{x\} \mathrel{\vert\!\sim}_K y$. More generally: whenever $A \mathrel{\vert\!\sim}_K x$ for all $x \in B$ and $A \mathrel{\vert\!\sim}_K y$ then $A \cup B \mathrel{\vert\!\sim}_K y$. In the succinct notation of operations: whenever $A \subseteq B \subseteq C_K(A)$ then $C_K(A) \subseteq C_K(B)$.

On the other hand, default-assumption consequence can fail compactness in quite a radical way. We illustrate this with an example of David Gabelaia (personal communication). Put $K = K_1 \cup K_2$ where $K_1 = \{p_i \wedge q : i < \omega\}$ and $K_2 = \{\neg p_i \wedge \neg q : i < \omega\}$. Put $A = \{p_i : i < \omega\}$. Then on the one hand $A \mathrel{|\!\!\sim}_K q$, while on the other hand $B \mathrel{|\!\!\not\sim}_K q$ when B is any proper subset of A (finite or infinite) as we now verify. To follow the details, it may help to draw a table in three columns for K_1, K_2, A and consider the case that $B = A - \{p_1\}$.

- The positive side $A \mathrel{|\!\!\sim}_K q$ holds because $K_1 \cup A \vdash q$ and K_1 is clearly the unique maximal A-consistent subset of K.

- The negative side $B \mathrel{|\!\!\not\sim}_K q$ can be checked as follows. Consider the set $K^* = \{\neg p_n \wedge \neg q : p_n \notin B\}$. Since $B \subset A$ there is an n with $p_n \notin B$ and so $\neg p_n \wedge \neg q \in K^*$. Also K^* is consistent with B and indeed $K^* \cup B \nvdash q$ — witness the valuation v with $v(p_n) = 1$ iff $p_n \in B$ and $v(q) = 0$. It remains only to check that in fact, K^* is a maximal B-consistent subset of K. Suppose $K^* \subset J \subseteq K$. Then there is some i with either $p_i \wedge q \in J$, or $\neg p_i \wedge \neg q \in J$ and $p_i \in B$. In the former case, since J also contains some $\neg p_n \wedge \neg q$ it is inconsistent (look at q) and so inconsistent with B. And in the latter case, J is again inconsistent with B (look at p_i).

The failure here is radical in that there is no proper subset B of A, whether finite or infinite, with $B \mathrel{|\!\!\not\sim}_K q$. In other words, default-assumption consequence also fails the following weakened form of compactness, which we might call the *redundancy property*: whenever $A \mathrel{|\!\!\sim} x$ and A is infinite, then there is a proper subset $B \subset A$ such that $B \mathrel{|\!\!\sim} x$.

On a more general level, we note some interesting relations between classical logic, pivotal-assumption consequence, and default-assumption consequence.

- We constructed default-assumption consequences C_K by adding a consistency constraint to the definition of the monotonic pivotal-assumption consequences Cn_K. These in turn were obtained by adding a set of background assumptions to the definition of classical consequence. The *order of construction*, or conceptual order, is thus: Cn, then Cn_K, then C_K. The monotonic supraclassical notion can thus be seen as a natural halfway house or stepping-stone between the classical and nonmonotonic ones.

- However, this order of construction is not the same as the *order of inclusion* between the three operations. We have $Cn \leq C_K \leq Cn_K$, for the simple reason that by the monotony of classical consequence, $Cn(A) \subseteq Cn(K' \cup A) \subseteq Cn(K \cup A)$ whenever $K' \subseteq K$. In other words, as João Marcos has expressed it (personal communication), we can think of classical consequence Cn as giving a lower bound on all of our operations C_K, and for each choice of K the pivotal-assumption consequence Cn_K gives an upper bound on C_K. In other words, the non-monotonic default-assumption consequence operation C_K is interpolated between classical and pivotal-assumption consequence. We will find this pattern of contrast between order of construction and order of inclusion repeated when we come to other ways of generating nonmonotonic inference operations.

- In the case that the current premiss set A is consistent with the set K of background assumptions, the definitions clearly tell us that $C_K(A) = Cn_K(A) = Cn(K \cup A)$, i.e. the two supraclassical operations get the same value for argument A. From the point of view of pivotal-assumption consequence this case is the principal one. But from the point of view of default-assumption consequence it is a limiting case, for all the interest of the default operation arises when A is inconsistent with K.

A Dilemma

Despite its naturalness, the notion of default-assumption consequence faces a pragmatic dilemma. The dilemma arises when we ask the question: what kinds of assumption set K may usefully be used in generating operations?

- On the one hand, when K is *not* closed under classical consequence, i.e. when $K \neq Cn(K)$, then the identity of $C_K(A)$ can be sensitive to the manner of formulation of the elements of K; in other words, it is syntax-dependent.

- On the other hand, when K *is* closed under classical consequence, i.e. when $K = Cn(K)$, then the operation $C_K(A)$ becomes devoid of interest, because in its principal case it collapses back into classical consequence.

We state these results more formally, prove them, and discuss their significance. First, the situation when it is allowed that $K \neq Cn(K)$.

Observation 2.6 Classically equivalent background assumption sets K, K' can give rise to quite different consequence operations C_K and $C_{K'}$.

Proof. We give a simple example. Put $K = \{p \to (q \wedge r), r \to \neg p\}$ where $\to$ is material implication, while $K' = \{p \to q, \ p \to r, \ r \to \neg p\}$. These are classically equivalent, indeed quite trivially so, by the properties of conjunction. Now put $A = \{p\}$. Then A is inconsistent with K, and the subsets of K maximally consistent with A are its two singletons $\{p \to (q \wedge r)\}$ and $\{r \to \neg p\}$. Clearly $q \notin Cn(p, r \to \neg p)$ so $q \notin C_K(A)$. In contrast, the subsets of K' maximally consistent with p are its two pairs $\{p \to q, p \to r\}$ and $\{p \to q, r \to \neg p\}$. The remaining pair $\{p \to r, r \to \neg p\}$ is evidently inconsistent with p. Thus $q \in Cn(K' \cup \{p\})$ for both of these values of K' and so $q \in C_{K'}(A)$.

Roughly speaking, q gets lost when we process K but not when we process the trivially equivalent set K', because K is more 'chunky' than K' and so forces us to discard more to ensure consistency with the current premises. Such syntax-dependence is often regarded as counter-intuitive and undesirable: surely the consequences of A given a background set K of assumptions should depend only on the content of K, not on the way in which it is formulated.

We now consider the other horn of the dilemma: the situation when K is closed under classical consequence, i.e. when $K = Cn(K)$. The unpleasant outcome may be stated as follows. Here, as always, 'consistency' means classical consistency. ∎

Theorem 2.7 *When* $K = Cn(K)$, *then* $C_K(A) = Cn(A)$ *whenever* A *is inconsistent with* K.

Of course, as already noted, when A is consistent with K, then we have $C_K(A) = Cn(K \cup A)$ whether or not K is closed under classical consequence. There is nothing untoward about that. The theorem considers the principal case, that A is inconsistent with K, and states that if K is closed under classical consequence then the nonmonotonic operation loses almost all of its power. The background assumption set K ceases to contribute anything, and we get nothing more than the classical consequences of A.

Proof. Suppose $K = Cn(K)$ and A is inconsistent with K. We want to show that $C_K(A) = Cn(A)$. The right-in-left inclusion is just supraclassicality, so we need only show that $C_K(A) \subseteq Cn(A)$. Suppose $x \notin Cn(A)$; we need to show $x \notin C_K(A)$. By the definition of C_K it suffices to find a maximal A-consistent subset K' of K such that $x \notin Cn(K' \cup A)$.

The argument uses the compactness of classical consequence and Zorn's Lemma to construct the maximal set. The key step is where we appeal to the hypothesis that $K = Cn(K)$ towards the end. Our presentation hops back and forth as convenient between operational and relational notations.

From the supposition of the case we know by compactness that there is a finite subset $A_0 \subseteq A$ that is inconsistent with K. Let a be the conjunction of all its finitely many elements. Then a is also inconsistent with K. To complete the proof we find a maximal A-consistent subset K' of K such that $\neg a \vee \neg x \in K'$. This will suffice, because given $\neg a \vee \neg x \in K'$ we have $K' \cup A \vdash a \wedge (\neg a \vee \neg x) \vdash \neg x$ so since $K' \cup A$ is consistent we have $x \notin Cn(K' \cup A)$ as was desired.

To find such a K', first note that $\neg a \vee \neg x$ is consistent with A; for otherwise $A \vdash \neg(\neg a \vee \neg x) \vdash a \wedge x \vdash x$ contrary to the hypothesis $x \notin Cn(A)$. Next we note that $\neg a \vee \neg x \in K$; for we know that a is inconsistent with K, so $K \vdash \neg a \vdash \neg a \vee \neg x$, and thus by the crucial hypothesis that $K = Cn(K)$ we have $\neg a \vee \neg x \in K$. Putting these two points together, we have established that the singleton subset $\{\neg a \vee \neg x\}$ of K is consistent with A. Since classical consequence is compact, we may now apply Zorn's Lemma to conclude that there is a maximal A-consistent subset K' of K such that $\{\neg a \vee \neg x\} \subseteq K'$, which is what we needed to show.   ■

Responses to the Dilemma

What are we to make of the dilemma? Is default-assumption consequence irrevocably flawed, or is there a way out?

Consider first the case that K is not closed under classical consequence. One reaction is to say that in this case the syntactical form of the assumptions in K *should indeed* have an impact on the conclusions that can be drawn, even though the syntactical form of the explicit premises in A should not have any such influence. This is a brave response, but rather difficult to swallow.

Another reaction is to reduce the amount of syntactic dependence by allowing as elements of the background assumption set only formulae that are expressed in a certain canonical way. For example, we might accept in K only formulae that are disjunctions of *literals*, i.e. disjunctions of elementary letters and their negations. In general, a single formula (e.g. $p \wedge q$) will be expressed by a set containing several such disjunctions (e.g. $p \vee q$, $p \vee \neg q$, $\neg p \vee q$), which makes it less 'chunky'. From classical logic we know that every formula may be expressed by a set of such disjunctions (remember conjunctive normal forms, and separate the conjunctions into separate items); so this restriction does not reduce expressive power. This regimentation will have the effect of reducing the level of syntax-dependence. Indeed, in the case of a finitely generated language, if one accepts in K

only disjunctions that use all the elementary letters of the language then the problem of syntax-dependence disappears. For if K, J are classically equivalent sets, all of whose elements are of this canonical form, then $K = J$ and so $C_K(A) = C_J(A)$.

In the case that $K = Cn(K)$, a quite different kind of response is needed. We need to modify the definition of default-assumption consequence in such a way as to avoid the collapse into classical consequence. There are many ways in which this can be done, and they will be the focus of the following section. Before leaving this section, however, we make some general remarks on terminology and on the notion of maximality.

Terminology: Consequence or Inference?

We are using the term 'consequence operation' to cover monotonic operations like Cn and Cn_K and also nonmonotonic ones like C_K. In this, we are following the usage of many investigators, including Kraus, Lehmann and Magidor (1990). But we are running against others, including Lindström (1991), Makinson (1994), Rott (2001) and Bochman (2001). They reserve the term 'consequence' operation' for the monotonic ones and speak of 'inference' operations for the nonmonotonic ones.

Such a terminological separation between 'consequence' and 'inference' is attractive in principle. But in practice it turns out to be rather cumbersome. This is partly because the verbal contrast is not rooted in ordinary usage, and partly because we sometimes wish to talk about the operations generated in a certain manner *before* finding out whether they are monotonic, or about families of operations *some* of which are monotonic and others not. In this presentation, therefore, we will use the term 'consequence' for *both the monotonic and nonmonotonic cases*. Nevertheless, as already remarked, we mark the difference in our notation by using $\vdash, Cn$ (with appropriate subscripts) in the monotonic case and $\vdash\!\!\!\sim, C$ when they are not known to be monotonic.

A Warning about Maxtalk

For those who are not accustomed to working mathematically with the notion of maximality, a word of warning may be useful. To say of a subset K' of K that it is maximally (such-and-such) and is also so-and-so is not at all the same thing as saying that it is maximally (such-and-such and so-and-so). The two must be distinguished carefully.

The former does imply the latter. For suppose K' is maximally a φ, and is also a ψ. Consider any $K'' \supseteq K'$ that is both a φ and a ψ. Then it will be a φ, so by the supposition it will be identical with K'.

But the latter does not in general imply the former. For suppose K' is maximally φ-and-ψ. Then there is no $K'' \supset K'$ that is *both* a φ *and* a ψ, but there may well be a $K'' \supset K'$ that is a φ without being a ψ; so that K' is not maximally a φ.

The point could be made in more set-theoretical language, writing $max_\subseteq(X)$ for the set of all items that are maximal, under the relation of set inclusion, among the elements of X, but the point should be clear enough without such formality. The important thing is to know what one intends to say in any context, and to express it unambiguously. This can require careful phrasing; some bracketing or hyphening can also help.

To illustrate the difference, suppose that K' is maximal among the proper subsets of K, and is consistent with A. This implies that it is maximal among the proper subsets of K that are consistent with A. But it is easy to construct an example where K' is maximal among the proper subsets of K that are consistent with A, but is not maximal among the proper subsets of K. For instance, put $K = \{a, b, (a \vee b) \to c\}$ and $A = \{\neg c\}$. Then K has two maximal (proper subsets consistent with A), namely $K_1 = \{a, b\}$ and $K_2 = \{(a \vee b) \to c\}$. Of these, K_1 is indeed a maximal (proper subset of K), but K_2 is not.

Nevertheless, in the case that $K = Cn(K)$ we have a special situation. Let A be a premiss-set inconsistent with K. It is easy to verify that since K is closed under classical consequence, so too is each maximal A-consistent subset of K. And we have the following important fact, closely related to Theorem 2.7 and also to Theorem 2.9 in the next section. Roughly speaking, it says that examples like that of the preceding paragraph are impossible when $K = Cn(K)$.

Observation 2.8 *Suppose $K = Cn(K)$ and let A be a set of formulae that is inconsistent with K. Then the following three conditions are equivalent, for any $K' \subseteq K$:*

    a. *K' is maximal among the subsets of K that are consistent with A.*

    b. *K' is maximal among the classically closed proper subsets of K that are consistent with A.*

    c. *K' is maximal among the classically closed proper subsets of K, and also K' is consistent with A.*

Historical Remarks

Default-assumption consequence has a rather long and complicated history. Veltman (1976; 1985) and Kratzer (1981) used closely related constructions in the logic of counterfactual conditionals. Alchourrón and Makinson (1982) defined the operation in a study of the revision of a belief set K by a new belief a, i.e. the introduction of new information into a belief set while preserving its consistency. The collapse into classical consequence when $K = Cn(K)$ was noted (in various forms, for singleton premiss sets), by all these authors. The family of all subsets of K maximally consistent with A was also studied by Poole (1988), but as part of a formal account of *abduction*, i.e. the formation of hypotheses to explain data.

Exercises

1*. Let $K = \{p \to q, q \to p, p \vee q\}$ and let $A = \{\neg p \vee \neg q\}$ where p, q are elementary letters. What are the maximal subsets of K consistent with A? Now let $K = \{p \leftrightarrow q, p \vee q\}$, let A be as before, and answer the same question.

2. Let $K_1 = \{p, q\}$, $K_2 = \{p \wedge q\}$, $K_3 = \{p \wedge q, p, q\}$, $K_4 = \{p \wedge q, p, q, p \vee q\}$. Let $A = \{\neg p\}$. For each K_i, what are the maximal subsets of K_i consistent with A?

3*. Consider the Boolean language generated by just two elementary letters p, q. Let $K = Cn(p, q)$ and let $A = \{\neg p\}$. What are the maximal subsets of K consistent with A?
   Hint: First enumerate all the elements (up to classical equivalence) of $Cn(p, q)$.

4. Show that default-assumption consequence relations are supraclassical, satisfy left classical equivalence (LCE) and right weakening (RW).

5. Show that notwithstanding the syntax-dependence of default-assumption consequence noted in the text, we have least the following degree of syntax-freedom. Let K, K' be background assumption sets with a one-one correspondence between them such that $Cn(a) = Cn(a')$ for all $a \in K$, where we write a' for the element of K' corresponding to a in K. Then for any premiss set $A, C_K(A) = C_{K'}(A)$.

6*. When a consequence operation satisfies both cumulative transitivity and cautious monotony it is said to be *cumulative*. Write out a single Horn principle, in both relational and operational notation, to express this condition.

7*. Verify the claim made in the text, that when $K = Cn(K)$ and A is inconsistent with K, then $K' = Cn(K')$ for every maximal A-consistent subset of K.

8. Show that compactness implies the redundancy property.

9. Check out the following counterexample to compactness for default-assumption consequence, devised (for a slightly different purpose) by A. Brodsky and R. Brofman as reported in Freund and Lehmann (1994). Put $K = \{\neg p_1 \wedge \ldots \wedge \neg p_{i-1} \wedge p_i : 1 \leq i \leq \omega\}$ and put $A = \{p_i \rightarrow q : i < \omega\}$.

Problems

1. Verify the claims made in the text that default-assumption consequence relations satisfy the following conditions: cumulative transitivity (CT), cautious monotony (CM), disjunction in the premises.

2*. Prove Observation 2.8.
   Hint: Cycle around the three conditions. The implications from (a) to (b), and from (c) to (a), are both straightforward, so begin with them. For the implication from (b) to (c) you will need to apply classical compactness. It is essential to be clear, at each step, what you are assuming and what you are trying to show.

3. Show that default-assumption consequence relations satisfy *consistency preservation*: whenever $Cn(A) \neq L$ then $C_K(A) \neq L$.
   Hint: Make use of the compactness of classical logic, say in the form of the general maximalizability principle given in section 1.2.

4. Give an example of a closure operation that shows that the redundancy property does not in general imply compactness.
   Hint: Forget about logic and find an abstract example.

2.3   Specializations, Variants and Generalizations

We open this section by describing a special case of the concept of default-assumption consequence that is of both historical and practical importance: the *closed world assumption* (CWA). We will then sketch some of the many variations and generalizations that may be found in the literature — about a dozen in total, depending on how you count them — beginning with those that most closely resemble our simple paradigm in the preceding section and then passing on to others more distantly related.

A Special Case: The Closed World Assumption

Default-assumption consequence as we have defined it in the preceding section, is an abstraction upon a much more specific notion, known as *inference using the closed world assumption* (briefly, CWA), introduced by Reiter (1978) — one of the earliest formal studies of nonmonotonic reasoning in a qualitative context.

To explain this kind of inference, we need the notion of a Horn formula of the language of classical logic. In section 1.2 we already introduced the notion of a Horn rule, as a special kind of rule formulated in the metalanguage in which we talk about inference relations. Now we need the corresponding concept for formulae in the object language, to describe a special class of Boolean formulae. A *Horn formula* is simply one of the form $(p_1 \wedge \ldots \wedge p_n) \to q$, where $p_1, \ldots p_n, q$ are all elementary letters and $n \geq 0$. Equivalently, using only the primitive connectives $\neg, \wedge, \vee$: it is a formula of the kind $\neg p_1 \vee \ldots \vee \neg p_n \vee q$, with the same ingredients. That is, a disjunction of literals, of which just one is positive.

Suppose that our current premiss set A consists solely of Horn formulae. Suppose also that our set K of background assumptions consists of the negations $\neg p$ of all the elementary letters of the language. In other words we wish to assume, as far as is compatible with our current premisses, that all elementary letters are false. The set K is evidently not closed under classical consequence, but the problem of syntax-dependence discussed in the preceding section does not arise as only this one choice of K is allowed: it is held fixed in all applications.

In this special case it is not difficult to show that there is a *unique* maximal subset K' of K consistent with A. Consequently the definition of default-assumption consequence, which was $C_K(A) = \cap \{Cn(K' \cup A) : K' \subseteq K$ and K' maxiconsistent with $A\}$, may be simplified to $C_K(A) = Cn(K' \cup A)$ where K' is the unique maximal subset of K consistent with A.

Exactly the same situation holds if, instead of elementary letters p_i, our language uses elementary formulae of the form $P\underline{t}$, where P is a predicate or relation symbol and $\underline{t} = t_1, \ldots, t_n$ is an n-tuple of individual names, with the remaining formulae of the language generated from them by Boolean operations only (no individual variables, no quantifiers). Suppose that K consists solely of the negations $\neg P\underline{t}$ of all elementary formulae, and our premiss set A consists only of formulae of the form $(P_1\underline{t_1} \wedge \ldots \wedge P_n\underline{t_n}) \to Q\underline{s}$, where $P_1\underline{t_1}, \ldots, P_n\underline{t_n}, Q\underline{s}$ are all elementary formulae. Then again the definition of default-assumption consequence simplifies to $C_K(A) = Cn(K' \cup A)$ where K' is the unique maximal subset of K consistent with A.

The motivation for this construction arises from the fact that we may be dealing with a database about a certain domain. The database may reasonably be thought of a set A of Horn formulae $(P_1 \underline{t}_1 \wedge \ldots \wedge P_n \underline{t}_n) \to Q\underline{s}$ (with $n \geq 0$) where the individual constants in the tuples $\underline{t}_1, \ldots, \underline{t}_n, \underline{s}$ designate specific elements of the domain and the symbols $P_1, \ldots, P_n, Q$ designate specific predicates and relations over that domain. Closed world inference amounts to assuming, within the limits of consistency with the database, that the predicates and relations $P_1, \ldots, P_n, Q$ are *as small as possible*.

In section 3.4 we will see how this particular kind of default-assumption consequence may also be formulated in semantic terms, and generalized to become a form of inference known as circumscription.

Variations and Generalizations: Three Broad Kinds

There are many variations and generalizations of default-assumption consequence. In all of them the notion of consistency continues to play an important and usually quite visible role. To bring some order into the affair, we may conveniently sort them into three main groups:

1. The *partial meet operations*, which intersect the output of only *some* of the maximal subsets of K consistent with the current premises.

2. The *submaximal operations*, which intersect subsets of K that are consistent with the current premises, but *not necessarily maximal*.

3. The *intersection-free operations*, which specify a unique output without the need for any kind of intersection.

They all have the advantage, over the simple paradigm presented in the preceding section, of allowing the set K of background assumptions to be closed under classical consequence without thereby collapsing the nonmonotonic operation into the classical one in the manner described in Theorem 2.7. We illustrate each of these kinds with examples from the literature.

Partial Meet Approaches

These approaches continue to work with maximal subsets of the background assumption set K that are consistent with the current premiss set A, but restrict attention to only some of them. In other words, they put $C(A)$ to be the intersection of sets $Cn(K' \cup A)$ for certain $K' \subseteq K$ that are maxiconsistent with A, but they differ in how they pick them out.

We will consider four of them, in roughly increasing order of generality. They are: *screened consequence* (treating some elements of K as inviolable); *layered consequence* (treating some elements of K as preferred to others); *relational partial meet consequence* (taking some A-maxiconsistent subsets of K as preferable to others); and consequence via *selection functions* (the most general form covering, as special cases, the other three as well as the paradigm default-assumption consequence defined in the preceding section).

Screened Consequence

We might wish to regard some of our background assumptions as unquestionable, no matter what premises come along. To express this in mathematical terms, we fix our set K of background assumptions, and also fix a distinguished subset $K_0 \subseteq K$ of *fully protected* assumptions. We then define an operation $C_{KK_0}(A)$ of *screened consequence* by the equation $C_{KK_0}(A) = \cap \{Cn(K' \cup A) : K_0 \subseteq K' \subseteq K$ and K' maxiconsistent with $A\}$. In this way, the protected assumptions in K_0 are maintained in the face of anything, while the remainder may be dropped when contradiction so requires.

This kind of operation was introduced by Makinson (1997) in the context of the logic of belief contraction and revision. In that context, it also carried an additional twist for the limiting case that the set K_0 of protected background assumptions is inconsistent with the current premiss set A. Clearly, in that case there are *no* maximal sets including K_0 consistent with A, so *every* formula in the language becomes a consequence of A under the definition above. This makes good sense when we are thinking of inference; but less so for revision, where we might refuse to revise a belief set K when the incoming information is in conflict with its protected core. For this reason, in the belief revision context of Makinson (1997), the output in the limiting case was taken to be just K itself.

We note that the inclusion sequence $Cn \leq C_K \leq Cn_K$ that was observed for default-assumption consequence becomes for screened consequence $Cn \leq Cn_{K_0} \leq C_{KK_0} \leq Cn_K$. In other words, the pivotal-assumption operation Cn_K continues to serve as upper bound for the nonmonotonic screened consequence operation, while the lower bound moves up from classical Cn to the pivotal-assumption operation Cn_{K_0}.

As the lower bound is no longer classical Cn, we no longer get the collapsing phenomenon that we noted in the previous section in the case that $K = Cn(K)$ and is inconsistent with the current premiss set A. But we do get a 'lesser collapse'. Under those two hypotheses, we have $C_{KK_0}(A) = Cn_{K_0}(A)$, which is nearly as bad: the only conclusions that may be drawn are those that follow from the current premisses taken together with the inviolable background assumptions. The proof is a straightforward re-run of the proof of Theorem 2.7. Thus we may say that this construction, without further refinements, is still not suitable for application to background assumption sets closed under classical consequence.

Layered Consequence

Another idea is to segment the set K of background assumptions into levels, $K_1, \ldots, K_n$, and then maximize in a stepwise manner, giving early levels preference over later ones. In other words, given a premiss set A we first take the maximal subsets of K_1 consistent with A, then extend each of them into a maximal subset of $K_1 \cup K_2$ consistent with A, and so on.

Formally, a *preferred subset of* K with respect to A (modulo the layering) is a set $J_1 \cup \ldots \cup J_n \subseteq K$ such that for each $i \leq n$, $J_1 \cup \ldots \cup J_i$ is a maximal A-consistent subset of $K_1 \cup \ldots \cup K_i$. Clearly, every preferred subset of K is in fact a maximal A-consistent subset of K, but not conversely. We are thus restricting attention to a subfamily of the latter.

This construction was introduced by Brewka (1989), where it was described as 'consequence via level default theories'. A variant, in which maximal cardinality replaces maximality under the subset relation, was introduced by Benferhat *et al.* (1993).

This approach is designed for background assumption sets K that are not closed under classical consequence. When they are so closed, and the levels K_i are also closed under Cn, then we have a kind of 'mini-collapse'. For in that case, when K is inconsistent with the current premiss set A, the conclusions obtainable will be just the classical consequences of A taken together with the highest K_i with which A is consistent (or with the empty set if none of them are). The proof is again essentially the same as that for Theorem 2.7.

Relational Partial Meet Consequence

An alternative procedure for selecting a subfamily of the maximal A-consistent subsets of K is to fix a relation $<$ between subsets K' of K, and pick out from the maximal A-consistent subsets of K those that are minimal under that relation. Placing constraints (such as rankedness) on the relation $<$ can give rise to greater regularity of behaviour in the induced consequence relation.

When applied to sets closed under classical consequence, this approach avoids the collapse phenomenon of the 'full meet' construction of the previous section and its lesser forms noted above for screened and layered sequence.

The construction is essentially the same as one effected in the AGM account of belief change, as developed by Alchourrón, Gärdenfors and Makinson (1985), and there called 'relational partial meet contraction and revision'. It is also closely related to a semantic approach to nonmonotonic reasoning called preferential inference, which we examine in detail in the next chapter.

Consequence via Selection Functions

A more general procedure is to use a *selection function*. This associates with each family $\mathcal{K}$ of subsets of K a subfamily $\delta(\mathcal{K}) \subseteq \mathcal{K}$ of 'distinguished' elements of $\mathcal{K}$. The selection function may be taken as arbitrary, or it may be constrained in various ways. It is usually required that $\delta(\mathcal{K})$ is non-empty whenever $\mathcal{K}$ is non-empty.

Using this concept, we define $C_\delta(A) = \cap \{Cn(K' \cup A) : K' \in \delta(\mathcal{K}_A)\}$, where $\mathcal{K}_A$ is the family of all subsets $K' \subseteq K$ maxiconsistent with A, and δ is a selection function. Like K, δ is fixed independently of the premiss sets A. Evidently, we get different consequence operations for different choices of δ, as well as for different choices of K.

In the limiting case that the selection function makes no real choice, always putting $\delta(\mathcal{K}_A) = \mathcal{K}_A$ (in other words, when it is the identity function) we are back with the basic notion of default-assumption consequence defined in the previous section. We have seen how this leads to counterintuitive results in the case that K is already closed under classical consequence, i.e. $K = Cn(K)$.

At the opposite end of the spectrum is another limiting case, where the selection function always gives us a singleton, i.e. $\delta(\mathcal{K}_A) = \{K'\}$ for some $K' \in \mathcal{K}_A$ whenever the latter is non-empty. Such a selection function is usually called a *choice function*, and the consequence operation $C_\delta(A)$ that it engenders is called a *maxichoice* default assumption consequence. In this case, for every premiss set A inconsistent with K, there is a subset $K' \subseteq K$ maxiconsistent with A such that $C_\delta(A) = Cn(K' \cup A)$.

This limiting case also leads to a counterintuitive result for background assumption sets K closed under classical consequence. When $K = Cn(K)$, the maxichoice consequence operations always give consequence-sets that are *complete*, in the sense that they contain at least one of $x, \neg x$ for every formula x of the language. This is a strange and undesirable inflation. The result was first proven by Alchourrón and Makinson (1982) in the context of the logic of belief change.

Theorem 2.9 *Let* $K = Cn(K)$ *and let* A *be a premiss set inconsistent with* K. *Then for any maximal* A-*consistent subset* K' *of* $K, Cn(K' \cup A)$ *is complete.*

Proof. Let $K = Cn(K)$ and let A be any premiss set inconsistent with K. Let K' be any maximal A-consistent subset of K. Let x be any formula. We want to show that either $x \in Cn(K' \cup A)$ or $\neg x \in Cn(K' \cup A)$. The argument has some elements in common with that for Theorem 2.7.

Since A is inconsistent with K, the compactness of classical logic tells us that there is a finite subset $A_0 \subseteq A$ that is inconsistent with K. Let a be the conjunction of the finitely many elements of A_0. Then $a \in Cn(A)$. To complete the proof it will suffice to show that either $\neg a \vee x \in K'$ or $\neg a \vee \neg x \in K'$, for then $K' \cup A \vdash a \wedge (\neg a \vee x) \vdash x$ or $K' \cup A \vdash a \wedge (\neg a \vee \neg x) \vdash \neg x$.

Suppose for *reductio ad absurdum* that both $\neg a \vee x \notin K'$ and $\neg a \vee \neg x \notin K'$. Since A_0 is inconsistent with K we know that a is also inconsistent with K, so $\neg a \in Cn(K)$, so both of $\neg a \vee x$, $\neg a \vee \neg x \in Cn(K) = K$ using the (crucial) supposition that K is closed under classical consequence. On the other hand, by supposition K' is maximal among the subsets of K consistent with A. So $K' \cup \{\neg a \vee x\}$ and $K' \cup \{\neg a \vee \neg x\}$ are both inconsistent with A. By the monotony of classical consequence it follows that $K' \cup \{x\}$ and $K' \cup \{\neg x\}$ are both inconsistent with A. In turn it follows that K' is inconsistent with A, giving us the desired contradiction. ∎

The moral of this story is that when our background assumption sets are closed under classical consequence, the selection function should not be extremal. We get one undesirable result when the selection function is just the identity function: this takes us back to the basic form of default assumption consequence — which as we saw in Theorem 2.7 collapses into classical logic in the case that $K = Cn(K)$. We get another undesirable result when we select a single maximal subset: this inflates the size of consequence sets, making them complete. The selection functions will have to be somewhere in the middle between these extremes, Goldilocks style.

The approach via selection functions is very general, and covers the three preceding ones as special cases. The connection with relational partial meet consequence has received particular attention. Given any well-founded relation $<$ between subsets of K, the function taking each family $\mathcal{K}$ of subsets of K to its $<$-minimal elements is clearly a selection function. Conversely, if sufficiently powerful constraints are imposed on a selection function δ, then it can be represented in this way, i.e. we can find a relation $<$ between subsets of K such that $\delta(\mathcal{K})$ consists of the minimal elements $K' \in \mathcal{K}$ under $<$. The relation thus uncovered is sometimes called a 'revealed preference', a term borrowed from the theory of choice between goods, in economics, where the interplay between preference relations and selection functions was first studied.

There is a systematic study of the relationships between constraints on selection functions and the possibility of representing them by preference relations, in Rott (1993; 2001).

Sub-maximal Approaches

All of the variants considered above worked with *maximal* premiss-consistent subsets of the background assumption set K. They differed only in which of those subsets they took into consideration. The following generalizations also allow us to take into account some of the less-than-maximal subsets of K.

Background Constraints

One idea, already considered by Poole (1988), is to add to the set K of background assumptions another set J of 'constraints'. In the best of circumstances, it is consistent with the explicit premisses of an inference. But it does not participate positively in the generation of conclusions. And when consistency fails, J is not diminished; in effect, it further reduces the background assumptions from K that may legitimately be used alongside A.

To be precise, the definition of default-assumption consequence is re-run as follows. Let $K, J \subseteq L$ be sets of formulae, which will play the role of background assumptions and constraints respectively. We define the relation $\vdash_{KJ}$ of *default-assumption consequence with constraints* by putting $A \vdash_{KJ} x$ iff $K' \cup A \vdash x$ for every subset $K' \subseteq K$ with K' maximal among the subsets of K that are consistent with $A \cup J$. Writing C_{KJ} for the corresponding operation, this says $C_{KJ}(A) = \cap\{Cn(K' \cup A) : K' \subseteq K$ and K' maxiconsistent with $A \cup J\}$.

If there are no such subsets K', this definition puts $C_{KJ}(A) = L$. Clearly, this happens when J itself is inconsistent with A, for then K' is inconsistent with $A \cup J$ even for $K' = \emptyset$. It is also possible to show the converse, using the compactness of classical consequence. Thus $C_{KJ}(A) = L$ iff J is inconsistent with A.

As one might expect, this kind of operation is rather less regularly behaved than the one without constraints. For example, it fails disjunction in the premisses. However, it does satisfy both cumulative transitivity and cautious monotony.

What, in this construction, is the difference between a background assumption and a constraint? Both are fixed independently of the premiss sets. But constraints are more 'protected' than background assumptions. In case of conflict with a premiss set, a background assumption may be withdrawn, but constraints are never dropped. Indeed, the presence of the constraints will tend to create inconsistencies where none existed between premisses and background assumptions alone, and so force the retraction of more background assumptions than would otherwise be the case. Constraints thus play a powerful negative role.

On the other hand, they have no positive role at all: they are never conjoined with the current premisses to obtain new conclusions. Thus the default consequence relation generated by a set of background assumptions plus a set of constraints is always weaker than (i.e. is a sub-relation of) the one determined by the background assumptions alone. If we give the constraints a positive as well as a negative role, by putting $C_{KJ}(A) = \cap\{Cn(K' \cup J \cup A) : K' \subseteq K$ and K' maxiconsistent with $A \cup J\}$, then the operation can be seen as just screened consequence, as defined above, with $K' \cup J$ now serving as the utilized subset of the background assumption set $K \cup J$, and J as the fully protected ones among them.

Maximally Informative Subsets

There is another way in which we might wish to relax the requirement of maximality. We might wish to consider not the *biggest* subsets, but the most *informative* subsets, of K that are consistent with the premisses. It is natural to assume that all of the maximally large subsets will also be maximally informative, but some among the non-maximal subsets may be just as informative as their maximal supersets. In this case, it is suggested, they should also be counted in the family scheduled for intersection, thus in turn diminishing the set obtained by that intersection.

Isaac Levi (1996) has argued for this approach, formulated in the context of belief revision but with an evident analogue for inference. Rott and Pagnucco (1999) have studied the formal properties of such consequence relations.

This construction may still be seen as considering the subsets of K that are maximally consistent with the current premisses, but with maximality now understood with respect to a relation $<$ of degree of informativeness rather than with respect to set inclusion.

When $<$ is a subrelation of $\subset$, then every $\subset$-maximal A-consistent subset of K is a $<$-maximal A-consistent subset of K, with the effect that in the case $K = Cn(K)$, intersection of all of the latter leads again to collapse into classical consequence. To avoid this, we would have to combine the idea with one of the partial meet approaches already considered, or else generalize by allowing the relation $<$ to be more loosely tied to set inclusion. Indeed, such a generalization would be appropriate if we reinterpret $<$ as representing the 'relative epistemic value' of subsets of K, calculated in some way that combines several competing factors, not all positively correlated with size. For example, it might balance size, informativeness, simplicity of formulation, simplicity of application, richness of connections, etc. Then, not all of the maximal subsets of K that are consistent with the premisses need be of maximal value, nor conversely.

Best Epistemic States

The 'ultimate' level of abstraction among partial meet approaches has been attained by Bochman (2001). Two ideas underlie his construction. One is to compare subsets of K by an *arbitrary* relation, abstracting entirely from set inclusion or relative epistemic value. The other is to allow some of the subsets of K to be omitted from consideration; in other words, as well as fixing K, we also fix some family $\mathcal{K} \subseteq 2^K$ of its subsets. We think of these as representing the range of all entertainable states of belief within the limits of K, and Bochman calls them *epistemic states*. We define $A \hspace{1pt}\vdash_\mathcal{K} x$ to hold iff $K' \cup A \vdash x$ for every epistemic state K' (i.e. element of $\mathcal{K}$) that is maximally A-consistent under the relation $<$.

Strictly speaking, Bochman does place some constraints on this construction. In particular, the elements K' of $\mathcal{K}$ are required to be closed under classical consequence, and the relation $<$ is required to be transitive and irreflexive. Moreover, for most purposes, a constraint like stoppering, alias smoothness (to be explained in section 3.2) is placed on $<$. But the definition remains very abstract. Bochman notes that once one fixes the family $\mathcal{K} \subseteq 2^K$ we have no more need for K itself, and may dispense with it.

We put the word 'ultimate' in inverted commas when introducing this approach, because in fact there is no such thing as a most general level of abstraction in these matters. For example, as Bochman (2001) notes, the consequence relations defined by Makinson (1989) are in some respects more abstract than his, but in other respects less so.

Approaches that do not need Intersection

All of the variants considered so far consider certain subsets K' of K that are consistent with the current premiss set A and, following the 'sceptical policy', intersect their respective outcomes $Cn(K' \cup A)$. We now consider certain approaches under which we can get a unique outcome without intersection.

Epistemic Chains

Suppose we take the very abstract construction of Bochman but, as in an Escher engraving, descend the stair of generalization in a new direction. Let us retain Bochman's idea of a family $\mathcal{K} \subseteq 2^K$ of subsets of K, but return to plain set-inclusion as the relation for comparing its elements. Thus $A \mathrel{\vrule height 1.2ex depth 0pt width 0.6pt\kern-0.6pt\sim}_{\mathcal{K}} x$ may be defined to hold iff $K' \cup A \vdash x$ for every epistemic state $K' \in \mathcal{K}$ that is consistent with A and maximally so among elements of $\mathcal{K}$.

This brings us closer to our paradigm notion of default-assumption consequence in section 2.2. The only difference is that we maximize over the $K' \in \mathcal{K}$, rather than over the $K' \subseteq K$. But this small change can have considerable effect. A maximally A-consistent subset K' of K may be absent from $\mathcal{K}$. Conversely, an A-consistent subset K' of K may be maximally so among elements of $\mathcal{K}$ without being maximally so among the entire collection of subsets of K, for there may be another K'' consistent with A with $K' \subset K'' \subseteq K$ but $K'' \notin \mathcal{K}$.

Now let us particularize further. Suppose that the set $\mathcal{K}$ of epistemic states contains the empty set as smallest element, and is *a chain under set inclusion* — that is, for all K', K'' in $\mathcal{K}$ either $K' \subseteq K''$ or $K'' \subseteq K'$. Suppose further that the language is finite. Since the language is finite, there are only finitely many non-equivalent formulae modulo classical equivalence. Without loss of generality, we may thus take $\mathcal{K}$ to be a set of formulae $k_1, ..., k_n$, linearly ordered by classical consequence, with the weakest one a tautology. These are called *epistemic chains*.

In this context, Bochman's definition of $A \mathrel{\vrule height 1.2ex depth 0pt width 0.6pt\kern-0.6pt\sim}_{\mathcal{K}} x$ reduces to the following: $A \mathrel{\vrule height 1.2ex depth 0pt width 0.6pt\kern-0.6pt\sim}_{\mathcal{K}} x$ iff either A is inconsistent, or else A is consistent and $\{k_i\} \cup A \vdash x$ where k_i is the strongest formula in $\mathcal{K}$ that is consistent with A. Equivalently, iff either A is inconsistent, or else A is consistent and $\{k_i\} \cup A \vdash x$ for *some* formula in $\mathcal{K}$ that is consistent with A.

This kind of consequence relation was introduced and studied intensively by Michael Freund (1998). As he has shown, the definition using epistemic chains is (in the finite case) the syntactic counterpart of a semantic one (namely ranked preferential consequence) that we will discuss in the following chapter.

It is interesting to compare this construction with the 'layered consequence' of Brewka described earlier in this section. They both make use of a collection $K_1, \ldots, K_n$ of subsets of K. Freund requires this to be a chain under set inclusion, whereas Brewka requires it to form a partition of K, i.e. a collection of disjoint non-empty substs whose union is K. However, on closer inspection it is apparent that this is largely a difference of presentation. More significant is the fact that Brewka looks for maximal A-consistent *subsets* of each K_i while Freund treats each K_i as *indivisible* and looks for the largest A-consistent one. When K is not closed under classical consequence, this difference typically changes the output. But when K and all the K_i are closed under classical Cn then, as we have seen, the K_i also become indivisible under the layered approach of Brewka, which in that case essentially reduces to Freund's epistemic chain system.

Safe Consequence

An interesting feature of Freund's construction is that it permits us to designate a special A-consistent subset of K without having to intersect maximals. The cost is that we must require the family of possible epistemic states to be linearly ordered under set inclusion. We now describe an approach that also obtains its output without intersection, but needs only an *acyclic* relation $<$ over K that is, one such that there are no propositions $a_1, ..., a_n$ in K with $a_1 < a_2 < ... < a_n < a_1$.

The essential idea is to keep only those elements of K that cannot reasonably be 'blamed' for the inconsistency of K with A. Suppose we are given a fixed relation $<$ over the set K of background assumptions representing some notion of degree of vulnerability, so that $k < k'$ means that k is more vulnerable than k'. Let A be the current premiss set. We say that a proposition $a \in K$ is *safe with respect to* A (modulo $<$) iff a is not a minimal element of any minimal subset K' of K that is inconsistent with A. Note carefully that there are *two dimensions of minimality* here. The first one is under the relation $<$ between elements of K, while the second one is under set-inclusion between subsets of K. It is not difficult to show that the set of all safe elements deserves its name:

Observation 2.10 *Let K be a set of background assumptions, and $<$ an acyclic relation over K. Let A be a consistent set of premisses. Then the set S_A of all safe elements of K with respect to A (modulo $<$) is consistent with A.*

Proof. The proof is a very elegant one, reminiscent of diagonal arguments in set theory. Suppose for *reductio ad absurdum* that A is consistent but S_A is inconsistent with A. Then by the compactness of classical consequence, there is a finite $S_1 \subseteq S_A$ that is inconsistent with A. Hence there is a minimal and finite $S_0 \subseteq S_1 \subseteq S_A$ that is inconsistent with A. Since A is consistent, S_0 is not empty. Since S_0 is non-empty and finite, and the relation $<$ is acyclic, there must be at least one $<$-minimal element s of S_0. Thus by the construction, s is a $<$-minimal element of a $\subseteq$-minimal A-inconsistent subset of K, and so by definition is not safe with respect to A. On the other hand, $s \in S_A$, and so by supposition it is safe with respect to A. This gives us a contradiction, completing the verification. ∎

The relation of *safe consequence* is then defined by putting $A \mid\!\!\sim x$ iff $A \cup S_A \vdash x$. This is evidently a kind of default-assumption consequence. From the set K of background assumptions it selects a special subset S_A of safe elements, whose identity depends in a motivated manner on the current premiss set A (as well as on a background acyclic relation $<$ over K). It then joins these special background assumptions to the premisses.

One attraction of safe consequence is that, like the others in this subsection, it does not require intersecting a family of output sets. A further attraction is the very weak requirement of acyclicity that is needed on the guiding relation $<$. Safe consequence has been studied in detail by Alchourrón and Makinson (1985; 1986), as a form of belief contraction and revision.

Comparative Expectation Inference

One may also elaborate the notion of background assumptions in a quite different way. Instead of representing them as a *set*, one may say that to be a background assumption is at heart *a matter of degree*. Any consistent proposition of the language may serve as an additional assumption, to a degree limited by its plausibility. Plausibility may be represented as a *relation* $<$ over all formulae of the language. Thus $z < y$ is read as saying that y is strictly more plausible (or: less unexpected) than z.

Given such a relation of plausibility, we can define an appropriate notion of consequence that allows sufficiently plausible propositions to be used as additional assumptions. One way of doing this, using a definition of Rott (1991), is to put $a \mid\!\!\sim_< x$ iff $x \in Cn(\{a\} \cup \{y : \neg a < y\}$. In words: $a \mid\!\!\sim_< x$ iff x is a classical consequence of premiss a supplemented by all those propositions that are strictly more plausible than $\neg a$. Thus, when the premiss is a, all propositions y with $\neg a < y$ are allowed to serve as background assumptions. This is called *comparative expectation inference*. If sufficient conditions are imposed on the relation $<$, it can be shown that the set $K_a = \{y : \neg a < y\}$ of all background assumptions (in the context of a) is classically consistent with a whenever a itself is consistent.

The construction has a number of attractions. One is that we do not need to intersect outputs. To the premiss a we simply add the *unique* set $K_a = \{y : \neg a < y\}$ and take the closure under classical consequence. Another gratifying feature is that the nonmonotonic inference relation $\mathop{\sim}\limits_{<}$ thus generated has very regular properties. It satisfies not only cumulative transitivity and cautious monotony but also a non-Horn condition of *rational monotony*: whenever $a \mathop{\sim} x$ and $a \not\mathop{\sim} \neg b$ then $a \wedge b \mathop{\sim} x$.

However, there is also a negative side. The requirements that we need to place on the relation $<$ are very demanding. In particular, to show that the additional assumptions are consistent with the premiss, we need the radical requirement that $\neg a < y_1$ and $\neg a < y_2$ together imply $\neg a < y_1 \wedge y_2$. To make the induced consequence relation well behaved, we also need $<$ to be not only transitive and irreflexive but also *ranked* (alias *modular*): whenever $a < x$ and $y \not< x$ then $a < y$.

Comparative expectation inference may be defined in another way: put $a \mathop{\sim}\limits_{<} x$ iff either $\neg a < \neg a \vee x$ or $\neg a \in Cn(\emptyset)$, where Cn is classical consequence. This definition is equivalent to the first one if sufficiently many constraints are placed on the relation $<$. With this definition, we no longer need any conditions on $<$ to show that the current premiss is consistent with background assumptions — for we no longer use additional assumptions! But the economy is an illusion. The same radical requirements on $<$ are still needed in order to ensure that $\mathop{\sim}\limits_{<}$ is reasonably well behaved. And conceptually, we lose the illuminating *Gestalt* of default assumptions that is apparent under Rott's definition.

Comparative expectation inference is investigated in detail in Gärdenfors and Makinson (1988; 1994), with a brief account in Makinson (1994) section 4.2. These presentations take as primitive a relation $\leq$, defining $x < y$ as $y \not\leq x$. But the basic idea goes back much further, and appears in a wide variety of guises, sometimes in dual form, in earlier studies of belief revision, conditionals, and generalizations of probability theory. The history is outlined in appendix A of Gärdenfors and Makinson (1994). We will explain the connection with probability in section 5.4. For detailed investigations of comparative expectation inference relations, with generalization to infinite premiss sets, see Rott (2001; 2003).

Final Remarks

We have deliberately left aside many issues of a technical nature. For example, we have mentioned only in passing the main Horn conditions (and the non-Horn condition of rational monotony) that are satisfied by the various kinds of consequence relation. This matter is studied systematically in Makinson (1994). On a more difficult level, we did not discuss the representation theorems that may be proven for some of them, nor the maps that can be constructed to embed structures of one kind in those of another. These questions have been investigated in the literature, and a number of results, some deep and difficult, have been obtained. Some of them are brought together in the books of Bochman (2001), Rott (2001) and Schlechta (2004). A sample representation theorem, for one of the kinds of default-assumption consequence, is also proven in section 6.3 below.

In addition to the basic form of default assumption consequence examined in the previous section, we have sketched nearly a dozen others from the literature, obtained by processes of specialization, variation, abstraction, and re-particularization. Evidently there are many other ways in which one might play with the notion of background assumptions, using consistency constraints, ordering principles and other devices to obtain yet other versions. Evidently too, one may combine the different variations into composite ones. There is no point in ringing out the changes systematically. It is enough, at least for this overview, to have indicated a simple paradigm and some of the main ideas for elaborating on it.

By now the reader may be rather dismayed by the multiplicity in face. Which if any of these kinds of default-assumption is *the right* one? Or, failing that, which is the best one to use?

We would suggest that none of them is *the* right one, and none of them is *always* the best to use. From a theoretical perspective, they are all interesting ways of generating nonmonotonic inference operations. They are all reasonably well behaved; in particular they are all supraclassical and satisfy left classical equivalence, right weakening and cumulative transitivity. When applied to background assumption sets already closed under classical consequence, they do not collapse into classical consequence as does the simple 'full meet' default-assumption consequence of section 2.2 — although two of them (screened consequence and layered consequence) do manifest a partial collapse in that context. From a practical perspective, they should be regarded as elements of a toolbox to be applied as suitable and convenient. For one purpose one may be more suitable than another; on other occasions the reverse. Sometimes the choice may not matter much; sometimes none may be what we are looking for.

Exercises

1*. *Closed world assumption*
   Suppose the language is based on the elementary letters p, q, r, s, t, u.
   Put $A = \{p, q, (p \wedge q) \to r, (p \wedge r) \to s, (s \wedge t) \to u\}$. Which literals may be inferred from A using the closed world assumption — i.e. which are in $C_K(A)$ when K is the set of all negative literals?

2. *Screened consequence*

(a)* Put $K = \{p \to q, q \to r, r \to s, s \to \neg p\}$ and let $A = \{p\}$ be a premiss set. Put $K_0 = \{p \to q\}$. Determine the maximal subsets K' with $K_0 \subseteq K' \subseteq K$ that are consistent with A. Identify in the most specific way that you can the screened consequences of A given K_0, K.

(b) Check out the details of the 'lesser collapse' phenomenon for screened consequence when $K = Cn(K)$, noted in the text.
    Hint: Take the proof of Theorem 2.7 and re-run it with appropriate editing.

3. *Layered consequence*

(a) Let K, A be as in exercise 2(a). Divide K into two layers, with $p \to q$, $q \to r$ in the first layer and $r \to s, s \to \neg p$ in the second. Determine the preferred subsets of K with respect to A (modulo the layering).

(b) Check out the details of the 'minor collapse' phenomenon for layered consequence when $K = Cn(K)$, noted in the text.
    Hint: As for Exercise 2(b) but with more editing.

4. *Relational partial meet consequence*
   Let K, A be as in exercise 2(a). Impose your own order (linear or otherwise) on all the subsets of K, under the constraint that it respects set-inclusion. Determine the family K_A of maximal subsets K' of K that are consistent with A. Identify the elements of K_A that are maximal under your ordering. Describe the relational partial meet consequences of A given your ordering.

5. *Background constraints*

(a) Let K, A be as in exercise 2(a), and put the constraint set J to be the singleton $\{r \vee s\}$. Determine the maximal subsets of K that are consistent with $A \cup J$. Describe $C_{KJ}(A)$.

(b) Give an example showing the failure of disjunction in the premisses for default assumptions with background constraints.
    Hint: Use a premiss set with two elements, and make one of them inconsistent with the constraints.

6. *Epistemic chains*

(a) Check the equivalence of the two definitions of the epistemic chain consequence $A \mathrel{|\!\!\sim}_K x$ given in the text.

(b) Let K, A be as in exercise 2(a). Let K be the sequence (t, a, b, c, d) where t is a tautology, a is the last element of K, b the conjunction of the last two, etc. What is the strongest formula in K that is consistent with A? Describe $C_K(A)$.

7. *Safe consequence*
   Put $K = \{p \to q, p, r, r \to q\}$ and let $A = \{\neg q\}$. Determine the minimal subsets K' of K that are inconsistent with A (i.e. that classically imply q). Let $<$ be the relation on K defined by the order in which its elements are presented above. Determine the $<$-minimal elements of each of the minimal K' above. Determine the safe elements of K. Describe $C_S(A)$.

8. *Comparative expectation inference*
   Show the equivalence of the two definitions of comparative expectation inference.
   Hint: Make use of all the requirements on the expectation relation $<$ that were mentioned in the text.

9. *Properties of consequence relations*

   (a) Check that each of the kinds of default-assumption consequence defined in section 2.3 is supraclassical. *Hint*: In most cases, this will be immediate from the definition.

   (b) Check that each of the kinds of default-assumption consequence defined in section 2.3 satisfies the rules of left classical equivalence (LCE) and right weakening (RW).

Problems

1*. *Closed world assumption*
   Prove the uniqueness property for inference under the closed world assumption, assuming that the premiss set A consists only of Horn formulae and the set K of background assumptions is made up of the negations of all elementary formulae.
   Hint: Exploit the two assumptions to the hilt, for they are both indispensable for the proof.

2. *Default-assumption consequence*

   (a) Show that whenever $C_{KJ}(A) = L$, then J is inconsistent with A. *Hint*: Prove the contrapositive by supposing that J is consistent with A and use the compactness of classical consequence to construct a suitable maximal set.

(b) Show that default-assumption consequence with constraints satisfies cumulative transitivity and cautious monotony.

(c) Let K be as in exercise 2(a). Give an example of a selection function on subsets of K that is not determined by any relation over K.

Project

Choose any one of the generalizations of default-assumption consequence that are outlined in this section, read the basic references indicated in the text and in the review section that follows to learn about its essential properties, and write a report on it.

2.4   Review and Explore

Recapitulation

The distinctive ingredient of pivotal-assumption consequence is its use of a fixed set K of background assumptions to amplify the effect of premises. The resulting operation is always monotonic, indeed paraclassical. Nonmonotonic consequence operations arise when we allow K, or rather the parts of it that we actually use, to vary in a principled way with the premises. The simplest idea is to require that when a set A of premises is inconsistent with K, then instead of the whole of K we use only the maximally A-consistent subsets of K to help obtain our conclusions. When there is more than one such subset, we intersect the outcomes.

In this way, the monotonic concept of pivotal-assumption consequences serves as a stepping-stone towards nonmonotonic default-assumption consequence. Ultimately, both reflect the ancient notion of an enthymeme.

However, the simplest form of default-assumption consequence faces a dilemma. When applied to background assumption sets K that are not closed under classical consequence, it is syntax-dependent; when applied to background assumption sets K with $K = Cn(K)$ it collapses into classical consequence in the principal case.

The basic notion of default-assumption consequence may be varied and generalized in many ways. They fall into three broad categories: those which intersect the output of only *some* of the maximal premiss-consistent subsets of K; those which also intersect some *non-maximal* premiss-consistent subsets of K; and *intersection-free operations*, which specify a unique output without the need for any kind of intersection. In all of them, both the notion of background assumptions and the decision to impose some kind of consistency constraint on their use, continue to play an important role.

Checklist of Concepts and Definitions for Revision

Section 2.1: Enthymeme, pivotal-assumption consequence, right weakening, free premises, compactness, representation theorems versus completeness theorems. *Section 2.2*: default-assumption consequence, maxiconsistency, cautious monotony, literals. *Section 2.3*: Horn formulae, closed world assumption (CWA), screened consequence, layered consequence, relational partial meet consequence, consequence via selection functions, background constraints, maximally informative subsets, Bochman's epistemic states, Freund's epistemic chains, safe consequence, comparative expectation inference.

Further Reading

- G. Brewka, J. Dix and K. Konolige. *Nonmonotonic Reasoning — An Overview*. CSLI Publications, Stanford, CA, 1997. Chapter 4.3.

- D. Makinson. General theory of cumulative inference. In *Nonmonotonic Reasoning*, M. Reinfrank *et al.*, eds., pp. 1–17. Vol 346 of *Lecture Notes on Artificial Intelligence*, Springer-Verlag, 1989.

- D. Makinson. General Patterns in Nonmonotonic Reasoning. In *Handbook of Logic in Artificial Intelligence and Logic Programming, Vol. 3*, Gabbay, Hogger and Robinson, eds., pp. 35–110. Oxford University Press, 1994. Especially sections 1, 2, and 3.3.

- D. Poole. A logical framework for default reasoning, *Artificial Intelligence*, **36**, 27–47, 1988.

For material focussed on particular generalizations and variants, see the reference calls in the relevant paragraphs of the text.

Chapter 3

Restricting the Set of Valuations

3.1 From Classical Consequence to Pivotal Valuations

So far, we have described one way of defining supraclassical consequence relations. The essential idea was to augment the current premisses A by a set K of background assumptions. This set K may be independent of A, in which case the generated supraclassical relation is monotonic, or may vary in a principled manner with A, producing a nonmonotonic consequence relation.

Definition and Basic Properties

This idea of adding background assumptions may be seen as a 'syntactic' manoeuvre. We now do almost the same thing in a 'semantic' manner. The basic idea is to *restrict the set of valuations* that are considered. In other words, we take a subset W of the entire set V of all Boolean valuations, and simply redefine consequence modulo W instead of modulo V.

It turns out that the consequence relations that can be so generated are almost the same as can be obtained by using pivotal assumptions; indeed, in the finite case they are exactly the same. But this way of proceeding points to quite different ways of allowing the new ingredient W to vary with A, leading to substantially different ways of generating nonmonotonic

59

relations. In this way an apparently small change on the monotonic level opens new perspectives for going nonmonotonic.

Definition 3.1 (Pivotal-Valuation Consequence) *Let $W \subseteq V$ be a set of Boolean valuations on the language L. Let A be any set of formulae, and let x be an individual formula.*

- *We say that x is a consequence of A modulo the valuation set W, and write $A \vdash_W x$ alias $x \in Cn_W(A)$, iff there is no valuation $v \in W$ such that $v(A) = 1$ whilst $v(x) = 0$.*

- *We call a relation or operation a pivotal-valuation consequence iff it coincides with $\vdash_W$ (resp. Cn_W) for some set W of valuations.*

Note again that there is not a unique pivotal-valuation consequence relation, but many — one for each value of W.

Immediately from this definition, pivotal-valuation consequence relations and operations are supraclassical, i.e. $Cn \leq Cn_W$ for any choice of W . They also satisfy inclusion, cumulative transitivity and monotony, and thus are closure operations. We are thus still in the realm of paraclassical inference. Pivotal-valuation consequence relations also have the property of disjunction in the premises. All these points are easily checked.

On the negative side, as we would already expect, pivotal-valuation consequence relations are not closed under substitution. Moreover — and this is a new feature compared to pivotal-assumption consequence — they are not always compact.

The following very simple example from the folklore illustrates the failure of compactness. Indeed, the example shows that pivotal-valuation consequence can even fail the weakened version of compactness that we called the redundancy property (section 2.2). Consider a language based on a countable set P of elementary letters. Let v_1 be the unique valuation that makes every elementary letter true. Let W be the set of all valuations except v_1 . Then we have $P \vdash_W (p \land \neg p)$, since there is no valuation in W that satisfies all the infinitely many letters in P , thus *a fortiori* none that does that and at the same time falsifies $(p \land \neg p)$. On the one hand, for no proper subset $Q \subset P$ do we have $Q \vdash_W (p \land \neg p)$, since W contains a valuation that makes all letters in Q true, and this valuation evidently makes $(p \land \neg p)$ false.

These observations are summarised in Table 3.1.

The failure of compactness shows that not every pivotal-valuation consequence operation is a pivotal-assumption one. For as we have seen, all of the latter are compact. On the other hand, the converse inclusion does

Table 3.1: Some Features of Pivotal-Valuation Consequence

Supraclassical		
Reflexive		
Cumulatively Transitive (CT)	Closure Relation	Paraclassical
Monotonic		
Disjunction in the Premisses (OR)		
(Not always compact)		

hold. This follows easily from the following simple lemma, where V is the set of all Boolean valuations.

Lemma 3.2 *Let K be any set of (Boolean) formula. Then $Cn_K = Cn_W$ where $W = \{v \in V : v(K) = 1\}$.*

Proof. Clearly, it suffices to show that for every valuation v and every premiss set $A, v(K \cup A) = 1$ iff $v \in W$ and $v(A) = 1$. But $v(K \cup A) = 1$ iff $v(K) = 1$ and $v(A) = 1$, and by the definition of W this holds iff $v \in W$ and $v(A) = 1$. ∎

Call a subset W of V *definable* iff there is a set K of formulae such that $W = \{v \in V : v(K) = 1\}$. Then:

Theorem 3.3 *Every pivotal-assumption consequence operation is a pivotal-valuation one. Indeed, the pivotal-assumption consequence operations are precisely the pivotal-valuation operations determined by a definable subset W of V.*

Proof. We already have the left-in-right inclusion by the Lemma. For the right-in-left inclusion, let Cn_W be any pivotal-valuation consequence operation where W is a definable subset of V. This means that there is a set K of formulae such that $W = \{v \in V : v(K) = 1\}$, so we may again apply the Lemma. ∎

Thus the family of pivotal-assumption consequence operations is strictly narrower than the family of pivotal-valuation ones. Can we say any more about the links between the two families? Is satisfaction of compactness enough to ensure that a pivotal-valuation consequence operation is a pivotal-assumption one? The answer is positive.

Theorem 3.4 *The pivotal-assumption consequence operations are precisely the pivotal-valuation ones that are compact.*

Proof. For the left-to-right implication, we have just shown in Theorem 3.3 that every pivotal-assumption consequence operation is a pivotal-valuation one. Also, we have already noticed in section 2.1 that pivotal-assumption consequence operations are always compact.

For the right-to-left implication, we have noted that any pivotal-valuation operation is a supraclassical consequence operation satisfying disjunction in the premisses. So the representation Theorem 2.2 tells us that if it is also compact then it is a pivotal-assumption relation. ∎

By a *finitely generated Boolean language* (or more briefly, a *finite language*), we mean one generated by Boolean connectives from a finite set of elementary letters. It is well known that in such a language there are only finitely many formulae that are mutually non-equivalent under classical consequence. The same is therefore also true under any supraclassical consequence operation. It follows that any paraclassical operation on a finite language is compact. It is also easy to show that any set of valuations over such a language is definable, indeed definable by a single formula — just take an appropriate formula in disjunctive normal form. By either route, we have the following as a corollary of Theorem 3.3 and of Theorem 3.4.

Corollary 3.5 *For finite Boolean languages the pivotal-assumption consequence operations are precisely the pivotal-valuation ones.*

For the computer scientist, who always works in a finitely generated language, pivotal-assumption and pivotal-valuation consequence are thus equivalent. For the logician, who takes perverse pleasure in the subtleties of the infinite, they are not. We persist with the infinite case from here to the end of the section; hard-line finitists will have to grin and bear it, or skip it.

The Representation Problem for Pivotal-Valuation Consequence

The question arises whether we can characterize the family of pivotal-valuation consequence operations over a countable Boolean language (i.e.

where we have countably many elementary letters) in terms of the properties that these operations satisfy. This would give us a representation theorem for the family, paralleling Theorem 2.2 for pivotal-assumption consequence operations.

It would be pleasant to be able to report that the family is fully characterized by the properties of being a closure operation, supraclassical, and satisfying disjunction in the premises. However, inspection of the proof that we gave for Theorem 2.2 should make us rather suspicious about such a conjecture. For half of that proof depends on applying the compactness property, which is no longer available. It was needed in order to make a single formula do the work of an infinite set A of premises in so far as any given conclusion x is concerned.

In fact, an elegant counterexample has been devised by Karl Schlechta. He has constructed a supraclassical closure operation satisfying disjunction in the premises (indeed, satisfying a more infinitary version of it than we have considered here) that is not a pivotal-valuation consequence operation. Schlechta's subtle construction shows even more: his example is not even a preferential consequence operation (to be defined in the next section); indeed, it is not even the intersection of any family of preferential consequence operations (see Schlechta (1992) or the alternative presentation in Makinson (1994, Observation 3.4.10)). But these features need not concern us for the present. All we need to know here is that his example is a supraclassical closure operation, satisfies OR, but is not equal to Cn_W for any $W \subseteq V$.

On the other hand, the failed representation theorem does hold in a finitary form, as follows.

Theorem 3.6 *Let Cn^+ be any supraclassical closure operation satisfying OR. Then there is a pivotal-valuation operation Cn_W that agrees with Cn^+ on finite sets, i.e. such that $Cn_W(A) = Cn^+(A)$ for all finite A.*

Proof. The proof is easy, given what we know already. Define an operation Cn^* from Cn^+ by the rule: $x \in Cn^*(A)$ iff $x \in Cn^+(B)$ for some finite $B \subseteq A$. Clearly, using monotony, $Cn^* \leq Cn^+$. Also, Cn^* agrees with Cn^+ on finite sets, and is compact. For this reason, we might call it the *compactification* of Cn^+. It is also easy to check that Cn^* inherits from Cn^+ the properties of supraclassicality, being a closure operation, and satisfying OR. Hence by the representation Theorem 2.2, Cn^* is in fact a pivotal-assumption operation Cn_K for some $K \subseteq L$, and so by Theorem 3.3 is also a pivotal-valuation operation Cn_W for some $W \subseteq V$. ∎

The question remains: Is there any 'strong' representation theorem for pivotal-valuation consequence, i.e. also covering infinite premiss sets? In other words, can we add further syntactic conditions, still satisfied by all pivotal-valuation consequence operations, such that every operation satisfying the enlarged collection of conditions is identical to some pivotal-valuation consequence? As far as the author knows, this question has not been answered, positively or negatively. Given the finitary result in Theorem 3.6, any such conditions would presumably need to be infinitary. Given the subtlety of Schlechta's example, they might also need to be rather complex

Notice that there is an epistemological asymmetry between the two sides of this open question. For a positive answer, we don't need a precise formal definition of what a representation theorem is. We just need to understand the notion well enough to recognize the one that we find. But to obtain a negative result we do need a precise formal definition of the concept.

Generalizing to Ideals

We now describe another, more abstract, way of restricting the set of valuations without losing monotony in the consequence operation. For finitely generated languages it is equivalent to pivotal-valuation consequence (and thus in turn to its pivotal-assumption counterpart). But it is rather more general in the infinite case. It will appeal particularly to those readers who have studied some abstract algebra or lattice theory, where the notion of an ideal is well established. Others may prefer to skip it. The notion of an ideal is dual to that of a filter, which is rather more familiar in logical studies. The definitions below could be formulated equivalently, but rather less intuitively, in terms of filters.

Recall that we defined $A \vdash_W x$ to hold iff:

- There is no valuation $v \in W$ such that $v(A) = 1$ whilst $v(x) = 0$.

Clearly this is equivalent to each of the following:

- Every valuation $v \in V$ such that $v(A) = 1, v(x) = 0$ is in $V - W$

- $\{v \in V : v(A) = 1, v(x) = 0\} \subseteq V - W$

- $\{v \in V : v(A) = 1, v(x) = 0\} \in 2^{V-W}$.

Now for any set $U \subseteq V$, its powerset 2^U has special properties. In particular, it contains the empty set, contains all subsets of each of its elements, and is closed under the union of any two of its elements (in fact, of any collection of them). We may generalize by introducing the abstract notion of an *ideal* over V. This is any family Δ of subsets of V such that $\emptyset \in \Delta, S \in \Delta$ whenever $S \subseteq T \in \Delta$, and $S \cup T \in \Delta$ whenever $S, T \in \Delta$.

An ideal is thus like a family of 'small' subsets, in so far as it contains the empty set and all of the subsets of any of its elements. But it is dissimilar from any numerical notion of smallness in two ways. First, an ideal over V need not contain all the subsets of V that are numerically as small as one of its elements; for example it may contain some singletons but not others. Second, by iterating indefinitely the last clause in the definition, an ideal contains the union of any finite number of its elements, and so may have elements of any finite size so long as there are enough smaller ones to join together.

Let Δ be any ideal over the set V of all valuations on the language L. Let A be any set of formulae, and let x be an individual formula. We say that x is a *consequence of A modulo the ideal* Δ, and write $A \vdash_\Delta x$ alias $x \in Cn_\Delta(A)$ iff the set of valuations that satisfy A but not x is 'Δ-small'. In other words, iff $\{v \in V : v(A) = 1 \text{ and } v(x) = 0\} \in \Delta$. We call a relation or operation a *pivotal-exception consequence* iff it coincides with $\vdash_\Delta$ (resp. Cn_Δ) for some ideal Δ over V. Note again that there is not a unique pivotal-exception consequence relation, but many — one for each value of Δ.

Any pivotal-valuation consequence operation is evidently a pivotal-exception one — given Cn_W, simply put $\Delta = 2^{V-W}$, and Δ will be an ideal over V with $Cn_\Delta = Cn_W$. Evidently, the converse also holds whenever the ideal Δ is *principal*, i.e. whenever there is a $U \subseteq V$ such that $\Delta = 2^U$. We can thus say:

Theorem 3.7 *The pivotal-valuation consequence operations are precisely the pivotal-exception ones generated by a principal ideal over V.*

Pivotal-exception consequences behave very much like pivotal-valuation ones. On the positive side, they are always closure operations and satisfy disjunction in the premises. On the negative side, they are not always compact, as can be seen by the same counterexample given earlier in this section. Indeed, when a pivotal-exception operation is compact, then it is a pivotal-valuation one. For by the representation Theorem 2.2 such an operation will be a pivotal-assumption consequence and thus by Theorem 3.3 a pivotal-valuation one.

Here too the question of a representation theorem arises. As for the less general class of all pivotal-valuation consequences, the question appears to open.

One could in principle generalize further by using *downsets* rather than ideals. These are families Δ of subsets of V such that $\emptyset \in \Delta$ and $S \in \Delta$ whenever $S \subseteq T \in \Delta$. In other words, the requirement of closure under union of pairs is dropped. However, the pivotal-exception operations generated by downsets will be less regularly behaved than those generated by ideals. In particular they will not in general be closure operations (cumulative transitivity can fail) and may fail the rule of conjunction in the conclusion.

Exercises

1*. Let the elementary letters of our language be $p_1, p_2, p_3, \ldots$ Let W be the set consisting of just the four valuations v_1, v_0, v_e, v_{10}, where:

v_1 makes every elementary letter true
v_0 makes every elementary letter false
v_e makes exactly the even elementary letters true
v_{10} makes exactly the elementary letters $p_1, \ldots, p_{10}$ true.

Put $A = \{\neg p_1 \wedge p_2\}$. Which of the following hold?

$A \vdash p_2$	$A \vdash_W p_2$
$A \vdash p_3 \vee \neg p_4$	$A \vdash_W (p_3 \vee \neg p_4)$
$A \vdash p_{11} \vee p_{12}$	$A \vdash_W (p_{11} \vee p_{12})$

2*. Why is it immediate from the definition that pivotal-valuation consequence operations are supraclassical, i.e. that $Cn \leq Cn_W$ for any choice of W?

3. Show that pivotal-valuation consequence relations satisfy inclusion, cumulative transitivity and monotony, and thus are closure operations.

4*. Show that pivotal-valuation consequence relations satisfy disjunction in the premisses.

5. It is possible to give a more general version of disjunction in the premisses. It says: $C(A) \cap C(B) \subseteq C(Cn(A) \cap Cn(B))$. Notice the pattern of Cn and C here: the condition relates whatever operation C is under consideration to classical consequence Cn. Notice too that it does not mention disjunction explicitly. Nevertheless, it covers disjunction implicitly, because whenever $a \in A$ and $b \in B$ then $a \vee b \in Cn(A) \cap Cn(B)$. With this in mind, show that (a) OR follows as a special case of this general principle, (b) classical consequence satisfies it, i.e. the principle holds when we put $C = Cn$, (c) every pivotal-valuation consequence operation Cn_W satisfies it.

6. In the text it was claimed that in a finitely generated Boolean language there are only finitely many formulae that are mutually non-equivalent under classical consequence. How many? It was also claimed that, as a result, any paraclassical operation on a finitely generated language is compact. Verify this fully using the definition of compactness. Identify the point at which your verification would fail if we assumed only supraclassicality instead of paraclassicality.

7. Fill in the details of the proof of Theorem 3.6.

8. Verify the remarks on downsets made in the last paragraph of this section.

3.2 From Pivotal Valuations to Default Valuations

How can we go from pivotal-valuation consequence to its default-valuation counterpart? The essential idea is to allow the restricted set W of valuations, or more precisely the part of it that we actually use, to vary with the premiss set A.

In principle, this could be done by taking the various maxiconsistent constructions and translating them into the language of Boolean valuations. In this translation, formulae and sets of formulae become sets of valuations (specifically, the set of all valuations making them true), intersections of sets of formulae become unions of the corresponding sets of valuations, and so on. But this is not the way in which the material actually developed, nor a good way of reviewing it. The paradigm default-valuation system is not a translation of the simple default-assumption system of section 2.2. It is a rather more sophisticated affair, involving not only a set of valuations but also a relation between valuations.

In the context of valuations, the basic default construction is due to Shoham (1988). His central idea was to focus on those valuations satisfying the premiss set A, that are *minimal* under some background ordering over the set of all valuations.

Definition 3.8 (Preferential models and preferential consequence) *A prefer-ential model is understood to be a pair $(W, <)$ where W is, as in the monotonic case, a set of valuations on the language L — not necessarily the entire set V — and $<$ is an irreflexive, transitive relation over W.*

- *Given a preferential model $(W, <)$ we say that a formula x is a preferential consequence of a set A of formulae and write $A \mathrel{\vvdash}_< x$ iff $v(x) = 1$ for every valuation $v \in W$ that is minimal among those in W that satisfy A. Here minimality is understood in the usual way: when U is a set of valuations, u is a minimal element of U iff $u \in U$ and there is no $v \in U$ with $v < u$.*

- *We call a relation or operation a preferential consequence (or default-valuation consequence) iff it coincides with $\mathrel{\vvdash}_<$ for some preferential model $(W, <)$.*

The definition of the consequence relation $\mathrel{\vvdash}_<$ makes it depend on both W and $<$, and strictly speaking the snake sign should also carry W as a subscript; but it is customary to omit it to simplify notation. When preferential consequence is read as an operation rather than a relation, we write it as $C_<(A)$. The relation $<$ over W should not be confused with any of the relations between formulae that were discussed in section 2.3, and which we also wrote as $<$ to keep notation simple. In the following section, we shall look at more general versions of the notion of a preferential model, notably ones that allow 'copies' of valuations, but for the present we remain with the basic version.

It is worth noting that the definition of minimality under $<$ makes perfect sense for an *arbitrary* relation over W. The notion of a preferential model is thus well defined even when we do not place any constraints on its relation, and in many presentations that is what is done. Nevertheless, the properties of preferential consequence become more regular when some such constraints are imposed, and to simplify life we do so here, requiring both irreflexivity and transitivity (and so also asymmetry).

It is easy to see that pivotal-valuation consequence $A \vdash_W x$ is a special case of preferential consequence. It is the case where all elements of W are minimal under $<$, i.e. where no element of W is less than any other, i.e. where $<$ is the empty relation.

It is sometimes convenient to express the definition in a more concise manner. As is familiar, in classical logic one often writes $v \vDash A$ to mean that the valuation v satisfies A, i.e. that $v(A) = 1$, i.e. that $v(a) = 1$ for every $a \in A$. We now also write $v \vDash_< A$ and say that v *preferentially satisfies* A to mean that $v(A) = 1, v \in W$, and there is no $v' \in W$ with $v' < v$ such that $v' \vDash A$. Again, strictly speaking the symbol $\vDash_<$ for preferential satisfaction should carry a further subscript, since it depends on W, but this is generally left as understood. In this notation the definition of preferential consequence says: $A \mathrel{\vvdash}_< x$ iff $v \vDash x$ whenever $v \vDash_< A$. This manner of expression tends to be handy when checking examples.

Another way of expressing the concept of preferential consequence more succinctly is to write $|A|_W$ for the set of all valuations in W that satisfy A, i.e. $|A|_W = \{v \in W : v(A) = 1\}$. Write $min_<|A|_W$ for the set of all minimal elements of $|A|_W$. In this notation we have $A \mathrel{\vdash_<} x$ iff $v \in |x|$ whenever $v \in min_<|A|_W$. Even more briefly: iff $min_<|A|_W \subseteq |x|_W$. This notation leaves nothing implicit, and tends to be useful when proving general observations about preferential models.

Preferential consequence relations/operations are nonmonotonic. For a simple example, consider a language with three elementary letters p,q,r. Put $W = \{v_1, v_2\}$ where these two valuations are defined by setting $v_1(p) = v_2(p) = 1, v_1(q) = 0, v_2(q) = 1, v_1(r) = 1, v_2(r) = 0$. Finally, order W by putting $v_1 < v_2$. Informally, we can describe this preferential model by saying: let p be true in both valuations, q true in just the top one, and r true in just the bottom one. We can also represent it by a diagram with levels:

Here the convention is that all points on a lower level are less than all those on a higher level, but incomparable among themselves (i.e. none is less than any other). We can also use a diagram in which lines represents the relation between valuations. This is potentially more general in that we can also use it with less well-behaved relations:

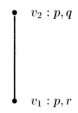

In both kinds of diagram, the convention is that at each point, i.e. at each element $v \in W$, we list only the elementary letters that v satisfies, omitting those that it makes false. This convention reduces clutter, but readers who find it irksome can simply add at each point the negations of the letters omitted.

In this preferential model, $p \mathrel{\vert\!\sim}_< r$ since the least valuation in which p is true is v_1, and r is also true there; but $p \wedge q \mathrel{\not\vert\!\sim}_< r$, since the least valuation in which $p \wedge q$ is true is v_2, and r is false there.

This example also shows that preferential consequence $\mathrel{\vert\!\sim}_<$ can fail transitivity — even though the relation $<$ of the model is transitive. For we have $p \wedge q \mathrel{\vert\!\sim}_< p$ and $p \mathrel{\vert\!\sim}_< r$ but $p \wedge q \mathrel{\not\vert\!\sim}_< r$. In general, it is important not to confuse the properties of the relation $<$ of the model with the properties of the consequence relation $\mathrel{\vert\!\sim}_<$ that it generates. Evidently, imposing constraints on $<$ will tend to yield additional properties of $\mathrel{\vert\!\sim}_<$, but not simply the same properties.

This example is rather special in that the relation $<$ is not only transitive and irreflexive but also *complete* in the sense that for all elements $v, v' \in W$, either $v < v'$ or $v' < v$ or $v = v'$. Briefly, it is *linear*. As a result, any minimal element u of a subset $U \subseteq W$ is a *least* element of U, in the sense that $u < u'$ for every $u' \in U$ with $u \neq u'$. Indeed, as the relation is also asymmetric, any minimal element u of U is *the unique least* element of U.

But in general, when the relation is not complete, there may be more than one minimal element of U. Consider for example a language with four elementary letters p, q, r, s and the preferential model presented by the following diagram:

• $v_{21} : p, q$	• $v_{22} : p, q, r$	
• $v_{11} : p, r$	• $v_{12} : q, s$	• $v_{13} : p, r, s$

In the corresponding line diagram, each element in the bottom layer is linked with all elements in the top layer. Here there are two minimal valuations satisfying p (v_{11} and v_{13}) and they both satisfy r, so $p \mathrel{\vert\!\sim}_< r$ holds in the model. There are also two minimal valuations satisfying $p \wedge q$ (v_{21} and v_{22}) and one of them fails to satisfy r, so that $p \wedge q \mathrel{\not\vert\!\sim}_< r$. The relation in this example is still quite regular: it is *ranked* (or *modular*) in the sense that we defined in section 2.3: whenever $v < v'$ and not $v'' < v'$ then $v < v''$.

Apart from failing monotony, preferential consequence relations are remarkably well behaved. They are supraclassical and satisfy disjunction in the premises. They also satisfy cumulative transitivity and inclusion (the last implied anyway by supraclassicality) and so are also idempotent.

However, they lack some of the properties of their assumption-based analogues. For example, they do not always satisfy *cautious monotony*, which is in effect, a converse of cumulative transitivity. We recall the definition from section 2.2. In the language of operations it says: $A \subseteq B \subseteq C(A)$ implies $C(A) \subseteq C(B)$. In terms of relations: whenever $A \mathrel{|\!\sim} b$ for all $b \in B$ and $A \mathrel{|\!\sim} x$ then $A \cup B \mathrel{|\!\sim} x$. In the case that A, B are singletons it says: whenever $a \mathrel{|\!\sim} b$ and $a \mathrel{|\!\sim} x$ then $\{a, b\} \mathrel{|\!\sim} x$, which in its conjunctive counterpart says: whenever $a \mathrel{|\!\sim} b$ and $a \mathrel{|\!\sim} x$ then $a \wedge b \mathrel{|\!\sim} x$.

Although this property sometimes fails, it always holds for finite preferential models. More generally, it holds whenever there are no infinite descending chains in the preferential model. More generally still, it holds whenever the model satisfies a condition known as *stoppering* (alias *smoothness*). This says that whenever $v \in |A|_W$ then either $v \in min_<|A|_W$ or there is a $u < v$ with $u \in min_<|A|_W$.

Another property that preferential consequence relations may lack is *consistency preservation*. This is the property that whenever $A \mathrel{|\!\sim} f$ then $A \vdash f$. Here, f is a classical contradiction and $\vdash$ is of course classical consequence. Equivalently: whenever $C(A)$ is classically inconsistent then so is A itself. This holds for default-assumption consequences $\mathrel{|\!\sim}_K$. But it can fail for preferential consequences $\mathrel{|\!\sim}_<$ essentially because some classical valuations may be missing from the model. When valuations making a proposition a true are missing from W, we will have $v(a) = 0$ for all $v \in W$ even though a is not a classical contradiction, so that also $min_<|a|_W = \emptyset$ and thus $a \mathrel{|\!\sim}_< f$.

Nevertheless, for models satisfying the stoppering condition, consistency is preserved with respect to a suitable paraclassical operation. Specifically, we may take this to be the pivotal-valuation consequence $\vdash_W$ determined by the set W of all valuations in the preferential model. In other words, for stoppered preferential models, we have: whenever $A \mathrel{|\!\sim}_< f$ then $A \vdash_W f$.

Preferential consequence relations have been studied quite extensively. We do not wish to lose the reader in details; for them see Makinson (1994). The main point of this section is that conceptually, monotonic pivotal-valuation consequences Cn_W serve as a natural bridge between classical Cn and the nonmonotonic operations $C_<$ known as preferential consequence operations. The definitions of Cn_W and $C_<$ both allow restriction of the set of classical valuations; for $C_<$ we also allow this restriction to vary with the premises.

Looking at the inclusion relations between operations, we see that the pattern for preferential consequence resembles the one that we observed for screened consequence, described in section 2.3. For preferential consequence we have the inclusions $Cn \leq Cn_W \leq C_< \leq Cn_{min(W)}$. In other words, the lower bound for the nonmonotonic consequence operation $C_<$ moves up from classical Cn to the pivotal-valuation operation Cn_W, while another pivotal-valuation operation $Cn_{min(W)}$ serves as upper bound.

In effect the small set $min(W)$ of valuations is the semantic counterpart of the large set K of background assumptions, while the large set W of valuations corresponds to the small set K_0 of protected background assumptions.   If we are to construct formal maps, we will put $K = \{x : v(x) = 1$ for all $v \in min(W)\}$, i.e. we take K to consist of the formulae that are true when all is normal, while we put $K_0 = \{x : v(x) = 1$ for all $v \in W\}$, i.e. we never entertain formulae that are false throughout W. This kind of opposition larger/smaller is typical of the duality between syntactic approaches with sets of formulae and semantic approaches with sets of valuations. Until one gets used to it, the reversal can be disorienting.

If one is to compare preferential consequence with any of the default assumption relations of the previous section, it is not with the basic one of section 2.2 but rather with a combination of screened and relational partial meet consequence from section 2.3. The sets W, $min(W)$ provide a lower and upper bound respectively, as did K_0 and K for screened consequence, while the consequence relations between those bounds are determined using a minimality rule as for partial meet consequence.

Exercises

1*. Explain why every irreflexive transitive relation is *asymmetry* (i.e. never both $v < v'$ and $v' < v$) and more generally *acyclic* (never $v_1 < v_2 < ... < v_n < v_1$ for $n \geq 1$).

2*. Draw a diagram for a preferential model consisting of an infinite descending chain, labelling the nodes with valuations in such a way that the model is not stoppered and cautious monotony and consistency preservation both fail.

3. Draw a diagram for a preferential model that contains an infinite descending chain, but is nevertheless stoppered.

4*. Show that every preferential consequence operation is supraclassical and satisfies cumulative transitivity.

5. Show that every preferential consequence operation satisfies disjunction in the premises.

6. Explain why every finite preferential model is stoppered. *Hint*: Show more generally that every non-stoppered preferential model contains an infinite descending chain of distinct elements.

7. Show that the consequence operation determined by any stoppered preferential model satisfies cautious monotony.

8. We defined a relation $<$ to be ranked (or modular) iff whenever $v < v'$ and not $v'' < v'$ then $v < v''$. Show that given transitivity and irreflexivity, this is equivalent to each of the following, where # means incomparability under $<$:

   (a) whenever $v < v'$ and $v'\#v''$ then $v < v''$

   (b) whenever $v\#v'$ and $v' < v''$ then $v < v''$.

9. Show that when a preferential model is ranked, it satisfies the non-Horn condition of *rational monotony* defined in Chapter 2: whenever $A \mathrel{|\!\sim} x$ and $A \mathrel{|\!\not\sim} \neg b$ then $A \cup \{b\} \mathrel{|\!\sim} x$.

10. Consider any stoppered preferential model over a set W of valuations. Show that whenever $A \mathrel{|\!\sim_<} f$ then $A \vdash_W f$, as claimed in the text.

11. Show that every preferential consequence $\mathrel{|\!\sim_<}$ satisfies the condition: whenever $A \cup \{x\} \mathrel{|\!\sim_<} y$ then $A \mathrel{|\!\sim_<} x \to y$. Construct a small finite model serving as a counterexample to the converse.

12*. Show that for ranked preferential models, whenever $|A|_{min(W)} \neq \emptyset$ then $C_<(A) = Cn_{min(W)}(A)$.

3.3   Specializations and Generalizations

We continue this account of default-valuation consequence operations by indicating briefly some of the better-known generalizations of our paradigm version of preferential consequence, including one that has acquired the position of 'industry standard'. But first we describe a special case of considerable importance.

Circumscription

The operation of circumscription was introduced by John McCarthy (1980). It may be seen as a transposition to the semantic level, with considerable broadening, of the closed world assumption, which we presented in section 2.3 as a special kind of default-assumption reasoning.

Circumscription is typically applied in the context of classical first-order logic, where we have predicates, relation symbols, individual constants, individual variables, and quantifiers binding those variables, as well as the Boolean connectives that we have been considering. The essential idea is that when we are presented with a set A of first-order premisses, we do not consider all the models of A but only those in which the extension of certain specified predicates are minimized, while the extensions of certain others are held constant and the remainder are allowed to vary freely. The consequences of A are just those formulae that hold in all the models of A that are in this sense minimal. No particular constraints are imposed on the form of the premisses in A; in particular, they need not be Horn formulae.

This may be given a precise definition as a special kind of default-valuation consequence, defined however on a classical language richer than propositional logic, so that the 'valuations' correspond not just to assignments of truth-values to elementary letters but to first-order models. Some forms of circumscription further refine the above definition of minimality — for example, by introducing an ordering on the predicates that are to be minimized, and performing the minimization lexicographically. Indeed, much of the literature on circumscription considers the question of what is the best definition of minimality to facilitate implementation and avoid unwanted consequences.

Another part of the literature investigates the extent to which the semantic definitions in terms of minimality may be recast as syntactic ones — in our terminology, as default-assumption consequence relations. In order to do this without loss of generality it is necessary to move up one more linguistic level, formulating the additional background assumptions in the language of second-order logic. The resulting theory is highly intricate.

We will not enter into the labyrinth of these investigations, referring the reader to the summary overviews in Brewka, Dix and Konolige (1997, section 2.2), Antoniou (1997, chapter 12), and the extended survey in Lifschitz (1994). But to help bring out the relationship of circumscription to the closed world assumption on the one hand, and to preferential entailment on the other, we briefly extract its Boolean content.

Suppose that in the semantics of our first-order language we restrict attention to a specific domain, perhaps infinite, and suppose that the language is equipped with an individual constant to serve as name for each element of the domain. Then, as is well known, a first-order model may be identified as an assignment of truth-values to the elementary formulae of the form $P\underline{t}$ where P is a predicate or relation symbol and $\langle \underline{t} = t_1, \ldots, t_n \rangle$ is an n-tuple of individual names. These formulae may in turn be associated with elementary propositional letters $p_{\underline{t}}$, which we may as well write without the subscripts.

On the Boolean level, a *circumscriptive model* may thus be understood as a preferential model $(V, <)$ in which V is the set of all Boolean valuations and $<$ is a relation between valuations defined in a particular way. The set S of all elementary letters is partitioned into three subsets S_1, S_2, S_3. For valuations v, v' we put $v \leq v'$ iff $v(p) \leq v'(p)$ for all $p \in S_1$ while

$v(p) = v'(p)$ for all $p \in S_2$. No constraints are placed on the values for letters p in S_3. We put $v < v'$ iff $v \leq v'$ but not conversely (so that $v(p) < v'(p)$ for some $p \in S_1$).

Each choice of the sets S_1, S_2 determines a circumscriptive relation $<$ defined in this way, and thus a circumscriptive model. Each circumscriptive model determines a consequence operation $\mathrel{\vdash_<}$ by the same rule as for preferential inference in general: $A \mathrel{\vdash_<} x$ iff $v(x) = 1$ for every valuation v that is $<$-minimal among those satisfying A. As the premise set A is allowed to be arbitrary (not just a set of Horn formulae), in general there need not exist a unique such valuation.

In the special case that $S_1 = S$ (so that $S_2 = S_3 = \emptyset$) and the premise set A consists only of Horn formulae, the $<$-minimal valuation will be unique, and the construction clearly generates the same inference operation as does the closed world assumption. In both cases we are limiting attention to the valuations that satisfy as few elementary letters as possible. Circumscriptive inference, in a purely Boolean context, is thus a special case of preferential inference, but a generalization of closed world inference.

Multiple Copies of Valuations

We pass now to generalizations. It is evident that not all situations can be fully described in a meagre Boolean language. It is therefore natural to wish to allow distinct possible worlds to satisfy exactly the same Boolean formulae. In other words, we may wish to permit as many 'copies' v_i of a valuation v as we like in a preferential model.

Technically, this can be done by indexing valuations v by elements s of an arbitrary index set S. Equivalently, one may take valuations to be functions $v(a, s)$ of two arguments instead of one, where a ranges over formulae of the propositional language L as before, and the new argument s ranges over the index set S.

To be sure, such a step could already have been taken in the monotonic case for pivotal-valuation semantics. But, as is almost immediate from the definitions, it would have made no difference there, generating exactly the same consequence relations with a more complex apparatus. In the nonmonotonic case, however, it makes a significant difference, even for finitely generated languages. This is because two copies of a single valuation may have quite different positions in the ordering. A simple example of this will be given shortly, after formulating the precise definition.

For the definition, consider a set S of arbitrary items, whose elements we will call *states*. Consider also an arbitrary relation over S, written as $<$. With each state $s \in S$ we associate a valuation v_s to the formulae of the language. The function that takes a state s to its associated valuation v_s is often called the *labelling function*. It need not be onto the entire set V of valuations (i.e. there may be some $v \in V$ such that $v \neq v_s$ for all $s \in S$), thus allowing us to work with a proper subset of the classical valuations. Nor need it be *injective* (i.e. we may have $v_s = v_{s'}$ although $s \neq s'$), thus offering the desired possibility of multiple copies of a valuation.

We remark in passing that terminology is fickle here, as it varies from author to author, and even between the papers of a single author. Usually, as here, the elements s of S are called 'states', but sometimes they are called 'worlds'. Other authors reserve the term 'worlds' for the associated valuations v_s (or for the sets of formulae that they make true). This ambiguity makes no difference when the labelling function is injective, since the elements of S may then be identified with their images under the labelling. But if care is not taken, confusion can arise in the non-injective case, where several elements of S may correspond to a single valuation.

When multiple copies are allowed, a *preferential model* is defined as a structure made up of the above ingredients: a set S, a relation $<$ over S, and a labelling function associating a classical truth-value assignment v_s to each $s \in S$. The consequence operation is defined by the rule: $A \hspace{1pt}\vert\!\!\sim_< x$ iff $v_s(x) = 1$ for every state s that is minimal among those making A true, i.e. among those with $v_s(A) = 1$. In another notation introduced in section 3.2: iff $s \vDash x$ whenever $s \vDash_< A$. In a third notation introduced there: iff $min_< |A|_S \subseteq |x|_S$, where this time $|A|_S$ means $\{s \in S : v_s(A) = 1\}$.

How can this introduction of 'copies' change anything? An elegant example due to Kraus, Lehmann and Magidor (1990) brings out the difference. It is a preferential model with just four states, two of which are labelled by the same valuation. We show that there is no preferential model without copies that determines the same consequence relation.

Example 3.9 *Consider the Boolean language with just two elementary letters p,q (and thus just four possible valuations). Take the preferential model defined by the following diagram, where we use the same conventions as in section 3.2 except that it will be clearer in this example to list the negative part of each valuation as well as the positive part.*

Note that this preferential model is *not ranked*. For instance, $s_1 < s_3$ and s_3 is incomparable with s_4 but $s_1 \not< s_4$. Note also that it is *not injective*: states s_3 and s_4 are labelled with the same valuation. We claim that for any preferential model defined for the same language with elementary letters p,q, if it generates the same preferential consequence relation as this one does, then it must contain two distinct states labelled by the same Boolean valuation.

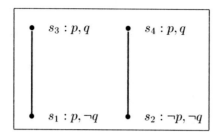

Verification. For simplicity of notation, we leave the subscript $<$ off the snake sign in what follows. First observe that in this preferential model we have $p \wedge q \not\hspace{-0.5ex}\vdash f$ (where f is any self-contradiction), $t \hspace{0.3ex}\vdash\hspace{-1.3ex}\sim \neg q$ (where t is any tautology), $p \not\hspace{-0.5ex}\vdash \neg q$ and $p \leftrightarrow q \not\hspace{-0.5ex}\vdash \neg p \wedge \neg q$ (where $\leftrightarrow$ is truth-functional co-implication). Now consider any preferential model generating the same consequence relation as this one. We want to show that it contains two distinct states labelled by the same Boolean valuation. We break the argument into cases.

Case 1. Suppose that the preferential model has more than four states. As there are only four valuations possible on our meagre language with just two elementary letters, there must be at least two states labelled by the same valuation.

Case 2. Suppose that the preferential model has at most four states. Then it has finitely many states, and so is stoppered. Since $p \wedge q \not\hspace{-0.5ex}\vdash f$ there is a state s with $s \vDash_< p \wedge q$, and thus $s \vDash p \wedge q$. Evidently too, $s \vDash t$. But since $t \hspace{0.3ex}\vdash\hspace{-1.3ex}\sim \neg q$ we know that s is not a minimal t-state. So by stoppering, there must be a minimal t-state s' with $s' < s$. Since $t \hspace{0.3ex}\vdash\hspace{-1.3ex}\sim_< \neg q$ we have $s' \vDash \neg q$. Now either $s' \vDash p$ or $s' \vDash \neg p$. We consider these sub-cases separately.

<u>Sub-case 2.1</u>. Suppose $s' \vDash p$. Then $s' \vDash p, \neg q$. But we know that $p \not\hspace{-0.5ex}\vdash \neg q$ so there is also a minimal p-state s'' with $s'' \vDash q$, so we have $s'' \vDash p, q$. We can picture this in the following diagram:

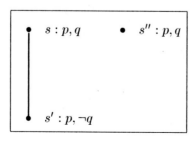

Thus s, s'' are labelled by the same valuation, for they satisfy the same elementary letters of our meagre language. But they must be distinct. For on the one hand s'' is a minimal p-state, while on the other hand s is not since $s' < s$ and by the supposition of the sub-case $s' \vDash p$.

<u>Sub-case 2.2</u>. Suppose $s' \vDash \neg p$. Then $s' \vDash \neg p, \neg q$ so also $s' \vDash p \leftrightarrow q$. But we know that $p \leftrightarrow q \not\vdash \neg p \wedge \neg q$ so there is a minimal $(p \leftrightarrow q)$-state s'' with $s'' \vDash \neg(\neg p \wedge \neg q)$. It follows that $s'' \vDash p, q$. The situation may be pictured as in the following diagram:

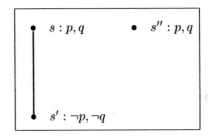

Thus again s, s'' are labelled by the same valuation, for they satisfy the same elementary letters of out meagre language. But they must be distinct. For on the one hand $s' < s$. On the other hand we do not have $s' < s''$, since s'' is a minimal $(p \leftrightarrow q)$-state and $s' \vDash p \leftrightarrow q$.

Given the existence of examples like this, the multiple copies version of preferential consequence has become the 'industry standard', and is often known as *KLM consequence* after the seminal paper of Kraus, Lehmann and Magidor (1990).

The reader may suspect that there is another way of handling such examples, using a syntactic rather than a semantic manoeuvre. Instead of allowing multiple copies of valuations, we could increase the supply of elementary letters in the language so as to make the same model injective for the enlarged language. Thus in Example 3.9 we might add a third letter r, label the two top nodes with the valuations p, q, r and $p, q, \neg r$ and assign r anything we like in the bottom nodes. Similarly for any other example. If there are at most n copies of a valuation in the preferential model, we will need at most $\lceil (\log_2 n) \rceil$ fresh letters to do the job. If there is no finite upper bound on the number of copies, we can still do it with countably many fresh letters.

Clearly, the consequence relation that the preferential model determines on the enlarged language agrees, over the original language, with the original consequence relation. However, in practice when working with preferential consequence operations it easier to hold the language constant and allow copies of valuations, rather than keep on expanding the language and the valuations labelling the model and restricting attention to the original language.

Suppose, now, that we wish to work only with the consequence operations generated by injective preferential models, but hold fixed the supply of elementary letters in the language. Do these consequence operations satisfy any special syntactic conditions? Can we prove a representation theorem for them? The answer is not entirely clear. The rather intricate story, up to the time of writing, is as follows.

- Lehmann and Magidor (1992) showed that when we restrict attention to ranked preferential models, the generated consequence operations can always be determined by an injective model.

- Freund (1993) strengthened this result. He showed that it holds for all 'filtered' preferential models, i.e. all those such that for any two states non-minimally satisfying a formula, there is a state that is less than both of them that satisfies the formula. Ranked models are always filtered, but not conversely. As we remarked earlier, ranked models always satisfy the non-Horn condition of rational monotony. Filtered models always satisfy the weaker condition of *disjunctive rationality*. This is the non-Horn condition: whenever $a \vee b \hspace{0.1em}\mid\!\sim x$ then either $a \hspace{0.1em}\mid\!\sim x$ or $b \hspace{0.1em}\mid\!\sim x$, or in the language of operations: $C(a \vee b) \subseteq C(a) \cup C(b)$.

- In the same paper (1993), Freund showed that when the language is finite, injective preferential models always satisfy the non-Horn condition $C(a \vee b) \subseteq Cn(C(a) \cup C(b))$. This is clearly weaker than disjunctive rationality, and we call it *Freund's condition*. Conversely, he showed that for a finite language we have a representation theorem: every preferential consequence relation satisfying this condition is generated by some injective preferential model.

- The restriction to finite languages in Freund's representation theorem was eliminated by Pino Pérez and Uzcátegui (2000), and also by Zhu *et al.* (2002). Using two different constructions, leading to distinct representations, these papers show, for both finite and infinite languages, that any inference relation satisfying Freund's condition may be represented by an injective preferential model.

- A gap remains: the soundness theorem can fail for infinite languages. For as Pino Pérez and Uzcátegui also show with an example, for an infinite language there are injective preferential models whose consequence operations do not satisfy Freund's condition. The issue of injectivity is thus quite complex, with a number of technical questions still unanswered in the infinite case.

Standing back from these technical issues, can we say what is the best framework for presenting preferential models? It is generally felt that the one chosen by Kraus, Lehmann and Magidor is the most convenient to work with. It allows copies of valuations in the preferential models. At the same time, attention is usually restricted to individual formulae as premisses, rather than sets of them. This is because the failure of compactness renders difficult the proof of representation theorems when infinite premiss sets are considered.

Selection Functions instead of Relations

Another line of generalization abstracts on the preference relation over W (or over S, if we are allowing copies), and works instead with a selection function γ over its power set, with $\gamma(U) \subseteq U$ for every $U \subseteq W$. This selection function may be constrained by suitable conditions as desired. If sufficiently powerful constraints are imposed, then a preference relation can be recovered from the selection function.

Evidently, this move runs parallel to one for partial meet default assumptions that we considered in section 2.3. In that case, we could work either with relations between subsets of the set K of background assumptions, or with selection functions on families of such subsets. Now, on the semantic level, we may work with relations between valuations (or states), or selection functions on families of them. On the abstract mathematical level, essentially the same questions arise.

Lindström (1991), Rott (2001) and Lehmann (2001) investigate in detail the approach using selection functions. As remarked in section 2.3, Rott (1993; 2001) looks deeply into the abstract connections between selection functions and preference relations.

Non-Classical Valuations

In all of the constructions of this section, we have been dealing with classical valuations, i.e. those functions on the set of formulae into $\{0,1\}$ that behave in the usual Boolean fashion. It is possible to relax this condition, either partially or entirely. Kraus, Lehmann and Magidor (1990) studied a partial relaxation. A more radical relaxation, taking valuations to be arbitrary functions on the set of formulae into $\{1,0\}$, was investigated by Makinson (1989) and more recently by Lehmann (2002).

Working with Ideals

In section 3.1 we looked at a variation on pivotal-valuation consequence, which we called 'pivotal-exception consequence', in which the set of all Boolean valuations is restricted by looking at an ideal. That was on the monotonic level. We may pass to the nonmonotonic level by allowing the identity of the ideal Δ to vary with the premiss set. Instead of taking Δ to be an ideal over the set V, we may take it to be one over the set $|A|$ of those valuations that satisfy the premiss set A.

In more detail, consider any function γ that associates with each set $|A|$ an ideal over $|A|$. Then we may say that x is a *default-exception consequence of A modulo* γ, and write $A \mid\!\sim_\gamma x$ alias $x \in Cn_\gamma(A)$, iff the set of valuations that satisfy A but do not satisfy x is an element of the ideal $\gamma(|A|)$ over $|A|$, i.e. iff $\{v \in V : v(A) = 1 \text{ and } v(x) = 0\} \in \gamma(|A|)$.

So defined, the relations $\mid\!\sim_\gamma$ remain supraclassical but become nonmonotonic. However, because the ideals associated with different sets $|A|$ need have no relationship to each other, properties such as CT and OR may also fail. In order to recover some or all of them, it is customary to add constraints on the relationship between the ideals $\gamma(|A|)$ for different values of A. We shall not enter into the details, referring the reader to the papers mentioned below.

This approach was developed by Ben-David and Ben-Eliyahu-Zohary (2000), Schlechta (1997), and Friedman and Halpern (2001), in a number of versions and with various names. Lehmann (2001) has made a detailed comparison with the default-valuation approach (in a version using selection functions and multiple copies of valuations).

Exercises

1*. Take the preferential model (with copies) in Example 3.9 (the Kraus, Lehmann and Magidor example) and consider the following orderings:

    (a) Like that of 3.9 but with also $s_1 < s_4$

    (b) Like that of 3.9 but with also $s_1 < s_4$ and also $s_2 < s_3$

    (c) Like that of 3.9 but upside-down

    (d) The transitive ordering $s_1 < s_2 < s_3 < s_4$

    (e) The transitive but cyclic ordering $s_1 < s_2 < s_3 < s_4 < s_1$

        (i) Which of these are ranked? Which contain infinite descending chains?

(ii) For each of these five preferential models (with copies), determine the status of the following consequences (whose status we checked in the text for Example 3.9 itself): $p \wedge q \mathrel{|\!\sim} f$ (where f is any self-contradiction), $t \mathrel{|\!\sim} \neg q$ (where t is any tautology), $p \mathrel{|\!\sim} \neg q$ and $p \leftrightarrow q \mathrel{|\!\sim} \neg p \wedge \neg q$.

2. Check that in the case of the pivotal-valuation semantics, it would have made no difference to allow copies of valuations. Specifically, show that for every set W of valuations with copies, the set U obtained by simply deleting copies determines the same consequence relation, i.e. $\vdash_W = \vdash_U$.

3. Show that when a preferential model is filtered, it satisfies the (non-Horn) condition of *disjunctive monotony*: whenever $A \cup \{x \vee y\} \mathrel{|\!\sim} z$ then either $A \cup \{x\} \mathrel{|\!\sim} z$ or $A \cup \{y\} \mathrel{|\!\sim} z$.

Problems

1. Verify that, as claimed in the text, in the special case that $S_1 = S$ and the premiss set A consists only of Horn formulae, circumscriptive inference and inference under the closed world assumption coincide.

2. Show that examples like 3.9 cannot exist with a ranked preference relation. In other words, show that for every ranked preferential model with copies, there is a ranked preferential model without copies that determines exactly the same consequence operation.

3. Show that default-exception consequence relations are supraclassical. What about left classical equivalence (LCE), right weakening (RW)? Give an example of the failure of cumulative transitivity (CT).

Project

Study in detail, through the references given, one of the specializations or generalizations of preferential consequence described in this section.

3.4   Review and Explore

Recapitulation

The main point of this chapter is that the syntactic step carried out in Chapter 2 to generate supraclassical consequence relations has a counterpart on the semantic level. Instead of adding background assumptions we reduce the set of valuations. If this reduction is constant, not depending on the premiss sets, then in the finite case we get an exact analogue of pivotal-assumption consequence. In the infinite case the constructions come apart, with pivotal-valuation consequence operations forming a broader class than their pivotal-assumption counterparts. The difference between the two classes is made up of just those pivotal-valuation relations that are not compact.

Despite this close parallel, the passage from a syntactic level to a semantic one is not just a technical exercise in saying the same thing in two ways. It has real utility, for it suggests new ways of going nonmonotonic. In the case of background assumptions, the paradigm for doing this was based on that of maximal consistency. In the case of reduced sets of valuations, it is based on the concept of minimality under a relation. The simplest way of doing this, which was also historically the first, gives rise to the class of preferential consequence operations. A number of other constructions in the literature refine or vary this paradigm, giving us other forms of default-valuation consequence, each with its own interest and special features. The most widely used is the KLM version, whose preferential models allow copies of valuations.

Checklist of Concepts and Definitions for Revision

Section 3.1: Pivotal-valuation consequence, definable sets of valuations, finitely generated Boolean language, weak representation, compactification, ideals, pivotal-exception consequence, principal ideals. *Section 3.2*: Preferential model, minimal elements of a set, least elements of a set, preferential consequence operation, complete relation, ranked (alias modular) preferential models, stoppering (alias smoothness) condition, cautious monotony, consistency preservation, rational monotony. *Section 3.3*: Circumscriptive model, multiple copies of valuations, injective preferential models, states, labelling functions, non-classical valuations, default-exception consequence, disjunctive monotony.

Further Reading

- G. Antoniou. *Nonmonotonic Reasoning*. MIT Press, Cambridge, MA, 1997. Chapter 13.5.

- G. Brewka, J. Dix and K. Konolige. *Nonmonotonic Reasoning — An Overview*. CSLI Publications, Stanford, CA, 1997. Chapter 2.

- S. Kraus, D. Lehmann and M. Magidor. Nonmonotonic reasoning, preferential models and cumulative logics, *Artificial Intelligence*, **44**, 167–207, 1990.

- D. Makinson. General Patterns in Nonmonotonic Reasoning. In *Handbook of Logic in Artificial Intelligence and Logic Programming, Vol. 3*, Gabbay, Hogger and Robinson, eds., pp. 35–110. Oxford University Press, 1994. Section 3.4.

- Y. Shoham. *Reasoning About Change*. MIT Press, Cambridge. MA, 1988. Chapter 3.

For material focussed on particular generalizations, see the reference calls in the relevant paragraphs of the text. An advanced mathematical treatment of the material of this chapter will be available in Schlechta (2004).

Chapter 4

Using Additional Rules

4.1 From Classical Consequence to Pivotal Rules

We come now to a third way of going supraclassical, monotonically and nonmonotonically. The basic idea is similar to that of adding background assumptions, but instead of adding *propositions* we add *rules*. This apparently small twist brings with it considerable divergence, which reveals itself even in the monotonic context — indeed in its finite case, where the pivotal-assumption and pivotal-valuation approaches are equivalent. In brief, *rules for propositions do not behave quite like propositions*.

By a rule for propositions (briefly, a *rule*) we mean any ordered pair (a, x) of propositions of the language we are dealing with. A set of rules is thus no more nor less than a binary relation R over the language, i.e. a set $R \subseteq L^2$. It must be confessed that although this terminology is standard in the area, it is a bit odd: it would be more natural to refer to the pairs (a, x) simply as pairs, and reserve the name 'rule' for the sets R of such pairs; but we follow the choice of words that is more common in the literature. It makes no difference to the content.

Given a set X of propositions and a set R of rules, we define the *image* of X under R, written as $R(X)$, in the standard manner of elementary set theory: $y \in R(X)$ iff there is an $x \in X$ with $(x, y) \in R$. A set X is said to be closed under R iff $R(X) \subseteq X$, i.e. iff whenever $x \in X$ and $(x, y) \in R$ then $y \in X$.

Let $R \subseteq L^2$ be a set of rules. Intuitively, they will be playing the role of a set of background 'inference tickets' ready for travel from any set of premises. Let A be a potential premiss set, and let x be a potential conclusion.

Definition 4.1 (Pivotal-Rule Consequence)

- *We say that x is a consequence of A modulo the rule set R, and write $A \vdash_R x$ alias $x \in Cn_R(A)$ iff x is in every superset of A that is closed under both Cn and the rule set R. In other words, iff x is in every set $X \supseteq A$ such that both $Cn(X) \subseteq X$ and $R(X) \subseteq X$.*

- *We call an operation a pivotal-rule consequence iff it is identical with Cn_R for some set R of rules.*

The definition of $A \vdash_R x$ requires x to be in *every* superset of A that is closed under both Cn and the rule set R. Trivially, at least one such set always exists, namely the entire language L. Moreover, the intersection of any non-empty family of sets, each of which is closed under Cn (resp. R), is itself closed under Cn (resp. R). It follows that there is always a unique least such set, namely the intersection of all of them. Thus the definition may be put as follows: $Cn_R(A)$ is *the least* superset X of A such that both $Cn(X) \subseteq X$ and $R(X) \subseteq X$.

It is immediate from the definition that $Cn \leq Cn_R$ so that every pivotal-rule consequence Cn_R is supraclassical. It is not difficult to verify that it is monotonic and also satisfies cumulative transitivity, so that it is a closure operation. We are thus still in the realm of paraclassical inference. Pivotal-rule consequence can also be verified to be compact — like its assumption-based counterpart but unlike the valuation-based one.

But it lacks an important property possessed by both pivotal-assumption and pivotal-valuation operations, namely disjunction in the premises. For example, if $R = \{(a,x),(b,x)\}$ then $x \in Cn_R(a)$ and also $x \in Cn_R(b)$ but $x \notin Cn_R(a \vee b) = Cn(a \vee b)$. This is because the last-mentioned set is vacuously closed under R, i.e. we have $R(Cn(a \vee b)) = \emptyset \subseteq Cn(a \vee b)$ since $a,b \notin Cn(a \vee b)$. We thus have the picture given in Table 4.1.

Pivotal-rule consequence also fails contraposition. This follows from the failure of disjunction in the premises, since any paraclassical operation satisfying the former must satisfy the latter. For a direct counterexample, put $A = \{a\}$ and $R = \{(a,x)\}$. Then $x \in Cn_R(a)$ but $\neg a \notin Cn_R(\neg x) = Cn(\neg x)$, because the last-mentioned set is vacuously closed under R, i.e. we have $R(Cn(\neg x)) = \emptyset \subseteq Cn(\neg x)$ since $a \notin Cn(\neg x)$. This contrasts with the situation for pivotal-assumption and pivotal-valuation consequence. They both satisfy contraposition — although, it should immediately be added to avoid confusion, their default versions do not.

What is the relationship between the pivotal-rule and pivotal-assumption consequence operations? As one might expect, it is as follows.

Table 4.1: Some Features of Pivotal-Rule Consequence

Supraclassical		
Reflexive	Closure Relation	Paraclassical
Cumulatively Transitive (CT)		
Monotonic		
(Does not always satisfy Disjunction in the Premisses (OR))		
Compact		

Theorem 4.2 *The pivotal-assumption consequence operations are precisely the pivotal-rule ones that satisfy disjunction in the premisses.*

Proof. On the one hand, every pivotal-assumption consequence operation is itself a pivotal-rule one — given Cn_K, simply put $R = \{(t,k) : k \in K\}$ where t is a tautology, and it is easily checked that $Cn_K = Cn_R$. Conversely, when Cn_R is a pivotal-rule consequence then as we have remarked it is a compact supraclassical closure operation. So when in addition it satisfies disjunction in the premisses, then by the representation Theorem 2.2 it is also a pivotal-assumption consequence operation.   ∎

Combining this with results from the preceding sections, we thus have the following curious relationship between the three kinds of pivotal inference.

Corollary 4.3 (to Theorem 4.2) *The set of pivotal-assumption consequence operations is the intersection of the set of pivotal-valuation and the set of pivotal-rule consequence operations.*

Proof. We have already shown that the left set is included in each of the two right ones (Theorems 3.3 and 4.2). For the converse, when an operation is in both of the two right sets then it is paraclassical and satisfies both disjunction in the premisses and compactness (Theorems 3.4 and 4.2), so that we may apply representation Theorem 2.2 again.   ∎

What happens if we try to get disjunction in the premisses back on board? What if we define $Cn_{R\vee}(A)$ to be the least superset of A that is closed under Cn, R and disjunction in the premisses? As the reader may suspect, this leads us straight back to pivotal-assumption consequence again. More specifically, we have the following identity, noticed in a more general context by Makinson and van der Torre (2000, section 6).

Theorem 4.4 $Cn_{RV}(A) = Cn(A \cup m(R))$ *where* $m(R)$ *is the set of materializations of pairs in* R, *i.e.* $m(R) = \{a \to x : (a, x) \in R\}$.

Proof. [Sketch] Clearly $Cn_{RV}(A) \subseteq Cn(A \cup m(R))$ since the right side includes A and is closed under Cn, R, and OR, while the left side is by definition the least such set. The interesting part is the converse. It can be proven in several different ways, each instructive.

One proof begins by noting that Cn_{RV} is by definition supraclassical and satisfies OR, and then checks that it is also a compact closure operation. We may thus apply the construction used in the proof of Theorem 2.2 to obtain $Cn_{RV}(A) = Cn(A \cup Cn_{RV}(\emptyset))$. We then check that $Cn_{RV}(\emptyset) = Cn(m(R))$, so that finally $Cn_{RV}(A) = Cn(A \cup Cn(m(R))) = Cn(A \cup m(R))$.

Another method is to argue from first principles. Use Zorn's Lemma to show that whenever $x \notin Cn_{RV}(A)$ then there is a maximal $B \supseteq A$ with $x \notin Cn_{RV}(B)$, and show that such a maximal B must be a maxiconsistent set, with $m(R) \subseteq B$, so that its characteristic function is a Boolean valuation satisfying $A \cup m(R)$ but not satisfying x. In effect, this argument mimics that for Theorem 2.2 itself.

Yet another argument can be constructed by supposing $x \in Cn(A \cup m(R))$, using the compactness of classical consequence to infer that $x \in Cn(A \cup m(R'))$ for some finite subset $R' \subseteq R$, and then arguing by induction on the number of elements of R'.   ∎

Theorems 4.2 and 4.4 together throw light on the subtle relations between rules and propositional assumptions.

- The two are not the same. In general, adding propositional assumptions gives us *more* than adding rules. In other words, $Cn_R(A) \subseteq Cn(A \cup m(R))$ and the inclusion will usually be proper. This is so, not only for classical Cn but any closure operation satisfying modus ponens.

- But when we are also given closure under OR, the two kinds of addition have exactly the *same* power. Rules collapse into their materializations, that is, $Cn_{RV}(A) = Cn(A \cup m(R))$.

We also have a representation theorem for pivotal-rule consequence.

Theorem 4.5 *For every compact supraclassical closure operation* Cn^+, *there is a relation* R *such that for all* $A, Cn^+(A) = Cn_R(A)$.

Proof. The construction is trivial, the proof easy. For the construction, simply put R to be Cn^+ restricted to singletons, i.e. put $R = \{(a, x) : x \in Cn^+(\{a\})\}$. The proof is in two parts. First we show that $Cn^+(A)$ is a superset of A and is closed under both classical Cn and R. Then we show that it is the least such superset.

For the first part, we have $A \subseteq Cn^+(A)$ since Cn^+ is a closure operation. Also $Cn(Cn^+(A)) \subseteq Cn^+(A)$ since by supraclassicality and idempotence of Cn^+ we have $Cn(Cn^+(A)) \subseteq Cn^+(Cn^+(A)) \subseteq Cn^+(A)$. Again, $R(Cn^+(A)) \subseteq Cn^+(A)$ by the definition of R together with the monotony and idempotence of Cn^+. This shows that $Cn^+(A)$ is a superset of A that is closed under both classical Cn and R.

To show that it is the least such superset, let X be another one; we need to check that $Cn^+(A) \subseteq X$. But if $x \in Cn^+(A)$ then by compactness of Cn^+ there is a finite $B \subseteq A$ with $x \in Cn^+(B)$. Also $Cn^+(B) = Cn^+(b)$ where b is the conjunction of all the finitely many elements of B, using supraclassicality and the supposition that Cn^+ is a closure operation. Since $x \in Cn^+(b)$ we have by the definition of R that $(b, x) \in R$, so $x \in R(\{b\}) \subseteq R(Cn(\{b\})) = R(Cn(B)) \subseteq R(Cn(A)) \subseteq R(Cn(X)) = R(X) = X$ since by hypothesis X includes A and is closed under both R and classical Cn. ∎

However, it would be mistaken to read much into this representation theorem. It is far less significant than Theorem 2.2 for pivotal-assumption consequences. The proof works only because the definition of a pivotal-rule consequence relation places no constraints on the relation R. This permits us to 'cheat' by taking R to be *the very consequence relation that we are seeking to represent*, restricted to singletons. Evidently, it would be more interesting to have representation results in terms of relations R that are constrained in some natural way. That is an area that does not seem to have been explored.

To end this section, we note a point that will be vital when we pass to default-rule consequence in the next section. It is possible to reformulate the definition of pivotal-rule consequence in an inductive manner. We have the following identity, whose verification uses the compactness of classical Cn.

Observation 4.6 $Cn_R(A) = \cup\{A_n : n < \omega\}$ *where* $A_0 = Cn(A)$ *and* $A_{n+1} = Cn(A_n \cup R(A_n))$.

Indeed, assuming that our language has at most countably many formulae so that R is also finite or countable, we can go further and reformulate the inductive definition so that it has only singleton increments in the induction step.

To do this, fix an ordering $\langle R \rangle$ of the set R of rules, indexing them with natural numbers $0, 1, 2, \ldots$. More precisely speaking, fix an ordering $r_i = (a_i, x_i)_{i < \alpha}$ of all the rules in R, without repetitions, with α a natural number if R is finite, or ω if R is countable.

Definition 4.7 (Singleton Increment given an Ordering)

- *Given such an ordering $\langle R \rangle$ of a rule-set R, we define the operation $Cn_{\langle R \rangle}$ by putting $Cn_{\langle R \rangle}(A) = \cup\{A_n : n < \omega\}$ with $A_0 = Cn(A)$ and $A_{n+1} = Cn(A_n \cup \{x\})$, where (a, x) is the first rule in $\langle R \rangle$ such that $a \in A_n$ but $x \notin A_n$. In the case that there is no such rule, we put $A_{n+1} = A_n$.*

To avoid a proliferation of letters, we are here using the same notation A_n for the terms of this sequence as for the previous sequence defining $Cn_R(A)$, but evidently it is quite a different one, making only singleton increments. Several features of the definition deserve special note.

- The sequence $A_0, A_1, \ldots$ is increasing, i.e. $A_n \subseteq A_{n+1}$ for all n.

- The construction does not require that rules are applied in the order in which they occur in $\langle R \rangle$. When we form A_{n+1}, we may be applying a rule (a, x) that occurs earlier in the sequence $\langle R \rangle$ than some rule that we have already applied, since its body a may become available only at A_n.

- By running through the sequence $\langle R \rangle$ from its beginning again at each stage of the construction, we ensure that no rule (a, x) is overlooked when its body eventually becomes available for use.

- By the terms of the definition, once a rule (a, x) is applied, it is never applied again, since its head x is in all the subsequent sets A_{n+k}. This prevents the sequence getting stuck with eternal reapplications of the same rule, unable to get over it to other ones.

Although the terms A_n of the sequence defining $Cn_{\langle R \rangle}(A)$ are not the same as those of the sequence defining $Cn_R(A)$, their union is the same. In other words:

Observation 4.8 $Cn_{\langle R \rangle}(A) = Cn_R(A)$.

This in turn implies also that the choice of ordering $\langle R \rangle$ of R makes no difference to the final result, which is in every case equal to $Cn_R(A)$.

These inductive definitions of pivotal-rule consequence may seem like long ways of expressing something that the original definition says quite briefly. And so they are! But we will see in the next section that they — and especially the singleton-increment one — provide a key for passing transparently to the nonmonotonic default-rule consequence operations.

Historical Remarks

The idea of using the monotonic operations Cn_R as a stepping-stone towards default-rule consequence is implicit in many papers, but rarely brought to the surface. One paper that does do so is Sandewall (1985). Sandewall presents the bridge system as a four-valued logic, but it can be translated into the language we are using. However the manner in which he then passes from the bridge system to the default one is quite different from the one that we will use in the following section, and is much closer to Reiter's fixed-point account.

Exercises

1*. Let R be the set of the following rules: $(p, r), (p \wedge q, s), (r, u), (w, v)$. Let $A = \{p, q, \neg v\}$. Determine each of $R(A), R(R(A)), R(A \cup R(A)), R(Cn(A \cup R(A)))$ and note the differences.

2*. Let R be any set of rules, in the sense defined in the text. Explain why $R(\emptyset) = \emptyset$. Explain why, for any set, whenever $x \in R(A)$ then there is an $a \in A$ with $x \in R(\{a\})$.

3. Explain why, as claimed in the text, the entire language L is closed under both classical consequence and any set R of rules.

4*. Let R be the set of the following rules: $(p, u), (p \wedge q, v), (s, w), (\neg y, w), (r \wedge q, \neg w)$. Let A consist of the three formulae $p \wedge q, r \wedge q, s \vee \neg y$. Calculate the sequences $A_0, A_1, A_2, \ldots$ and their union for the first of the inductive definitions given in this section. Then, taking R in the order written, calculate $A_0, A_1, A_2, \ldots$ and their union under the second of the inductive definitions given. Comment on the differences.

5. Show, as claimed in the text, that the intersection of any non-empty family of sets of Boolean formulae, each of which is closed under a rule-set R, is itself closed under R. Then do the same for Cn.

6. Explain why, as claimed in the text, it is immediate from the definition of Cn_R that $Cn \leq Cn_R$.

7. Show, as claimed in the text, that pivotal-rule consequence is monotonic and satisfies cumulative transitivity.

8. Show, as claimed in the text, that any paraclassical (i.e. supraclassical closure) operation satisfying contraposition also satisfies disjunction in the premisses.
   Hint: You will need to make use of the fact that any such operation satisfies both left classical equivalence and right weakening, as established in the Lemma for Theorem 2.2.

9. Check the claim made in the proof of Theroem 3.4, that $Cn_K = Cn_R$, where $R = \{(t, k) : k \in K\}$.

Problems

1. Establish Theorem 4.4 using any of the three lines of argument sketched in the text.

2. Prove Observation 4.6.
   Hint: Show the two inclusions separately. For the right in left, show by induction on n that each set A_n is included in $Cn_R(A)$, and then conclude. For the left in right, show that $\cup\{A_n : n < \omega\}$ includes A and is closed under both classical consequence (this is where you will need compactness of classical consequence) and all rules in R, and conclude using the definition of $Cn_R(A)$.

3. Prove Observation 4.8.
   Hint: Two strategies are possible — a proof from first principles paralleling that of the previous exercise, and one showing that the right set in this exercise coincides with the right set in the previous exercise. If you follow the second strategy, re-label the sets A_n as say B_n to avoid confusion, and show each of the two inclusions by an induction on n.

4*. Show, as claimed in the text, that pivotal-rule consequence is compact.
   Hint: Make use of the characterization of pivotal-rule consequence given by Observation 4.6.

4.2   From Pivotal Rules to Default Rules

The consequence operations Cn_R defined in the preceding section by pivotal rules are, as we have seen, monotonic.   Once again we may obtain nonmonotonicity by allowing the set R of rules, or more precisely, the ones among them that may be applied, to vary with A.

As we are working on a syntactic rather than a semantic level, it will not be surprising to learn that this may be done by means of consistency constraints. There are a number of different ways of going about it. Roughly speaking, they are of two main kinds: those that impose consistency constraints on the rules themselves, and those that place constraints on their step-by-step application.

Formulated in such general terms, this may seem a rather nebulous and inconsequential distinction to make. But in fact it marks a real difference, and leads to different consequence relations, with quite different behaviour. The literature focuses mainly on the latter kind, where the rules are left untouched but their application is constrained, and we will do likewise. We will begin by describing one of the best-known accounts, due to Reiter (1980), referred to as his system of 'normal defaults'. In the following section we will explain how this may be generalized to cover also his 'non-normal defaults', and will also outline an approach that restricts the rules themselves.

We take as our starting point the inductive characterization of pivotal-rule consequence using singleton increments under the guidance of an ordering $\langle R \rangle$ of the rules in R, which we gave in Definition 4.7. Recall that this put $Cn_R(A) = \cup\{A_n : n < \omega\}$ where $A_0 = Cn(A)$ and $A_{n+1} = Cn(A_n \cup \{x\})$, where (a, x) is the *first* rule in $\langle R \rangle$ such that $a \in A_n$ but $x \notin A_n$. In the limiting case that there is no such rule, we put $A_{n+1} = A_n$.

The essential idea now is to monitor these singleton increments, and allow rules to be applied only when they do not generate inconsistency.

Definition 4.9 (Ordered Default-Rule Consequence with Normal Rules)

- As before, we fix a finite or ω-ordering $\langle R \rangle$ of the given set R of rules. Still as before, we put $C_{\langle R \rangle}(A) = \cup\{A_n : n < \omega\}$, and set $A_0 = Cn(A)$.

- As before, we break the definition of A_{n+1} into two cases. But now the cases invoke a consistency check.

  Case 1. Suppose there is a rule (a, x) in R such that $a \in A_n$ but $x \notin A_n$ and x is consistent with A_n. Then choose the first such rule and put $A_{n+1} = Cn(A_n \cup \{x\})$ as before.
  Case 2. Suppose there is no such rule. Then put $A_{n+1} = A_n$ as before.

Thus the only change in definition, compared to that for pivotal-rule consequence in the form given by Definition 4.7, is the introduction of the consistency check as a requirement for entering into the first case of the induction step: the head of the rule must be consistent with the material constructed so far. But this small addition has many effects.

- One is that choice of ordering now makes a difference. In other words, the content of $C_{\langle R \rangle}(A)$ varies with the particular ordering $\langle R \rangle$ of R. Roughly speaking, this is because the application of an earlier rule may introduce material that makes a later rule fail its consistency check.

  For example, if $A = \{a\}$ and $R = \{(a, x), (a, \neg x)\}$, then if we order R in the manner written, we get $C_{\langle R \rangle}(A) = Cn(a, x)$ while if we take the reverse order we get $C_{\langle R \rangle}(A) = Cn(a, \neg x)$. Reason: in the former case we have $A_1 = Cn(A_0 \cup \{x\})$ since x is consistent with A_0, while $A_2 = A_1$ since $\neg x$ is inconsistent with A_1. In the other case, it is the reverse.

- This means, in turn, that even when the set R of background rules is fixed, there will be not one but many consequence operations $C_{\langle R \rangle}(A)$. Roughly speaking, there will be one for each ordering $\langle R \rangle$, although of course different orderings may happen to give rise to the same operation.

- Another effect of the consistency constraint is that the operations $C_{\langle R \rangle}(A)$ are nonmonotonic. Roughly speaking, this is because an increase in the premises may introduce material that makes some rules fail their consistency checks.

  For example, if $A = \{a\}$ and $R = \{(a, x)\}$ then $C_{\langle R \rangle}(A) = Cn(a, x)$, but when A is increased to $B = \{a, \neg x\}$ then $C_{\langle R \rangle}(B) = Cn(B) = Cn(a, \neg x)$. Reason: in the case of $A = \{a\}$ we again have $A_1 = Cn(A_0 \cup \{x\}) = Cn(a, x)$ since x is consistent with $A_0 = \{a\}$, while $A_2 = A_1$ since already $x \in A_1$. But in the case of $B = \{a, \neg x\}$ we have $B_1 = B_0 = Cn(B) = Cn(a, \neg x)$ since x is inconsistent with B and thus with B_0.

This inductive definition of the sets $C_{\langle R \rangle}(A)$ was first formulated explicitly by Brewka (1994), although with hindsight one might say that it is extractable from Reiter's own discussion of derivations for normal default systems, in the later sections of his seminal (1980) paper. It is equivalent to Reiter's original definition, in that the sets $C_{\langle R \rangle}(A)$ for the separate orderings $\langle R \rangle$ of R coincide with what Reiter called the 'extensions' of

A under the normal rules R. More explicitly, a set E of formulae is an extension, in the sense of Reiter, of A under the set R of normal rules iff $E = C_{\langle R \rangle}(A)$ for *some* well-ordering $\langle R \rangle$ of R. This result is a particular case of a more general theorem, covering also non-normal rules, stated and proven as Theorem 4.12 in the following section.

The notation used here is a little simpler than Reiter's. Whereas he writes a normal default rule as $a : Mx/x$, we write it simply as an ordered pair (a, x). On our presentation, therefore, normal default rules are just the same things as plain rules; the difference lies in the way that they are used. There is also some variation in terminology. In a normal default rule (a, x) alias $a : Mx/x$ Reiter calls a the *prerequisite* of the rule and x its *conclusion*; we will also use the same terms as we did for plain rules — *body* and *head* respectively.

Much more interesting than these details, however, is the fact that the definition above differs in its structure from that of Reiter. In Reiter's original paper (1980), a set E is called an extension of A under R iff it is a *fixpoint* under a certain operation Γ, meaning that it coincides with the value of that operation with itself as argument — briefly, iff $E = \Gamma(E)$. It is important to realize that fixpoint definitions do not in general guarantee the uniqueness or even the existence of the objects being defined. In the particular case of normal default rules, Reiter's fixpoint definition does ensure existence, but not uniqueness. That is, a given set A of premises always has at least one extension under a given set R of normal default rules, but may have many of them. For non-normal default rules, neither uniqueness nor existence is guaranteed.

Reiter (1980) also shows that his extensions may be defined using what is sometimes called a *quasi-induction* or, in the terminology of Makinson (1994), an *end-regulated induction*. This looks like an ordinary inductive definition except that the induction step makes reference to the object to be defined — the definition of A_{n+1} calls not only on the values of A_m for $m \leq n$, but also on the value of the final product $\cup \{A_n : n < \omega\}$. While end-regulated inductions are similar in their appearance to genuine inductions, logically they behave like fixpoint definitions.

We have proceeded inductively for several reasons. With such a definition, it is much easier to get an intuitive feeling for what is going on. In practice, whenever teachers try to convey the general ideas of default-rule reasoning in the classroom, they use some kind of vague, quasi-inductive language before switching over to their official fixpoint definitions. In effect, we are showing that such inductive language can be used accurately and with a clear conscience. At the same time, we are making clear the way in which default-rule operations may be seen as natural elaborations of the perfectly monotonic pivotal-rule operations of the preceding section.

The reader may be puzzled how the inductive definition manages to give the same result as a fixpoint definition if the former gives a unique output and the latter allows multiple outputs. The job is done by the orderings $\langle R \rangle$ of the rules. In effect, the inductive definition transforms the multiplicity of extensions into uniqueness, *modulo the choice of ordering* $\langle R \rangle$. Thus different orderings in general give different extensions. When we generalize to non-normal rules in the next section, and not only uniqueness but also existence may fail, the inductive definition will need to be given a further twist.

The operations $C_{\langle R \rangle}$ are themselves of interest, Indeed, if one is equipped with a preferred ordering $\langle R \rangle$ of R, one may wish to go no further than the operation $C_{\langle R \rangle}$ defined modulo that particular choice of order. But one can also define a consequence C_R that is independent of any particular order, by formulating a policy for amalgamating (or 'flattening', as is sometimes said) all the operations $C_{\langle R \rangle}$ for different values of $\langle R \rangle$.

If we are to respect a principle of equal treatment for all orderings, then only two such policies seem possible: union and intersection of values. In the present context, the union of extensions is hardly acceptable for a notion of consequence, for it will give us an inconsistent output whenever there was more than one extension to begin with. This is because, as is well known, the union of any two distinct Reiter extensions of A under R will be inconsistent. The usual policy is therefore that of intersecting, just as it was when analogous questions arose for default-assumption consequence — and in effect also for default-valuation, where we considered the propositions true under *all* the minimal valuations satisfying the premises. Such a policy for amalgamating multiple outputs is usually called the *sceptical* one, and is expressed in the following definition.

Definition 4.10 (Sceptical Default-Rule Consequence) *We define default-rule consequence (under the sceptical policy for amalgamating multiple outputs) by putting* $C_R(A) = \cap\{C_{\langle R \rangle}(A) : \langle R \rangle$ *a finite or ω-ordering of $R\}$. In relational notation: $A \hspace{1pt}\vdash_R x$ iff $A \hspace{1pt}\vdash_{\langle R \rangle} x$ for every such ordering.*

As we have remarked, this coincides with what is usually known as 'consequence using normal Reiter default rules with the sceptical policy on extensions'.

Since the default-rule operations $C_{\langle R \rangle}$ are in general nonmonotonic, it follows that the sceptical operations C_R are also in general nonmonotonic. Indeed, the simple example given above may be used again, for there R is a singleton and so $C_{\langle R \rangle} = C_R$.

Continuing on the negative side, we note that default-rule operations C_R may also fail cautious monotony. This was noticed by Makinson (1989) with a simple example, although with hindsight one can also use example 6.1 of Reiter (1980) to the same end. The following even simpler example is taken from Makinson (1994, section 3.2). Let R consist of three rules: $(t,a),(a,b),(b,\neg a)$ where t is a tautology. It is easy to check that no matter what the ordering of R, the premiss set $\{t\}$ has the same extension $Cn(a,b)$ under that ordering. On the other hand, $\{b\}$ has two extensions: $Cn(a,b)$ under e.g. the ordering as listed, and $Cn(\neg a,b)$ under e.g. the reverse ordering. Thus $t \mathrel{\vert\!\sim}_{\langle R \rangle} a$ and $t \mathrel{\vert\!\sim}_{\langle R \rangle} b$ but $b \mathrel{\vert\!\not\sim}_{\langle R \rangle} a$, where $\langle R \rangle$ is the reverse ordering. Likewise for the sceptical relation $\mathrel{\vert\!\sim}_R$ we have the same pattern. So both of them fail cautious monotony.

Still on the negative side, as we would expect from the behaviour of the underlying pivotal-rule operations, default-rule operations C_R may also fail the rule of disjunction in the premisses (OR). Indeed, the same trivial example may be used to illustrate the failure.

Finally, default-rule operations C_R may fail compactness. This can be shown by taking the same example used in section 2.2 to illustrate non-compactness for default-assumption consequence and translating it into the language of rules, replacing the set K of background assumptions by the corresponding set of rules with tautologous bodies, i.e. by putting $R = \{(t,k) : k \in K\}$.

On the positive side, the default-rule operations $C_{\langle R \rangle}$ and their 'meet' versions C_R are of course supraclassical, and it is easy to check that they satisfy the conditions of right weakening (RW) and left classical equivalence (LCE). They also satisfy cumulative transitivity, as was in effect proven by Reiter (1980), and verified explicitly in Makinson (1989; 1994).

Looking now at the relationship between classical, pivotal-rule, and default-rule consequence, we see a familiar pattern reappearing. The order of construction was: first classical consequence Cn, then pivotal-rule consequence Cn_R, then default-rule consequence C_R. The monotonic Cn_R is thus a conceptual bridge between the classical and nonmonotonic operations. However, the order of inclusion between the operations is different: we have $Cn \leq C_R \leq C_{\langle R \rangle} \leq Cn_{\langle R \rangle} = Cn_R$. In brief, picking out the key items, $Cn \leq C_R \leq Cn_R$. In other words, classical consequence Cn gives a lower bound on our default operations C_R, while pivotal-rule consequence Cn_R gives an upper bound, with the non-monotonic operations intermediate between the two.

In the case that the set $heads(R)$, consisting of all heads of rules in R, is consistent with the premiss set A, we have $C_R(A) = Cn_R(A)$, reaching the upper bound. For in that case the consistency check in the inductive definition of an extension is always satisfied, so that the unique extension of A under R is the least superset X of A such that both $Cn(X) \subseteq X$ and $R(X) \subseteq X$, i.e. $Cn_R(A)$. At the opposite extreme, when every head of every rule in R is inconsistent with A, we have $C_R(A) = A_0 = Cn(A)$, down at the lower bound.

Exercises

1*. Assume that p, q, r are the only elementary letters in the language. Consider the rule set $R = \{(p, q), (q, r), (q, \neg r)\}$, and the premiss set $A = \{p\}$. List all possible orderings $\langle R \rangle$ of R. For each ordering, determine the extension $C_{\langle R \rangle}(A)$. Finally, determine $C_R(A)$.

2*. Consider the rule-set $R = \{(p, q), (q, r), (r, s), (s, \neg p)\}$ and the premiss set $A = \{p\}$. Show that $C_{\langle R \rangle}(A) = Cn(\{p, q, r, s\})$ irrespective of the ordering $\langle R \rangle$ of R, so that also $C_R(A) = \cap\{C_{\langle R \rangle}(A)\} = Cn(\{p, q, r, s\})$. This example is a rule-based form of the *Möbius strip* (with four elements), already considered in a propositional form (with three elements) in Chapter 2.2.

3*. (a) Explain why the set $C_{\langle R \rangle}(A)$ is well-defined for every set A of formulae, i.e. why the definition guarantees that it exists.

   (b) Show that the operations $C_{\langle R \rangle}$ are *consistency-preserving*, in other words, that $C_{\langle R \rangle}(A)$ is consistent whenever A is consistent.

   (c) Explain why it follows that the sceptical operation C_R is also consistency-preserving.

4. Let R, S be sets of rules. Suppose that R is finite. Show that for every ordering $\langle R \rangle$ of R there is an ordering $\langle R \cup S \rangle$ of $R \cup S$ such that $C_{\langle R \rangle}(A) \subseteq C_{\langle R \cup S \rangle}(A)$.

5. We know from the previous section that pivotal-rule consequence can fail disjunction in the premisses (OR). Check that the same example shows the same failure for default-rule consequence with normal rules.

6. Verify right weakening and left classical equivalence for default-rule consequence with normal rules.

7. In the counterexample to cautious monotony given in Makinson (1989), R consisted of just two rules (t, b) and $(a \lor b, \neg b)$. Check it out.

8. Show that default-assumption consequence may be seen as a special case of default-rule consequence in the following sense: for every set

K of background assumptions there is a set R of normal rules such that for every premiss set $A, \{Cn(A \cup K') : K'$ an A-maxiconsistent subset of $K\} = \{Cn_{\langle R \rangle}(K) : \langle R \rangle$ an ordering of $R\}$.

Hint: Adapt the idea used for the pivotal consequence relations in an exercise of the previous section.

9. Complete the proof, sketched in the text, that default-rule consequence is not compact.

Problems

1. Show that $Cn \leq C_R \leq C_{\langle R \rangle} \leq Cn_{\langle R \rangle} = Cn_R$.

2. Let R be a set of default rules, and let $\langle R \rangle$ be an ordering of R. Let A be an initial premiss set. With these elements fixed, the passage from A_n to A_{n+1} may be seen as an operation F, with $A_{n+1} = F(A_n)$. Show that $X = \cup\{A_n : n < \omega\}$ is a *fixpoint* of the operation F, in the sense that $X = F(X)$.

3. Show that default-rule consequence with normal rules satisfies cumulative transitivity (CT).

4.3 Generalizations and Variants

We begin with the best-known generalization of the normal default-rule consequence relations that were defined in the preceding section – its broadening to cover what are called 'non-normal' default rules.

Non-normal Default Rules

In his paper of 1980, Reiter already considered default rules of a much more general kind, termed 'non-normal'. They are no longer pairs (a, x) but triples (a, P, x), where a and x are Boolean formulae and P is a finite, possibly empty, set of formulae.

As already mentioned in the preceding section, Reiter calls a the *prerequisite* of the rule, and x its *conclusion*; we will also continue to call them *body* and *head* respectively. The new ingredient is the set P. Reiter calls its elements the *justifications* of the rule. We would prefer to call them *constraints*, because their only role is to figure in consistency checks; but in deference to tradition we continue to use Reiter's terminology.

Normal rules, used in the preceding section, may be identified with those triples (a, P, x) in which P consists of the head x alone. Plain rules without consistency checks, as studied in section 4.1, may be identified with triples (a, P, x) in which P is empty.

In allowing the set P of justifications to be empty we are following a convention that is by now consensual. Strictly speaking, Reiter himself required all rules to have a non-empty set of justifications; but allowing the empty set as limiting case facilitates our formulations.

The essential idea involved in applying a non-normal default rule $r = (a, P, x)$ is to pass from a to x whenever this can be done without leading to violation of any elements of P. Notoriously, this turns out to be an intricate notion, and admits many variations. We will focus on the version of Reiter, and will continue to use an inductive approach rather than one in terms of fixpoints. In effect, we have two problems to face in constructing an inductive definition: how to take account of multiplicity now that we are in the broadened context of non-normal default rules, and how to deal with possible non-existence of extensions.

We continue to handle the first problem by means of well-orderings of the rule-set, as we did in the normal case, but with the assistance of auxiliary sets R_n whose job is to track the rules applied in the course of the induction. This device has been used for various purposes by a number of authors, e.g. Łukaszewicz (1984/8) and (1990), Brewka (1991), and Remmel as reported in Marek and Truszczyński (1993), and was employed to obtain essentially the same result in Antoniou (1997).

We deal with the second problem by using an abort clause at an appropriate point in the definition. The idea is to insert a sub-clause into the construction of A_{n+1}, telling us that in certain situations A_{n+1} does not exist and the construction self-destructs. For the definition to be a genuine induction, the abort clause must not refer to what is still to be constructed, but only to what has already been built.

Definition 4.11 (Ordered Default-Rule Consequence with Non-Normal Rules)

- *As before, we fix a well-ordering $\langle R \rangle$ of the set R of rules, of order type at most ω.*

- *As before, we put $C_{\langle R \rangle}(A) = \cup \{A_n : n < \omega\}$, and we set $A_0 = Cn(A)$.*

- *Simultaneously with the sets A_n we define a sequence of sets R_n to record the rules applied in the course of the induction. We set $R_0 = \emptyset$.*

- *For the induction step defining A_{n+1} and R_{n+1}, we proceed as follows, where $just(R_n)$ stands for the set of all justifications of rules in R_n:*

  Case 1.   Suppose there is a rule $r = (a, P, x)$ in R such that $a \in A_n, r \notin R_n$, and A_n is consistent with each separate $p \in P$. Take the first such rule, and consider two sub-cases.

  Sub-case 1.1: Suppose that also $A_n \cup \{x\}$ is consistent with each separate $p \in just(R_n) \cup P$. Then we put $A_{n+1} = Cn(A_n \cup \{x\})$ and $R_{n+1} = R_n \cup \{r\}$.

  Sub-case 1.2: Suppose otherwise. Then the construction aborts in the sense that A_{n+1} and R_{n+1} are left undefined and we continue no further, taking all subsequent A_m and the union $\cup\{A_n : n < \omega\}$ alias $C_{\langle R \rangle}(A)$ also to be undefined.

  Case 2.   Suppose there is no rule as required for case 1. Then we put $A_{n+1} = A_n$ and $R_{n+1} = R_n$.

Following the terminology of Reiter, we will often refer to $C_{\langle R \rangle}(A)$, when it exists, as an *extension*, more fully as the extension of A generated by the ordered set $\langle R \rangle$ of rules.

Roughly speaking, the entry condition for Case 1 tells us that if everything is in order when we compare the part of the extension so far constructed with the justifications of the current rule, then we are forced to *try* to apply the rule. We cannot back out. But, having got so far, if the further test for entry into Sub-case 1.2 is not satisfied, then we are *condemned* – we are shunted into Sub-case 2.2 and the construction aborts. This second test takes into account the head of the current rule as well as the part of the extension constructed so far, and past as well as present justifications.

As mentioned in the previous section, the first inductive definition of normal Reiter extensions was given by Brewka (1994). For non-normal systems, it is implicit in the 'operational semantics' for default logic devised by Antoniou (1997). Although Antoniou presents matters in a procedural perspective using other terms, his construction is in effect inductive and, as he shows, equivalent to the Reiter fixpoint definition. The present formulation was given (with an error of detail) in Makinson (2003a).

Examples

To reduce notation, in these examples when P is a singleton $\{p\}$ we write the rule $(a, \{p\}, x)$ as (a, p, x).

1. Consider the simple example where $A = \{a\}$ and R consists of the single triple $(a, \neg x, x)$, so that there is just one well-ordering of R. As always, $A_0 = Cn(a)$. To identify A_1, note that the premiss a of the rule is in A_0, the rule itself is not in $R_0 = \emptyset$, and its justification $\neg x$ is consistent with A_0. Thus we are in Case 1. On the other hand, the conclusion x of the rule is inconsistent with the justification $\neg x$, and so we are in Sub-case 1.2. Thus A_1 is undefined and the construction aborts. As R consists of just one rule, with only one possible well-ordering, this means that the example has no extensions.

2. It is instructive to compare this with the example where $A = \{a\}$ and R consists of the single triple $r = (a, \neg a, x)$, so that the justification now contradicts the premiss of the rule rather than its conclusion. Again, $A_0 = Cn(a)$. To identify A_1, we observe that the premiss a of r is in A_0 and $r \notin R_0 = \emptyset$, but the justification $\neg a$ of r is inconsistent with A_0. Thus we are in Case 2 and hence $A_1 = A_0 = Cn(a)$.

3. Finally, we look at the example where $A = \emptyset$ and R contains two rules $r_1 = (t, q, x \wedge \neg p)$ and $r_2 = (t, p, x)$ where t is a tautology. If we order the rules as numbered, then we get the extension $Cn(x \wedge \neg p)$. If we reverse the order, the construction of an extension aborts.

If one is fanatic about parsimony, one can streamline the above definition a little. A straightforward induction tells us that the sets A_n are fully determined by the corresponding sets R_n; specifically, $A_n = Cn(A \cup heads(R_n))$, where $heads(R_n)$ is the set of heads of rules in R_n. One can therefore define just the sequence R_n inductively, then use the equality to get the corresponding A_n.

As in the case of normal rules, the inductive definition gives us exactly the extensions in the sense of Reiter. In other words:

Theorem 4.12 *Let R be any set of (normal or non-normal) default rules, and A any premiss set. Then the Reiter fixpoint extensions of A under R are precisely the sets $C_{\langle R \rangle}(A)$ for well-orderings $\langle R \rangle$ of R of order-type at most ω. That is:*

1. *For every well-ordering $\langle R \rangle$ of R of order-type $\leq \omega$, if the set $C_{\langle R \rangle}(A)$ is well-defined then it is a Reiter extension of A under R.*

2. *Every Reiter extension of A under R is a well-defined set $C_{\langle R \rangle}(A)$ for some well-ordering $\langle R \rangle$ of R of order-type $\leq \omega$.*

As the proof is quite intricate and takes us out of the main flow of our exposition, we place it in Appendix A.

Other Variants in the Reiter Tradition

Many variants of the Reiter default systems have been studied in the literature. We mention a few of the most important among them.

Some vary the *policy for amalgamating multiple extensions*. One idea is to use *partial meets* rather than full meets when managing multiple extensions. Recall that given a set R of rules, the 'sceptical' operation C_R was defined as the meet of the values of the default-rule operations $C_{\langle R \rangle}$ for all possible well-orderings $\langle R \rangle$ of R. That is, we put $C_R(A) = \cap \{ C_{\langle R \rangle}(A) : \langle R \rangle$ an ordering of $R \}$. As in the analogous cases of default-assumption and default-valuation consequence, one could replace this full meet by a partial meet, intersecting only a selected subfamily of the sets $C_{\langle R \rangle}(A)$.

Indeed, there are several ways in which this may be done. One would be to allow only those orderings $\langle R \rangle$ that include some given transitive irreflexive relation $<$ over R. In this way we obtain the *prioritized default logic* (acronym PDL) defined by Brewka 1994. Another approach would be to introduce a preference relation between orderings, and intersect only those sets $C_{\langle R \rangle}(A)$ such that $\langle R \rangle$ is a *minimal* ordering of R under that preference relation. Other devices are also possible; see e.g. Tan and Treur (1992).

Some other variants are motivated by examples that, arguably, are mistreated by the Reiter systems. Two are particularly well known.

Poole (1989) suggested that when building an extension we should require *joint consistency* of the justifications, rather than their separate consistency, with other material. It is easy to see how the definitions of $C_{\langle R \rangle}(A)$ given above, for normal and for non-normal rules, may be modified in this way – just replace the words 'each separate' with 'the conjunction of all' in them. Alternatively, one can simply replace the finite justification set of each rule by its conjunction and then apply the definition without modification.

Łukaszewicz (1984/8; 1990) expressed dissatisfaction with the way in which the Reiter construction can abort in the context of non-normal rules, leaving us without extensions. He proposed a revised formulation of Reiter's fixpoint definition of an extension, which *guarantees that extensions always exist* even when the default rules are non-normal.

The idea may be seen most clearly in terms of our inductive approach. Whenever our inductive generation of a Reiter extension of A under $\langle R \rangle$ succeeds, then it is also a Łukaszewicz extension. If on the other hand it aborts, say in the passage from A_n to A_{n+1}, then we also get A_n as a Łukaszewicz extension. We can obtain the Łukaszewicz extensions by suitably simplifying the induction clause of our definition. We drop the Sub-cases in the induction step, and reformulate Case 1 as follows: "Suppose there is a rule $r = (a, P, x)$ in R such that $a \in A_n, r \notin R_n$ and

$A_n \cup \{x\}$ is consistent with each $p \in \mathit{just}(R_n) \cup P$. Then we take the first such rule, and put $A_{n+1} = Cn(A_n \cup \{x\})$. We also set $R_{n+1} = R_n \cup \{r\}$."

Which of the definitions — of Reiter, Poole, Łukaszewicz or other — gives the right treatment of the controverted examples? In the author's view, it would be misleading to insist on this question, for it has no answer. There is no 'correct' account of Poole's 'broken-arm' example, Łukaszewicz' 'fishing' examples, or others like them, for intuitions are too variable and confused to provide clear verdicts. This is why we have not gone into the details of the examples themselves. It should also be said that the use of everyday language in examples can distort vision, for the language employed usually carries trails of unsuspected implicit assumptions influencing our intuitive judgement.

On the other hand, in specific contexts we may find it more convenient to use one variant than another, without erecting this preference into a doctrine of correctness.

We remarked in section 4.2 that although Reiter default-rule inference systems satisfy cumulative transitivity, they can fail the converse *cautious monotony*, even when all rules are normal. The same is true of the systems of Poole and Łukaszewicz, and indeed appears to be endemic to systems in which consistency constraints are imposed on the application of rules in derivations. Nevertheless, systems have been introduced that restore the validity of cautious monotony by the trick of 'upping the ontology'. The essential idea is that the premisses and conclusions that occur in a derivation are no longer just Boolean formulae, but rather Boolean formulae indexed by traces of the justifications used in their derivations. Systems of this kind were developed by Brewka (1991) for default-rule reasoning, and by Brewka, Makinson and Schlechta (1991) for logic programming.

Computational Aspects of Fixpoint and Inductive Definitions

In the preceding section we explained why we prefer an inductive account to a fixpoint one: essentially, they are easier to grasp, work with, and communicate.

On the other hand, it may be argued that from a computational point of view the passage from fixpoints to induction is a step backwards rather than forwards. Every extension of A under default rules R is known to be of the form $Cn(A \cup \mathit{heads}(S))$ for some subset $S \subseteq R$. So when the set of default rules is finite with n elements, to determine the family of extensions of A under R, it suffices to take the 2^n subsets S of R and check them, one by one, to see whether $Cn(A \cup \mathit{heads}(S))$ is a fixpoint of the operator Γ used to define extensions. If done haphazardly, this is a guess-and-test procedure; carried out systematically, it is a list-and-test one.

In contrast there are $n!$ well-orderings of an n-element set R and to determine the extensions inductively we need to take these orderings one by one, apply the induction, see which abort before completion, and retain the surviving constructions. But as is notorious, we have $n! > 2^n$ for all $n \geq 4$. Indeed, the function $n!$ grows faster than 2^n in the sense that $\lim_{n \to \infty}(2^n/n!) = 0$; in the usual shorthand, $2^n = o(n!)$ (see e.g. Hein (2002, section 5.5.2)).

Prima facie, this suggests that using an inductive definition to calculate the set of all extensions of a given finite system (A,R), is less efficient than using a fixpoint one. However, the situation is not quite so clear-cut, as there are some other relevant factors.

- The most important is that in practice we may not wish to find the set of *all* extensions. As pointed out by Brewka (1994), the specific problem in hand may naturally delimit a relatively small subset of the possible well-orderings — for example, all those that include some nearly-complete ordering — and we may be interested only in the extensions determined by them.

- Even when we wish to determine the set of all possible extensions, there may be some mitigating factors. In particular, if the set of all well-orderings of R is itself suitably well-ordered, information about the construction using an earlier ordering may perhaps be recycled towards the construction based on a later ordering. We do not attempt to resolve these computational questions here.

Induction versus Fixpoints

Our presentation of Reiter default inference and some of its variants suggests a general questions about the relationship between definition by fixpoints and using standard mathematical induction. When may the former be reduced to the latter?

We have seen how the two principal difficulties were overcome in the case of Reiter default logic. The multiplicity of extensions was handled by introducing an ordering $\langle R \rangle$ of R as an additional parameter (and, in the non-normal context, tracking rules used); their non-existence was dealt with by introducing an appropriate escape clause into the induction step. Similar steps work, as we remarked, for the variants of Poole and of Łukaszewicz. But what are the limits? Without attempting to answer this question in its generality, we mention a further case known to be positive, another that we conjecture to be positive, and a third that seems to be negative.

The construction of Theorem 4.12 may be used to cover logic programs with negation as failure under the 'answer-set semantics'. Such a program is a set of expressions of the form $x \leftarrow a_1, \ldots a_n$, *not* $(a_{n+1}), \ldots, not(a_{n+m})$ where x and all the a_i are literals (i.e. elementary letters or their negations). These expressions may be seen as rules about a perfectly classical though very restricted object language. More specifically, they may be read as non-normal default rules with the literal x as head (conclusion), the conjunction of the elementary letters $a_1, \ldots a_n$, as body (prerequisites, in Reiter's terminology), and the negated literals $not(a_{n+1}), \ldots, not(a_{n+m})$ as corresponding to justifications $\neg a_{n+j}$ of the rule. Theorem 4.12 can then be applied to cover such logic programs.

Logic programs have been generalised to allow disjunctions of literals in the head. These disjunctions are not understood in a simple truth-functional manner, but as presenting alternative possible conclusions open for choice. We conjecture that such programs may be reduced to families of programs without disjunctive heads, thereby permitting an inductive definition of their answer sets.

In the area of default logic, the 'weak extensions' of Marek and Truszczyński (1989; 1993) are of interest, both in their own right and because, as those authors have shown, they correspond to the expansions of autoepistemic logic. It appears difficult to give an inductive account of the fixpoints defining these extensions. Intuitively, they are not visibly grounded in their premiss-sets. Mathematically, they can exceed their unconstrained counterparts. Recall that for Reiter systems, whatever can be obtained by applying rules *with* their consistency constraints can already be obtained by applying the same rules *without* any consistency constraint. In other words, when E is any Reiter default extension of the premiss set A under a rule-set R, then $E \subseteq Cn_R(A)$, where $Cn_R(A)$ is the (unique) closure of A under both classical consequence and all of the plain rules obtained by dropping the constraint sets from rules in R. This inclusion fails for weak extensions. To take a trivial example, when $R = \{(p, p, p)\}$ and $A = \emptyset$, then both $Cn(\emptyset)$ and $Cn(p)$ are weak extensions E of A under R, while $Cn_R(A) = Cn(\emptyset)$. Thus for $E = Cn(p)$, the inclusion $E \subseteq Cn_R(A)$ fails.

However, neither of these two considerations is conclusive. The former is little more than a vague feeling; and while the latter is a mathematical fact, it does not constitute a proof of the point at issue. Indeed, there is a trivial sense in which weak extensions *can* be given an inductive definition. Instead of inducing modulo well-orderings of the rule set R, do so modulo its subsets. For a given $S \subseteq R$, it is trivial to give a two-step inductive definition that puts $A_0 = Cn(A)$; puts $A_1 = S$ if S is a fixpoint of the Marek and Truszczyński version of the Γ function and aborts otherwise; and if A_1 is well-defined, puts each following $A_n = A_1$. Formally speaking, this is an inductive definition, but evidently it is quite uninteresting. The problem therefore has to be reformulated: is there a non-trivial and interesting inductive definition of weak extensions? Evidently, the terms of the question are not very precise.

Maxfamilies of Rules

A quite different approach to default rules is to use consistency constraints to cut back on the set R itself, rather than restrict its step-by-step application. Following the pattern for default-assumption consequence in section 2, one can form a family of suitably maximal subsets of R.

Consider any set R of normal default rules (a, x). For each premiss set A we consider the family of all maximal subsets $S \subseteq R$ such that the pivotal-rule consequence $Cn_S(A)$ is consistent. This is called the *maxfamily* of A under R. We define $C_{\underline{R}}(A)$ (this time with subscript underlined) to be the intersection of the sets $Cn_S(A)$ for all S in the maxfamily of A.

These operations are not the same as the default-rule consequences C_R for normal rules given in section 4.2. To illustrate the difference, consider the Möbius strip example, where $R = \{(p, q), (q, r), (r, \neg p)\}$. On the one hand, the premiss set $\{p\}$ gives rise to exactly one default-rule extension, namely $Cn(\{p, q, r\})$. On the other hand, we have three maxfamilies S, namely the three two-element subsets of R. These yield three sets $Cn_S(A)$ — namely $Cn(p), Cn(\{p, q\})$, and $Cn(\{p, q, r\})$, which form a chain under set inclusion and have just $Cn(p)$ as their intersection. In general, there are more maxfamilies than extensions, and so the intersection of the maxfamilies will be smaller than the intersection of the extensions.

It should be noted, however, that the output obtained still differs from the one we saw when we used maximal subsets of a background assumption set K. If we translate the rules in R into material conditional formulae in K, the possibility of applying modus tollens as well as modus ponens to material conditional propositions gives us larger extensions, with a larger intersection. This can be seen in detail by comparing the Möbius strip example above with its counterpart in section 2.2.

In summary, while the distinction between the default-rule consequence operations $C_{\underline{R}}$ and the maxfamily consequence operations C_R is subtle, it leads to significantly different outcomes. In effect, we are looking at two strategies for guarding against contradictions when applying rules to a set of premisses. One restricts the *generating process*, giving us the operations $C_{\langle R \rangle}$ for well-orderings $\langle R \rangle$ of R. The other constrains the *generating apparatus*, giving us the operations $Cn_S(A)$ for sets $S \subseteq R$ in the maxfamily of A.

Maxfamily operations are studied by Makinson and van der Torre (2000) in a broader context where inputs (premisses) are not necessarily authorized to reappear as outputs (conclusions).

Exercises

As in the text, to reduce notation when P is a singleton $\{p\}$ we write the rule $(a, \{p\}, x)$ as (a, p, x).

1*. Let $A = \{a\}$. In the examples below, for each possible ordering of the rules in R, determine whether $C_{\langle R \rangle}(A)$ exists. If $C_{\langle R \rangle}(A)$ does not exist, identify the exact point in its construction where it aborts, and why. If it does exist, say what it is.

  (a) $R = \{(a, t, \neg a)\}$
  (b) $R = \{(a, x, x), (x, t, \neg a)\}$
  (c) $R = \{(a, x, x), (x \vee y, t, y), (y, t, \neg x)\}$
  (d) $R = \{(t, x \wedge y, \neg x)\}$
  (e) $R = \{(a, x, y), (y, t, \neg x)\}$

2*. When the initial premiss set A is inconsistent and every rule has a non-empty set of justifications, what is $C_{\langle R \rangle}(A)$? Illustrate with a simple example.

3*. When every rule has an inconsistent justification, what is $C_{\langle R \rangle}(A)$? Illustrate with a simple example.

4. Verify the claim made in the text, that normal rules may be identified with triples $(a, \{x\}, x)$. Verify also that plain rules, as studied in section 4.1, may be identified with triples $(a, \emptyset, x)$.

5. What are the extensions of A under R when $A = \{a\}$ and R is the singleton containing just the triple $(a, b, c \wedge \neg c)$.

6. What are the extensions of A under R when $A = \{a\}$ and $R = \{r_1, r_2\}$ where $r_1 = (t, b, a)$ and $r_2 = (t, c, \neg b)$?

7. We observed in section 3.1 that pivotal-rule consequence can fail the rule OR, and in 3.2 that the same is true for sceptical Reiter default consequence, even when normal. Show that in the non-normal case we may even have the following strange situation: $a \mathrel{\vert\!\sim}_R x, b \mathrel{\vert\!\sim}_R x$, but $a \vee b \mathrel{\vert\!\sim}_R \neg x$.
   Hint: Put R to consist of the three rules $(a, t, x), (b, t, x)$, $(a \vee b, \{\neg a, \neg b\}, \neg x)$.

Problems

1. Let A be a premiss set and $\langle R \rangle$ a well-ordered rule-set. Show that $A_n = Cn(A \cup heads(R_n))$.

2. Show that default-rule consequence with non-normal rules satisfies cumulative transitivity (CT).

4.4   Review and Explore

Recapitulation

By working with any fixed set of rules we may define a natural supraclassical consequence operation, which is monotonic and indeed a closure operation, and which we have called pivotal-rule consequence. In contrast to the pivotal-assumption and pivotal-valuation consequence   operations, it fails the rule of disjunction in the premisses.   Like them, it may be seen as a stepping-stone to the nonmonotonic realm. Specifically, by fixing a well-ordering of the rules in R and placing a suitable consistency constraint on their application, we may define certain quite natural nonmonotonic consequence operations in an inductive manner. They coincide with Reiter extensions with normal default rules, originally (and more commonly) defined as fixpoints.

The inductive definition can be generalized to cover extensions under what are known as 'non-normal' default rules. These contain a set of constraints (alias 'justifications') as well as body and head. By introducing an appropriate abort clause into the induction step we can handle cases where extensions do not exist, and again obtain exactly the Reiter extensions defined as fixpoints.

It is also possible to apply consistency constraints in a quite different way, restricting the generating apparatus rather than the generating process, giving us the maxfamily consequence operations, which give significantly different outcomes.

Checklist of Concepts and Definitions for Revision

Section 4.1: Closure of a set under a rule, pivotal-rule consequence, materialization of a rule, ordered rule-set, singleton increments. *Section 4.2*: Consistency constraints on the application of rules, normal default rules, ordered default-rule consequence, principle of equal treatment, sceptical default-rule consequence; fixpoint definitions, end-regulated inductions, standard mathematical inductions. *Section 4.3*: Non-normal default rules, constraints (alias justifications) in rules, book-keeping sets, abort clause; Poole's extensions, Łukaszewicz' extensions, Marek's 'weak' extensions, maxfamilies, constraining the generating process versus constraining the generating apparatus.

Further Reading

- G. Antoniou. *Nonmonotonic Reasoning.* MIT Press, Cambridge, MA, 1997. Chapters 3–8.

- G. Brewka, J. Dix and K. Konolige. *Nonmonotonic Reasoning — An Overview.* CSLI Publications, Stanford, CA, 1997. Section 4.1.

- W. Łukaszewicz. *Non-Monotonic Reasoning–Formalization of Common-sense Reasoning.* Ellis Horwood, 1990. Chapter 5.

- D. Makinson.   General Patterns in Nonmonotonic Reasoning.   In *Handbook of Logic in Artificial Intelligence and Logic Programming, Vol. 3*, Gabbay, Hogger and Robinson, eds., pp. 35–110. Oxford University Press, 1994. Section 3.2.

- V. W. Marek and M. Truszczyński. *Nonmonotonic Logic: Context Dependent Reasoning.* Springer, Berlin, 1993. Section 2.8, chapter 3, sections 4.1–2.

- R. Reiter. A logic for default reasoning, *Artificial Intelligence*, **13**, 81–132, 1980. Sections 1–3.

Chapter 5

Connections between Nonmonotonic and Probabilistic Inference

Up to now, we have not said a single word about probability, concentrating on getting a clear overview of the three main qualitative bridges to nonmonotonic consequence operations. It is now time to do so, for it is clear that there are connections, of some kind, between them.

On the one hand, there is an element of uncertainty in nonmonotonic inference: being supraclassical, there possible situations in which a conclusion is false although all premises are true. On the other hand, there is something nonmonotonic about probabilistic reasoning. To begin with, there is the notorious fact that the conditional probability of a proposition x given another one a, may fall, just as it may rise, when we are given additional information b to conjoin with a. In other words, we may have $p_{a \wedge b}(x) < p_a(x)$ where p_a is the conditionalization of the probability function p on the proposition a.

What then is the relation between probability and nonmonotonic logic? That is our principal question in the following sections. But behind it lie a number of other questions that need to be untangled.

- What, after all, is the relation between probability and *classical* consequence?

- In what ways do probabilistic considerations lead to supraclassical inference relations, and how do they compare with the qualitatively

111

defined ones that we have considered so far?

- Are all the probabilistic consequence relations nonmonotonic, or are there any natural probabilistic bridge-systems, akin to the qualitative ones outlined earlier?

In section 5.1 we recall and comment on the basic concepts and principles of probability theory, focussing on the Kolmogorov axioms and the notion of conditional probability. In section 5.2 we examine the relationship between probability and classical logic, showing in particular that classical consequence may be characterized in probabilistic terms — indeed, in a number of different but equivalent ways. In section 5.3 we show how these equivalent characterizations come apart from each other when we rework them to generate supraclassical consequence operations, with the most interesting one among them becoming nonmonotonic. In all cases, however, the supraclassical operations are quite different from those that we have so far considered; in particular, they fail the principle of conjunction in the conclusion. In section 5.4 we discuss this failure, and look at ways in which the probabilistic approach may be reconstructed to make it behave more like the qualitative one.

5.1   Basic Concepts and Axioms for Probability

The Kolmogorov Postulates

As with most branches of mathematics, probability was used and studied long before it was axiomatized. The standard axiomatization is that of the Russian mathematician Kolmogorov, published in German in 1933 but most accessible in the translation Kolmogorov (1950). It defines the notion of a (finitely additive) *probability function* or, as it is often called, *probability measure*.

Like all functions, these have a domain and a codomain. The codomain is the real interval $[0, 1]$: every probability function is into the set of all real numbers from 0 to 1 inclusive. The domain can be expressed in several different ways. Probability theorists usually take it to be an arbitrary *field of sets*, that is, as a non-empty family of subsets of some fixed set X, such that whenever A, B are in the family then so too are $A \cap B$, $A \cup B$ and $X - A$. Equivalently, the domain may be taken to be an arbitrary *Boolean algebra*, for every field of sets is a Boolean algebra and conversely, by Stone's representation theorem, every Boolean algebra is isomorphic to a field of sets. A less common alternative, but which we will follow here to make more transparent our comparison with logic, is to take the domain to be the set of all Boolean formulae of a propositional language. This may be done because the quotient structure of such a language under the relation of classical equivalence is a Boolean algebra, and conversely every Boolean algebra is a homomorphic image of such a quotient structure for some propositional language with sufficiently many elementary letters.

There are many minor variations in the formulation of the axioms, equivalent when the axioms are taken together but not when the axioms are considered separately. It will be convenient for us to use the following one.

Definition 5.1 (Probability Function) *A probability function is any function defined on the formulae of a language closed under the Boolean connectives, into the real numbers, such that:*

(K1) $0 \leq p(x) \leq 1$

(K2) $p(x) = 1$ *for some formula* x

(K3) $p(x) \leq p(y)$ *whenever* $x \vdash y$

(K4) $p(x \vee y) = p(x) + p(y)$ *whenever* $x \vdash \neg y$.

Here Cn alias $\vdash$ is, as always, classical consequence. Thus postulate (K1) tells us that the range of any probability function is a subset of the real interval $[0,1]$. (K2) tells us that 1 is in that range. (K3) says that $p(x) \leq p(y)$ whenever x classically implies y; and (K4) tells us that $p(x \vee y) = p(x) + p(y)$ whenever x is classically inconsistent with y.

Strictly speaking, these postulates, known as the Kolmogorov axioms, define the notion of a *finitely additive probability function*. They can be extended by strengthening (K4) to tell us something about infinite sums of probabilities. To do this one needs to enrich the background domain, working either with a field of sets closed under countable (or more) unions, or with a Boolean algebra likewise closed under infinite joins, or with a propositional language admitting infinite disjunctions. Such an extension is indeed necessary for many developments of probability theory, but will not be needed for our purposes.

Some further comments on the Kolmogorov postulates will help in our task of understanding the relations between probability and logic.

- The formulation of the axioms assumes concepts of classical logic — indeed two out of the four make explicit use of the notion of classical consequence. Of course, this dependence disappears, or rather takes a different form, if probability theory is formulated in terms of Boolean algebras or fields of sets. The axioms then make use of the subset relation $\subseteq$ between sets or the corresponding relation $\leq$ in Boolean algebra. Even when one retains Boolean formulae as domain, one can eliminate explicit reference to classical consequence by using a rather more extensive list of axioms, devised by Stalnaker (1970). But we have no quarrel with classical logic, and make free use of it whenever convenient.

- The real interval $[0,1]$ is infinitely larger and much more finely structured than is the two-element set $\{0,1\}$. Thus a probability function $p : L \to [0,1]$ can be much richer in information than a Boolean valuation $v : L \to \{0,1\}$. Accordingly probability theory is much more complex than truth-functional logic.

- Nevertheless, the Boolean valuations of classical logic are themselves limiting cases of probability functions, as they satisfy all four of the axioms, as can easily be verified.

- Conversely, any probability function whose values are all in the two-element set $\{0,1\}$ is a Boolean valuation. This is also easy to verify.

- The last two postulates are both conditionals. They are not biconditionals. Nor do their converses follow from what is given: each converse admits exceptions for suitably constructed probability functions.

- From the first three axioms it follows that $p(x) = 1$ whenever $x \in Cn(\emptyset)$. Here too the converse does not hold. The converse is sometimes added as a further condition defining a special class of probability functions, but that will not concern us here.

Unique Extension Properties for Logic and for Probability

Despite the close connections, there are also important differences. For those whose background is in logic, there is a habit of mind that must be broken from the beginning.

We know that in classical propositional logic, any assignment of truth-values to elementary letters can be extended in a unique way to a Boolean valuation over all formulae. But probability is not like that. There are assignments to elementary letters of real numbers in the interval $[0,1]$ that can be extended in more than one way to a function p on the entire Boolean language into $[0,1]$ that satisfies the Kolmogorov axioms.

For example, consider the language with just two elementary letters. To avoid possible confusion, as we are using the letter p in this section to stand for an arbitrary probability function, we will no longer use it for an elementary letter of a Boolean language, so we call the two letters of the example q, r. Consider the assignment f that puts $f(q) = f(r) = 0.5$. There are many ways in which this can be extended to a probability function $p : L \to [0, 1]$. In one of them, call it p_1, we have $p_1(q \wedge r) = p_1(\neg q \wedge \neg r) = 0.5$ and $p_1(q \wedge \neg r) = p_1(\neg q \wedge r) = 0$; while in another, call it p_2, we have $p_2(q \wedge r) = p_2(q \wedge \neg r) = p_2(\neg q \wedge r) = p_2(\neg q \wedge \neg r) = 0.25$.

The same point can be put in another way. The example shows that probability functions are not compositional: there is no function $* : [0, 1]^2 \to [0, 1]$ such that for all probability functions p and all formulae $a, b, p(a \wedge b) = p(a) * p(b)$. For in the example we have $p_1(q) = p_2(q)$ and also $p_1(r) = p_2(r) = 0.5$, so for any function $*$ whatsoever, $p_1(q) * p_1(r) = p_2(q) * p_2(r)$. If compositionality held, we would thus have $p_1(q \wedge r) = p_1(q) * p_1(r) = p_2(q) * p_2(r) = p_2(q \wedge r)$, whereas in fact $p_1(q \wedge r) = 0.5 \neq 0.25 = p_2(q \wedge r)$.

Yet another way of putting this is that probability functions are not many-valued truth-functions, created by expanding the set of truth-values from $\{0, 1\}$ — even if we take as our truth-values the uncountably many elements of the real interval $[0, 1]$. Whatever the number of values, and whatever the rules of truth for connectives, many-valued truth-functions give compound formulae values that are uniquely determined by the values of their constituents. Failure to see this clearly has led to many quixotic enterprises.

Nevertheless, when a probability function is defined over a finitely generated Boolean language, it does have a quite different 'unique extension property'. The simplest way of formulating this property is in terms of finite Boolean algebras; but to maintain the uniformity of our presentation we will explain it within our logical framework.

Consider classical propositional logic formulated with just n elementary letters $q_1, \ldots, q_n$. A *state-description* for that language is understood to be any conjunction of n terms in a fixed order, the i-th term being either q_i or its negation $\neg q_i$. For example, in the language with just two elementary letters q, r, the four formulae $q \wedge r$, $q \wedge \neg r$, $\neg q \wedge r$, $\neg q \wedge \neg r$ mentioned above are its state-descriptions. In general, when there n elementary letters there will be 2^n state-descriptions. Further, every non-contradictory formula x is classically equivalent to a disjunction of a non-empty subset of the state-descriptions. Finally, the conjunction of any two distinct state-descriptions is a contradiction. State descriptions on the level of formulae correspond to atoms on the level of Boolean algebras.

Now consider any function f on the 2^n state-descriptions of L into the real interval $[0, 1]$, such that their values sum to 1. Such a function is often called a *probability distribution*. Then we have the following 'unique extension property': *f can be extended in a unique way to a probability function* $p : L \to [0, 1]$ *satisfying the Kolmogorov axioms*.

The proof is simple. For each non-contradictory formula x, take the disjunction $s_1 \vee \ldots \vee s_k$ of all the state descriptions that classically imply it, and put $p(x) = f(s_1) + \ldots + f(s_k)$. When x is contradictory, put $p(x) = 0$. Then it is easy to check that p is a probability function, and that any probability function on L that agrees with f on the state-descriptions is identical with p.

This is an important feature of probability on finitely generated languages, and is used in many proofs and calculations. But it is also important to understand clearly the difference between this unique extension property and the homonymous property for Boolean valuations. One is based on state descriptions, the other on elementary letters.

Unfortunately, it is all too easy to be led into confusion by a terminological conflict between different communities. Algebraists use the term *atom* to stand for minimal non-zero elements of a Boolean algebra, and thus for state-descriptions (strictly, for the equivalence classes of state-descriptions under the relation of classical equivalence). From the algebraic point of view, elementary letters (strictly their equivalence classes under classical consequence) are the free generators of a free Boolean algebra. On the other hand, many computer scientists and some logicians, particularly those working in logic programming, call the elementary letters of propositional logic 'atomic formulae' or even 'atoms', because they are syntactically indivisible units.

The two terminologies should not be confused. We will always use the term 'atom' in the algebraist's sense, and reserve the term 'elementary letter' for the syntactically simple units of a propositional language. Readers will end up speaking the language of the tribe they associate with, but should also be alert to the potential confusion.

Conditionalization

One of the most basic and useful concepts of probability theory is that of *conditional probability*, or *conditionalization*. It will also play a central role in our story. It is a limited kind of revision. If p is a probability function giving proposition a some value in the interval $[0, 1]$, and we learn that a is in fact true, how should we modify p to take account of that information? The traditional answer is that, in the case $p(a) \neq 0$, we should pass from p to the function p_a defined by putting $p_a(x) = p(a \wedge x)/p(a)$. The function p_a is called the *conditionalization of p on a*.

Some comments may help appreciate the contours of this very important concept. First, we note three important mathematical properties of conditionalization.

- Given that p is a probability function and $p(a) \neq 0$, p_a is evidently also a function on the same Boolean language into the interval $[0, 1]$. More significantly, it is itself a probability function, i.e. satisfies the Kolmogorov axioms, as is easily checked from the definition with the help of some elementary arithmetic.

- There is a sense in which the passage from p to p_a is the most conservative change possible that brings the probability of a up to 1 (and so by axioms (K3) and (K1) does the same for all b with $a \vdash b$): it preserves untouched the ratios of probabilities of all propositions b with $b \vdash a$. To be precise, whenever p is a probability function and $p(a) \neq 0$ then it is not difficult to show that p_a is the unique probability function satisfying the following two conditions: (1) $p_a(a) = 1$, (2) for all b, b', if $b \vdash a$ and $b' \vdash a$ then $p_a(b)/p_a(b') = p(b)/p(b')$.

- Conditionalization is also conservative in another sense. It never diminishes the 'full belief' set $B_p = \{x : p(x) = 1\}$ determined by the probability function. In other words, when p_a is well defined then for any formula x, if $p(x) = 1$ then $p_a(x) = 1$. Using terminology from the logic of belief change, conditionalization serves as an *expansion* of the full belief set B_p, rather than a revision of B_p, even though it can be said to *revise* p itself.

  On the other hand, if we define 'threshold' or 'partial' belief sets $B_{p,k}$ by setting $B_{p,k} = \{x : p(x) \geq k\}$ where k is a fixed real less than 1, then they can lose as well as gain elements when p is conditionalized. Some ideas for redefining conditionalization to allow B_p itself to lose as well as gain when p is conditionalized, are canvassed in chapter 5 of Gärdenfors (1988).

The limited range of the definition also deserves note. The conditionalization p_a of p on a is *defined only when* $p(a) \neq 0$, i.e. p_a is left undefined when $p(a) = 0$. One cannot simply drop this restriction while retaining intact the defining equation, because notoriously division by zero is itself undefined in arithmetic. This can be bothersome when constructing proofs, because it obliges us to check that the condition is satisfied whenever we wish to define a conditional probability function, to be sure that it is well-defined. It is also rather disappointing intuitively. Surely we should also be able to revise a probability function on learning new facts, even when those facts contradict the function in a radical way. In other words, we would like to be able to revise p by a even when $p(a) = 0$.

For these reasons, there have been proposals to *extend the definition to ensure that p_a is defined in all cases* while agreeing with the usual definition in the principal case that $p(a) \neq 0$. A simple device sometimes used is to introduce the absurd probability function $p^\perp$, defined by putting $p^\perp(x) = 1$ for all propositions x. Once that is done, p_a may be set as $p^\perp$ in the limiting case that $p(a) = 0$. The cost of this manoeuvre is that the postulate (K4) must then be weakened, placing it under the condition that $p \neq p^\perp$. In any case, the irritating check to determine whether $p(a) \neq 0$ does not really disappear. It still needs to be made when defining a conditional function, not to determine whether the function is well-defined but in order to determine whether it is an ordinary one, with one kind of behaviour, or the absurd one, with a quite different behaviour. More discriminating definitions have also been suggested, allowing different values for $p_a(x)$ when $p(a) = 0$ — see for example the discussion in chapter 5 of Gärdenfors (1988). However we will not need to use such extensions, and will remain with the traditional definition.

Another kind of generalization is also possible. Conditionalization is appropriate when we wish to give a proposition a probability 1 upon learning that it is true. Evidently, this is a special case of a more general question: how should we revise a probability function p to a new one $p_{a=t}$ that ascribes probability t to a given proposition a, where t is an arbitrary element of the interval $[0,1]$? A well-known answer to this problem was introduced by Jeffrey (1965) and is called *Jeffrey conditionalization*. It is defined by the equality $p_{a=t}(x) = t \cdot p_a(x) + (1 - t) \cdot p_{\neg a}(x)$, where p_a and $p_{\neg a}$ are well-defined plain conditionalizations. To mark the contrast, the plain version is sometimes called *Bayesian conditionalization*. It can be seen as Jeffrey conditionalization in the limiting case that $t = 1$. However once again we will not need to use this kind of generalization, and we will remain with the initial Bayesian version.

Conditional Probability versus Probability of a Conditional

We end this section with a remark on notation, which at the same time brings to the surface a very deep conceptual issue. We have written $p_a(x)$ for the function defined by the ratio $p(a \wedge x)/p(a)$. It is common, indeed customary, to write $p(x|a)$ for the same function. However, such a notation can be highly misleading.

If we start from a probability function $p : L \to [0,1]$, then clearly its conditionalization as defined above is *a probability function on the same domain L*. It is not an extension of the initial probability function p to a wider domain consisting of the formulae in L plus new 'conditional objects' $x|a$ for formulae a, x in L. But that is just what the notation $p(x|a)$ suggests. For if we read the functional expression in the usual way, it tells us that $p(x|a)$ is of the form $p(y)$. In other words, it presents the conditionalization of p as the same function p applied to a new argument, the 'conditional object' $x|a$.

Once this notation is used, it leads almost irresistibly to the feeling that these 'conditional objects' have some kind of existence, and are in effect, conditional propositions. In other words, it is felt that there must be a conditional connective $\Rightarrow$ such that for every probability function p on the language with $p(a) \neq 0$, the conditional probability $p_a(x)$ alias $p(x|a)$ of x given a is equal to the probability $p(a \Rightarrow x)$ of the conditional proposition $a \Rightarrow x$. This is sometimes known as the *CP=PC property*, where the acronym abbreviates 'conditional probability = probability of a conditional'.

Such is the cognitive force of a bad notation that this feeling became a conviction among some investigators concerned with probability theory. The problem, as they saw it, was to find what, exactly, this conditional connective is. It is easy to see that it cannot be the ordinary truth-functional conditional $a \to x$, whose behaviour is incompatible with the properties desired. So, the line of thought went, it must be some kind of non-classical conditional.

This project received a severe setback from a celebrated result of David Lewis (1976). Lewis showed the impossibility, in a language that maintains the classical logic of the truth-functional connectives $\neg, \wedge, \vee$, of defining or even introducing a conditional connective with the CP=PC property. Lewis' paper was followed by others, establishing the same point in different ways. Some of them have slightly stronger formulations — see e.g. the review by Hájek (2001).

For most investigators, Lewis' 'impossibility theorem' put an end to the dream of a conditional with the CP=PC property. But not all have accepted defeat. Following an idea going back to de Finetti (1936), it has been proposed to replace classical two-valued logic by a three-valued one, within which one may seek to define a conditional with the CP=PC property. In such a three-valued logic, certain of the familiar principles of the classical logic of $\neg, \wedge, \vee$ will necessarily be lost. This program has been pursued by Dubois, Prade and colleagues in Europe, and by Calabrese in the USA. See e.g. Dubois and Prade (1994) and Calabrese (2003).

In the view of the present author, even if this program can be carried through without technical snags, to give up the simplicity of two-valued logic for the connectives $\neg, \wedge, \vee$ in favour of a weaker three-valued logic is an unpalatable price to pay for a dubious gain. At best, we become able to identify the probability of a conditional with a conditional probability, but we give up the simplicity of classical propositional logic, and lose some of its basic principles. Few logicians would be willing to follow this expensive path.

In the author's opinion, this issue illustrates a very general methodological point. It can be misleading to pose questions like the above as matters of doctrine, arguing that one point of view is correct and another incorrect. It can be a matter of cognitive convenience: we may think and talk coherently in various different ways, but some of them are ever so much more complicated and unmanageable than others.

Exercises

1*. Show, as claimed in the text, that the Boolean valuations of classical logic satisfy all four of the Kolmogorov axioms for probability functions.

2*. Verify the claim made in the text that from (K1), (K2), (K3) we may infer that $p(x) = 1$ whenever $x \in Cn(\emptyset)$.

3*. Show each of the following, which will be used in the next section, from the Kolmogorov axioms.
   Hint: Make use of the result of exercise 2 whenever appropriate.

   (a) $p(a) = p(b)$ whenever a and b are classically equivalent
   (b) $p(\neg a) = 1 - p(a)$
   (c) $p(a \wedge \neg a) = 0$
   (d) $p(a \wedge b) \leq p(a) \leq p(a \vee b)$
   (e) $p(a) > p(b)$ iff $p(\neg b) > p(\neg a)$.
   (f) $p(a) = p(a \wedge b) + p(a \wedge \neg b)$
   (g) $p(a \vee b) = p(a) + p(b) - p(a \wedge b)$
   (h) $p(a) + p(b) = p(a \vee b) + p(a \wedge b)$

4. Show, as claimed in the text, that any probability function whose values are all in the two-element set $\{0, 1\}$ is a Boolean valuation.
   Hint: You will find it convenient to use some of the results of exercise 2.

5. Show that whenever $p(a) \neq 0$ then $p_a(a) = 1, p_a(\neg a) = 0$.

6. Show that $p(a \wedge b) = p(a).p_a(b)$. From this, show that $p(a).p_a(b) = p(b).p_b(a)$.

7. Show, as claimed in the text, that whenever $p(x) = 1$ then $p_a(x) = 1$.

8. Verify that Bayesian conditionalization p_a coincides with Jeffrey conditionalization $p_{a=t}$ in the limiting case $t = 1$.
   Hint: Consider separately three cases $p(a) \notin \{0, 1\}, p(a) = 0, p(a) = 1$.

Problems

1. Some axiom-chopping:

   (a) Show that in the Kolmogorov postulates as we have formulated them, we may weaken (K3) to the rule (K3′) : $p(x) = p(y)$ whenever $Cn(x) = Cn(y)$, without affecting the joint power of the postulates.
   Hint: The easy half of the answer is given in exercise 3(a).

   (b) Suppose that we strengthen postulate (K2) to (K2′) : $p(x) = 1$ whenever $x \in Cn(\emptyset)$. We know from exercise 2 that this does not change the power of the axiom system as a whole. Show that it would nevertheless render postulate (K3) redundant, and would also make redundant the mention of 1 as an upper limit in postulate (K1).

2. Prove the unique extension property for probability functions. That is show, as claimed in the text, that when p is defined from f in the manner described it satisfies all of the Kolmogorov axioms, and that any function $p' : L \rightarrow [0, 1]$ that satisfies the Kolmogorov axioms and agrees with f on the state-descriptions is equal to p.

3*. In the text we gave an example of a function f on elementary letters into $[0, 1]$ that can be extended in at least two ways to a probability function $p : L \rightarrow [0, 1]$, i.e. uniqueness of extensions from elementary letters can fail. Show that nevertheless the *existence* of such extensions never fails for finite languages. That is, show that every function f on the finitely many elementary letters of the language into $[0, 1]$ has at least one extension to a probability function $p : L \rightarrow [0, 1]$.
   Hint: By the unique extension property for probability with respect to state-descriptions, it will suffice to find a function g on state descriptions into $[0, 1]$, summing to unity, such that for each elementary letter q_i, $f(q_i) = \Sigma(g(s) : s$ a state description with $s \vdash q_i)$.

5. Verify the claim made in the text that when $p: L \to [0,1]$ is a probability function with $p(a) \neq 0$ then p_a is also a probability function. To do this, show that p_a satisfies the Kolmogorov axioms. Better, show that it satisfies the following four conditions, where those subscripted with the letter a are evidently stronger than the Kolmogorov ones.

(K1) $0 \leq p_a(x) \leq 1$

(K2) $p_a(x) = 1$ for some formula x

(K3$_a$) $p_a(x) \leq p_a(y)$ whenever $x \wedge a \vdash y$

(K4$_a$) $p_a(x \vee y) = p_a(x) + p_a(y)$ whenever $a \wedge x \vdash \neg y$

6*. Verify the claim made in the text that if p is a probability function and a is a formula with $p(a) \neq 0$, then p_a is the unique probability function satisfying the following two conditions: (1) $p_a(a) = 1$, (2) for all b, b', if both $b \vdash a$ and $b' \vdash a$ then $p(b)/p(b') = p_a(b)/p_a(b')$.

7. Give an example to show that, as claimed in the text, $p_a(x)$ cannot be identified with $p(a \to x)$, where $\to$ is material implication.

Projects

1. Study Lewis (1976), Hájek (2001), Dubois and Prade (1994), Calabrese (2003) and other sources mentioned in these papers, on the issue of representing conditional probabilities as probabilities of conditional propositions, and write a report.
   Warning: This issue quickly becomes highly technical. Explore it only if you are strongly motivated.

2. Write a report on Adams (1998) and Edgington (2001), focussing on Adams' view that 'if...then...' assertions of ordinary non-mathematical discourse should not be understood as conditional propositions at all, but rather as assertions of the high conditional probability of the consequent given the antecedent.
   Warning: You will need considerable sensitivity to the subtleties of ordinary language.

5.2   Probabilistic Characterizations of Classical Consequence

What does classical consequence look like from a probabilistic perspective? Can it be characterized in terms of probability functions?   We say 'characterized' rather than 'defined' because, as noticed in the preceding section, the definition of a probability function, as given by the Kolmogorov axioms, already makes essential use of the relation of classical consequence, so that any reduction of the latter to the former would be circular. While reduction is not on the agenda, it nevertheless remains very interesting to know whether characterization is possible, and more broadly how classical consequence appears in probabilistic terms. As well as giving new ways of looking at classical logic, it will help prepare the way for our analysis, in the following sections, of the relations between probabilistic and nonmonotonic inference.

As we have already noticed, the real interval $[0,1]$ is infinitely larger and much more finely structured than is the two-element set $\{0,1\}$. Thus a probability function $p : L \to [0,1]$ is much richer in content than a Boolean valuation $v : L \to \{0,1\}$, and accordingly probability theory is much more complex than truth-functional logic. One effect of this is that there is not just one way of characterizing classical consequence in probabilistic terms; there is a multiplicity of them. In this section we present some of the best known.

The first characterization is almost immediate from the Kolmogorov axioms, yet involves a subtlety that should not be overlooked.

Observation 5.2 *Let a, x be any Boolean formulae. Then $a \vdash x$ holds iff for every probability function $p : L \to [0,1]$, $p(a) \le p(x)$.*

Proof. The implication from left to right is given by the Kolmogorov axiom (K3). Suppose that $a \nvdash x$. Then there is a Boolean valuation $v : L \to \{0,1\}$ with $v(a) = 1, v(x) = 0$. As noted in section 5.1, v is itself a probability function, and clearly $v(a) > v(x)$. ∎

Observation 5.2 should not be surprising, for it already has an analogue in the qualitative sphere. Quantifying over all probability functions is like quantifying over, say, all preferential models. Neither gives more than classical logic, since classical evaluation can be seen as a limiting case of evaluation in a preferential model, and likewise as a limiting case of probabilistic valuation.

It is important to note the positioning of the universal quantifier 'for every probability function p' in Observation 5.2. We have not proven that for every probability function $p : L \to [0,1]$, $a \vdash x$ holds iff $p(a) \le p(x)$, where the universal quantifier takes the whole biconditional as its scope. Indeed, the latter claim is wildly false. It does hold from left to right by (K3) again; but not from right to left. For example, let q, r be distinct elementary letters, and consider the Boolean valuation that puts $v(q) = 1, v(r) = 0$.

Once again, v is itself a probability function and $v(q) > v(r)$. But clearly since q, r are distinct elementary letters we do not have $q \vdash r$.

This kind of pattern will repeat itself many times in what is to follow. In general, we must distinguish carefully between two different relationships, where the quantification $\forall p$ is understood to range over the domain of all probability functions.

- If every probability function $p : L \to [0,1]$ satisfies a certain condition, then so-and-so holds. Schematically: $(\forall p \varphi(p)) \to \psi$, where p does not occur free in ψ.

- For every probability function $p : L \to [0,1]$, if p satisfies a certain condition then so-and-so holds. Schematically: $\forall p(\varphi(p) \to \psi)$, where p does not occur free in ψ.

The difference is in the scope of the universal quantifier. The latter implies the former but not conversely. The right-to-left half of Observation 5.2 is of the form $(\forall p \varphi(p)) \to \psi$ and not of the form $\forall p(\varphi(p) \to \psi)$. As shown, the latter statement is false.

In addition to the probabilistic characterization of classical consequence given in Observation 5.2, several others are of interest. The following table adds to our first condition four more that do the same job. There is nothing sacred about the number — others may easily be formulated. But these five are particularly simple and well known.

Number	Condition
1	$p(a) \le p(x)$
2t	if $p(a) \ge t$ then $p(x) \ge t$
3t	$p(a \to x) \ge t$
4t	$p_a(x) \ge t$ or $p(a) = 0$
5	$p(\neg x) \le \Sigma(p(\neg a_i) : i \le n)$

In conditions (2t) through (4t), t is any real number in $[0,1]$ with $t \ne 0$, called the *threshold* of the condition. Thus to be strict, these are not single conditions, but families of conditions, each family having infinitely many members, one for each non-zero value of t. An important instance is the one where $t = 1$. In that case, condition $(2t)$ for example says: if $p(a) = 1$ then $p(x) = 1$.

Conditions (1) and $(2t)$ are straightforward. Condition $(3t)$ could evidently be formulated equivalently as $p(\neg a \vee x) \geq t$, or as $p(a \wedge \neg x) \leq 1 - t$, and in the limiting case that $t = 1$, as $p(\neg a \vee x) = 1$ or $p(a \wedge \neg x) = 0$. Condition $(4t)$ makes use of the notion of (Bayesian) conditionalization, defined and discussed in the preceding section.

Condition (5) needs some explanation. It is understood for the situation where we may have finitely many premisses $a_1, \ldots, a_n$. Evidently, we could simply take the conjunction $a = \wedge a_i$ of all of them to do the work of the whole set. But when n is large, we may have information about the separate probabilities $p(a_n)$, but no direct knowledge of the probability $p(a)$ of their conjunction. In such a situation, condition (5) can be useful. Informally, it says that the improbability of the conclusion x is no greater than the sum of the improbabilities of the various separate premisses.

This condition has been highlighted by Ernest Adams (1975; 1998). However, the reader should be careful with terminology. Adams paraphrases the condition as saying that the uncertainty of the conclusion x should be no greater than the sum of the uncertainties of the separate premisses. This can be misleading since the term 'uncertainty' is already employed with another meaning in probability theory. More recent expositions of his ideas, such as that in Edgington (2001), therefore use the term 'improbability'.

Theorem 5.3 *Each of the quantified conditions $\forall p(1)$ through $\forall p(5)$, with p ranging over the set of all probability functions, characterizes classical consequence. They are thus also equivalent to each other. In full detail: let t be any real number in $[0, 1]$ with $t \neq 0$. Let a, x be any formulae, and suppose for condition 5 that $a = a_1 \wedge \ldots \wedge a_n$. Then $a \vdash x$ holds iff $\forall p(\varphi)$ holds, where φ is any one of conditions $1, 2t, 3t, 4t, 5$.*

Proof. Two strategies of proof suggest themselves. One is to prove separately the equivalence of each of the probabilistic items to the logical one $a \vdash x$. Another is to construct a cycle of implications, with the logical condition $a \vdash x$ one of those in the cycle. The former uses more logic, the latter more probability theory. The former can be longer, for if there are n probabilistic conditions then there are n equivalences to verify, and if (as usual) most have to be proven as co-implications, then we have up to $2n$ implications to check. Using a cycle, there are only $n + 1$ implications to prove.

We will follow a slightly mixed strategy, making use of the fact that we already know by Observation 5.2 that the logical condition $a \vdash x$

is equivalent to condition $\forall p(1)$. So we need only cycle around the probabilistic conditions in the table. As we do so, we take the opportunity to prove stronger implications whenever they hold, as they will be useful in the following section.

(i) We want to show $\forall p(1) \Rightarrow \forall p(2t)$. In fact we have the stronger implication $\forall_{p \in P}(1 \Rightarrow 2t)$. Suppose that $p(a) \le p(x)$. Then immediately if $t \le p(a)$ then $t \le p(x)$ and we are done.

(ii) We want to show $\forall p(2t) \Rightarrow \forall p(3t)$. It will be useful for later work to show a little more generally that $\forall p_{\in Q}(2t) \Rightarrow \forall p_{\in Q}(3t)$, where Q is any set of probability functions that is closed under conditionalization (i.e. whenever $p \in Q$ and $p(a) \ne 0$ then $p_a \in Q$). We argue contrapositively. Let Q be such a set and suppose that $p(a \to x) < t$ for some $p \in Q$. Then $p(a \land \neg x) = p(\neg(a \to x)) = 1 - p(a \to x) > 0$ so $p_{a \land \neg x}$ is well-defined. But clearly $p_{a \land \neg x}(a) = 1 \ge t$ while $p_{a \land \neg x}(x) = 0 < t$ as required.

(iii) We want to show $\forall p(3t) \Rightarrow \forall p(4t)$. Again we show that $\forall p_{\in Q}(3t) \Rightarrow \forall p_{\in Q}(4t)$, where Q is any set of probability functions closed under conditionalization. We argue contrapositively. Let Q be such a set and suppose that $p(a) \ne 0$ and $p_a(x) < t$ for some $p \in Q$. Clearly $p_a(\neg a) = 0$. Hence $p_a(a \to x) = p_a(\neg a \lor x) \le p_a(\neg a) + p_a(x) = p_a(x) < t$ as desired.

(iv) We want to show $\forall p(4t) \Rightarrow \forall p(5)$. Again we show that $\forall p_{\in Q}(4t) \Rightarrow \forall p_{\in Q}(5)$, where Q is any set of probability functions closed under conditionalization. Again we argue contrapositively. Let Q be such a set, let $p \in Q$, and suppose that $p(\neg x) > \Sigma(p(\neg a_i) : i \le n)$, where $a = a_1 \land \ldots \land a_n$. Now $\Sigma(p(\neg a_i) : i \le n) \ge p(\neg a_1 \lor \ldots \lor \neg a_n) = p(\neg(a_1 \land \ldots \land a_n)) = p(\neg a)$. So $p(\neg x) > p(\neg a)$ and thus $p(a) > p(x) \ge p(a \land x)$. Since $p(a) = p(a \land x) + p(a \land \neg x)$, it follows that $p(a \land \neg x) > 0$. Hence $p_{a \land \neg x}$ is well-defined, and clearly $p_{a \land \neg x}(a) = 1 \ne 0$ while $p_{a \land \neg x}(x) = 0 < t$ as required.

(v) To complete the cycle, we need to show that $\forall p(5) \Rightarrow \forall p(1)$. We show that $\forall p_{\in Q}(5) \Rightarrow \forall p_{\in Q}(1)$, where Q is as before. Once more we argue contrapositively. Let Q be such a set and suppose that for some $p \in Q, p(a) > p(x)$ where $a = a_1 \land \ldots \land a_n$. Then $p(a) \ne 0$ so so p_a is well-defined. We have $p_a(a) = 1$, so $p_a(a_i) = 1$ for all $i \le n$, so each $p_a(\neg a_i) = 0$, so $\Sigma(p_a(\neg a_i) : i \le n) = 0$. It remains to check that $p_a(\neg x) > 0$. Now $p_a(\neg x) = p(a \land \neg x)/p(a)$ so it suffices to show $p(a \land \neg x) > 0$. But $p(a) = p(a \land x) + p(a \land \neg x)$ so since by the supposition $p(a) > p(x) \geq p(a \wedge x)$ we have $p(a \wedge \neg x) > 0$ as desired and the proof is complete. ∎

Exercises

Although, as we have shown in Theorem 5.3, the universal closures of the conditions listed in the table are all equivalent to each other, they are not themselves universally equivalent. The following exercises look at the details.

1*. Show that the implication $\forall p(2t \Rightarrow 1)$ can fail. To put this in context, recall that in the text we have shown the converse $\forall p(1 \Rightarrow 2t)$ and also that $\forall p(2t) \Rightarrow \forall p(1)$.

2*. Show that the implication $\forall p(1 \Rightarrow 5)$ holds but that its converse $\forall p(5 \Rightarrow 1)$ can fail.

3. Show that condition (1) neither universally implies nor is universally implied by conditions $(3t), (4t)$.

4. Check out the universal implications between $(2t), (3t), (4t), (5)$.

5.3 Supraclassical Probabilistic Consequence Relations

Given the probabilistic characterizations of classical consequence expressed in Theorem 5.3, it is natural to ask what twists on them would make us go supraclassical, and eventually nonmonotonic.

A simple idea for going supraclassical, reminiscent of what we did with Boolean valuations in section 3.1, is to restrict the set of probability functions. Instead of quantifying over the set P of *all* probability functions on the language, we may take *some non-empty proper subset* $Q \subset P$ and quantify over it.

This will certainly give us properly superclassical consequence relations for a wide range of choices of Q. For example, in the case of condition 1, if there is some Boolean formula x that is not a tautology but such that $p(x) = 1$ for every $p \in Q$, then we have $t \hspace{1pt}\vert\hspace{-5pt}\sim x$ even though $t \nvdash x$.

However, the superclassical relation will remain monotonic for each of the conditions (1), $(2t)$, $(3t)$ and (5). Consider for example condition 1. Suppose $p(a) \leq p(x)$ for all $p \in Q$. Then immediately by postulate (K3), $p(a \wedge b) \leq p(a) \leq p(x)$ for all $p \in Q$. Similarly for the other conditions mentioned, quantified over an arbitrary domain $Q \subset P$.

The position with condition $(4t)$ is subtler. Fix a domain $Q \subset P$. Suppose on the one hand that Q is closed under conditionalization. Then as is apparent from the proof of Theorem 5.3, the condition $\forall_{p \in Q}(4t)$ is equivalent to the others and so monotonic. But when Q is not closed under conditionalization, monotony can fail. In particular, it can fail when Q is a singleton $\{p\}$. To show this, we need only find appropriate Boolean formulae a, b, x and a suitable probability function p with $p(a \wedge b) \neq 0$ (so that both p_a and $p_{a \wedge b}$ are well-defined) such that $p_a(x) \geq t$ while $p_{a \wedge b}(x) < t$. For example, suppose that the language has just two elementary letters q, r. Consider the probability distribution that gives each of the four atoms $q \wedge r, \ldots, \neg q \wedge \neg r$ equal values 0.25, and choose the threshold value $t = 0.5$. Put $a = q \vee \neg q, x = q \vee r$, $b = \neg q \wedge \neg r$. Then $p(a) = 1$ so $p(a \wedge x)/p(a) = p(x) = p(q \vee r) = 0.75 \geq t$ while $p(a \wedge b \wedge x)/p(a \wedge b) = 0 < t$.

Condition $(4t)$ is often regarded as in the most interesting probabilistic condition for defining consequence. So far, we have observed three points about it.

- When quantified over all probability functions, it gives us exactly classical consequence.

- When quantified over a domain of probability functions closed under conditionalization, it gives a supraclassical but still monotonic consequence relation.

- When instantiated to a specific probability function p (or, more generally, when quantified over a domain of probability functions not closed under conditionalization), the consequence relation typically becomes nonmonotonic.

However in probabilistic contexts the question of nonmonotonicity tends to leave centre stage, which is occupied by another property — conjunction in the conclusion (alias AND). To simplify the exposition, we write $(4tp)$ for the condition $(4t)$ instantiated to a specific probability function p; and likewise for the other conditions. The consequence relations determined by these instantiated conditions *all fail conjunction in the conclusion*, irrespective of whether or not they are monotonic. Thus they differ in a very important respect from their qualitative cousins studied in earlier sections.

As the nonmonotonic condition $(4tp)$ is the most interesting one for defining consequence, we verify explicitly the failure of AND in its case. For a trivial example, take again the language with just two elementary letters q, r, and probability function that gives each of the four atoms $q \wedge r, \ldots, \neg q \wedge \neg r$ equal values 0.25. Put a to be any tautology, $x = q$,

$y = r$ and set the threshold value t at 0.5. Then $p_a(x) = p(x) = 0.5 \geq t$ and likewise $p_a(y) = p(y) = 0.5 \geq t$ so by condition (4tp), we have $a \mathrel{\vert\!\sim} x$ and $a \mathrel{\vert\!\sim} y$. But $p_a(x \wedge y) = p(x \wedge y) = 0.25$, so that $a \mathrel{\not\vert\!\sim} x \wedge y$.

The failure of AND gives rise to other failures. There are rules that imply AND as a limiting case, and so also fail. One of these is right weakening (RW) in the generalized form: whenever $A \mathrel{\vert\!\sim} b$ for all $b \in B$ and $B \vdash x$ then $A \mathrel{\vert\!\sim} x$. In terms of operations, it can also be expressed as: $C(A) = Cn(C(A))$. Right weakening is valid for all the qualitative consequence relations, whether monotonic or nonmonotonic, that we have considered. Another rule that implies AND as a limiting case, assuming supraclassicality, is cumulative transitivity (CT) in its general form: whenever $A \mathrel{\vert\!\sim} b$ for all $b \in B$ and $A \cup B \mathrel{\vert\!\sim} x$ then $A \mathrel{\vert\!\sim} x$.

It may be argued that this is to the honour of the probabilistic approach, and that the qualitative one is misguided in validating the rule of conjunction in the conclusion. For while the rule may appear innocent when applied to the case of just two conclusions, it can become quite counterintuitive when applied by iteration to a large number of them. This is the message of the 'lottery paradox' of Kyburg (1961; 1970), and of the 'paradox of the preface' of Makinson (1965).

The *lottery paradox* observes that if a fair lottery has a large number n of tickets then, for each ticket it is highly probable that it will not win, and thus rational to believe that it will not do so. At the same time, it is certain (again, given that the lottery is assumed to be fair) that some ticket among the n will win, and so again rational to believe so. But these $n + 1$ propositions are inconsistent. We thus have a situation in which on the one hand, it is rational to believe in each element of a large finite set of $n + 1$ propositions, but on the other hand is not rational to believe in the conjunction of all of them, since it is a logically inconsistent proposition. Yet this is what the rule of conjunction in the conclusion would authorize us to do.

The *paradox of the preface* is similar in structure and conclusion, except that it makes no reference to probabilities. As author of a book making a large number of assertions, I may have checked and rechecked each of them individually, and be confident of each that it is correct. But sad experience in these matters may also teach me that it is inevitable that there will be some errors somewhere in the book; and in the preface I may acknowledge and take responsibility for this (without being able to put numbers on any of the claims). Then the totality of all assertions in the main text plus the preface is inconsistent, and it would thus be irrational to believe their conjunction; but it remains rational to believe each one of them individually. Thus again, the rule of conjunction in the conclusion appears to lead us astray.

This is a difficult philosophical question, and it cannot be said that a consensus has been reached on it. The author's tentative opinion is that there is a tension between two components of rationality — *coherence* and *practicality*. The criterion of coherence would lead us to abandon the rule of conjunction; that of practicality encourages us to manage our beliefs with minimal bookkeeping and calculation, which is facilitated by the rule of conjunction. Probabilistic inference favours the coherence criterion while qualitative nonmonotonic logics lean towards the practicality criterion.

We end this section with two further remarks on the consequence defined by condition $(4tp)$. For clarity, we repeat the full definition. For any given real number $t \in [0,1]$ with $t \neq 0$, and any given probability function p, the relation $a \mathrel{|\!\sim}_{tp} x$ is defined to hold iff either $p_a(x) \geq t$ or, in the limiting case, $p(a) = 0$.

It should be appreciated that this definition expresses a notion of *sufficient* probability of x given a. It should not be confused with a corresponding notion of *incremental* probability of x given a, which would be defined by putting: $a \mathrel{|\!\sim}_{tp}^{+} x$ iff $p_a(x) \geq p(x)$, in the principal case that $p(a) \neq 0$. This expresses the very different idea that the condition a leads to a probability of x that is higher than it would have in the absence of that condition. Clearly, this incremental inference relation is also nonmonotonic.

In the qualitative case, our nonmonotonic consequence relations were defined by relativizing the underlying supraclassical monotonic relations to the current premiss set A. The relativization was effected by various means — consistency constraints on background assumptions, minimality conditions, and consistency checks on the application of rules. But this is not how we proceeded with the definition of the relations $\mathrel{|\!\sim}_{tp}$. It is therefore natural to ask whether there is some monotonic notion that can serve as a stepping-stone to the nonmonotonic one $\mathrel{|\!\sim}_{tp}$ in much the same manner as in the qualitative arena?

The answer is positive. The monotonic condition $(3pt)$, i.e. $p(a \rightarrow x) \geq t$ for a specified probability function p, may be viewed in this light.

This can be seen clearly if we reformulate the two probabilistic conditions $(3pt)$ and $(4tp)$ in slightly different but equivalent ways. On the one hand, condition $(3tp)$ may equivalently be written as $p(a \wedge \neg x) \leq 1 - t$. On the other hand, in the principal case that $p(a) \neq 0$, condition $(4tp)$ may equivalently be written as $p(a \wedge \neg x)/p(a) \leq 1 - t$. Comparing these, we see that the latter uses the arithmetic operation of division to make the left-hand side depend on the probability of the premiss. In other words, division by the probability of the premiss serves to relativize condition $(3pt)$ into $(4tp)$. In this way, in probabilistic contexts the consequence relation defined by

$(3pt)$ serves as a (supraclassical, monotonic) bridge between classical and nonmonotonic inference.

We summarize the section. By taking any of the five probabilistic conditions that we listed as characterizing classical consequence, and restricting the set of probability functions, we get supraclassical consequence relations. When the chosen set is closed under conditionalization, all five conditions are equivalent, and all of them are monotonic. But when we look at instantiations of the conditions, one of them, namely $(4tp)$, is notoriously nonmonotonic. All of the instantiated conditions lead to failure of the rule of conjunction in the conclusion, and thus of several other rules implying it. There are arguments to suggest that this failure is just what is needed, but opinion is unsettled. Finally, although the order of our presentation did not put the fact into the limelight, there is a monotonic version of probabilistic consequence that may be seen as a natural stepping-stone to the nonmonotonic one, in much the same manner as for the qualitative relations.

Exercises

1*. Show that each of the conditions $(2tp), (3tp), (5p)$ is monotonic in the premiss formula a.

2*. Show that none of the conditions $(1p), (2tp), (3tp), (5p)$ satisfies AND.

3. Show that any relation satisfying RW (in the generalized form mentioned in the text) satisfies AND.

4. Show that any supraclassical relation satisfying CT (in the generalized form mentioned in the text) satisfies AND.

5. Show that condition $(3tp)$ may equivalently be written as $p(a \wedge \neg x) \leq 1 - t$. Likewise, show that in the principal case that $p(a) \neq 0, (4tp)$ may be rewritten as $p(a \wedge \neg x)/p(a) \leq 1 - t$.

5.4 Bringing Probabilistic and Qualitative Inference Closer Together

The results of the previous section lead to a further question: is there any way of bringing the probabilistic and qualitative approaches closer together? In particular, is there any way of adjusting the former so that the consequence relations that it engenders are more regularly behaved — specifically, so that the rule of conjunction in the conclusion (AND) is satisfied? Several ideas for such a rapprochement may be found in the literature. We outline two of them, quite different from each other.

One of them takes the concept of probability unchanged in its standard form as defined by the Kolmogorov postulates, but applies it in a more sophisticated manner so as to ensure satisfaction of AND. This is the *limiting probability* approach. The other transforms the notion of a probability function itself, replacing it by another kind of function into the real interval $[0, 1]$ in which, roughly speaking, the operation of maximality takes over the role played by addition in standard probability. These are often called *possibility functions*, also known in a dual form as *necessity* or *plausibility* functions.

In this section we will sketch both of these ideas and the kinds of nonmonotonic consequence relation that they give rise to.

Limiting Probabilities

This approach uses ideas of Adams (1966; 1975) and was set out systematically by Pearl (1988; 1989) and Lehmann and Magidor (1992). It exists in two versions: one using epsilon/delta constructions, and the other using non-standard analysis, i.e. infinitesimals. They differ in certain respects. In particular, the version using infinitesimals validates the non-Horn rule of rational monotony, while the epsilon/delta one does not. We describe the epsilon/delta version. For simplicity we continue to assume that the Boolean language is finitely generated.

The construction takes as input any relation R over Boolean formulae, whose elements (b, y) are thought of as forming *the base* for our construction. We wish to define as output a nonmonotonic supraclassical relation $\vdash^R$ with $R \subseteq \vdash^R$.

Fix such an initial relation R, and let ε be any non-zero real in the interval $[0, 1]$. We put $P_{R\varepsilon}$ to be the set of all probability functions p such that for every pair $(b, y) \in R, p(b) \neq 0$ (so that p_b is well-defined) and $p_b(y) \geq 1 - \varepsilon$. Roughly speaking, $P_{R\varepsilon}$ is the set of all those probability functions that bring the conditional probability of every element of R ε-close to unity. We could call it the set of all probability functions that are *epsilon-good for R*. We can now define the relation $\vdash^R$ of 'limiting probability consequence', by the following rule:

$a \vdash^R x$ iff for every $\delta > 0$ there is an $\varepsilon > 0$
such that for every probability function $p \in P_{R\varepsilon}$,
if p_a is well-defined then $p_a(x) \geq 1 - \delta$.

In effect, $a \vdash^R x$ iff the conditional probability $p_a(x)$ can be brought arbitrarily close to 1 by bringing all the conditional probabilities $p_b(y)$ of base pairs (b, y) sufficiently close to 1. We have written the index as a superscript rather than a subscript so as to avoid any confusion with the consequence relations defined using default rules.

It is almost immediate from the definition that every such relation $\mathrel{\vert\!\sim}^R$ is supraclassical. Moreover, for finite languages it is not difficult to show, using suitable arithmetic manipulations, that $\mathrel{\vert\!\sim}^R$ satisfies conjunction in the conclusion, cumulative transitivity, cautious monotony and disjunction in the premisses (see e.g. the verifications in section 3.5 of Makinson (1994)). For infinite languages, however, the generalized versions of the last three rules may fail. Finally, for finite languages, Adams (1975) and Lehmann & Magidor (1992) have proven a converse serving as a representation theorem.

Thus this construction, while remaining probabilistic, leads to nonmonotonic consequence relations which, for finite languages, have essentially the same properties as those generated in a qualitative manner. To be precise, for such languages it leads to exactly the same consequence relations as did the stoppered preferential models (with copies).

Possibility Functions

The other way of making the probabilistic approach satisfy conjunction in the conclusion, and generally behave like a qualitative approach, is to modify the Kolmogorov postulates defining probability functions, essentially by substituting maximality for addition. Such functions are often called possibility functions, as they are thought of as representing degrees of possibility in some sense of the term. This approach has been studied in a number of publications by Dubois, Prade and their co-authors, e.g. Dubois, Lang and Prade (1994), Dubois and Prade (2001). To avoid confusion with probability functions in the ordinary sense of the term, we will write possibility functions as π rather than p. Again, we work with finite languages.

A *possibility function* may be defined to be any function π on the Boolean language into the real numbers satisfying the following conditions:

(π1) $0 \leq \pi(x) \leq 1$

(π2) $\pi(x) = 1$ for some formula x

(π3) $\pi(x) \leq \pi(y)$ whenever $x \vdash y$

(π4) $\pi(x \vee y) = \max(\pi(x), \pi(y))$

This is not the most parsimonious axiomatization, but it brings out forcefully the relationship with ordinary probability. The first three postulates are just the same as (K1) to (K3) for probabilities. The difference lies in the last one. Whereas probability required that $p(x \vee y)$ is the sum of $p(x)$ and $p(y)$ whenever x is classically inconsistent with y, these functions require that $\pi(x \vee y)$ is the greater of $\pi(x)$ and $\pi(y)$, and does so without any proviso at all.

From the first three postulates we have that $\pi(x) = 1$ whenever $x \in Cn(\emptyset)$, just as for probability. But from this and postulate $(\pi 4)$ it follows that for any formula x, either $\pi(x) = 1$ or $\pi(\neg x) = 1$, which is quite unlike the equality $p(\neg x) = 1 - p(x)$ for probability. Disjunction thus becomes homomorphic with taking *max*, but negation ceases to be homomorphic with difference from unity. We gain one homomorphism but lose another.

Just as with probability functions, we have an extension property based on state-descriptions. Let f be any function on the state-descriptions of L into the real interval $[0, 1]$, such that their maximum is unity, i.e. such that $f(s) = 1$ for at least one state-description s. Such a function may be called a *possibility distribution*. Then f can be extended to a possibility function $\pi : L \to [0, 1]$ satisfying the above axioms. The construction parallels that of the probabilistic case. For each non-contradictory formula x, take the disjunction $s_1 \vee \ldots \vee s_k$ of all the state descriptions that classically imply it, and put $\pi(x) = \max(f(s_1), \ldots, f(s_k))$. When x is contradictory, put $\pi(x) = 0$. Then it is easy to verify that π is a possibility function, and that any possibility function on L that agrees with f on the state-descriptions is identical with π, except possibly in the value that it assigns to contradiction (which, due to the replacement of (K4) by $(\pi 4)$, need not be zero). The extension is thus 'almost unique'.

It remains to define the consequence relations determined by possibility functions. For any possibility function π, we define the relation $\mid\!\sim_\pi$ by the rule:

$a \mid\!\sim_\pi x$ iff either $\pi(a \wedge \neg x) < \pi(a \wedge x)$ or, as limiting case, $\neg a \in Cn(\emptyset)$.

Equivalently, given the properties of the function π and the irreflexivity of $<$:

$a \mid\!\sim_\pi x$ iff either $\pi(a \wedge \neg x) < \pi(a)$ or, as limiting case, $\neg a \in Cn(\emptyset)$.

Then it is not difficult to show that every such relation $\mid\!\sim_\pi$ is supraclassical and, for finite languages, satisfies conjunction in the conclusion, cumulative transitivity, cautious monotony, disjunction in the premises, and the non-Horn rule of rational monotony. Here again it is possible to prove a converse as a representation theorem.

Although the definition of a possibility function is quantitative in appearance, a little reflection indicates that it is essentially qualitative in nature. It makes no use of arithmetic operations such as addition or multiplication. Instead it uses the operation of choosing the *maximum* of two items, which makes perfectly good sense in any chain. Also, the presence of the number 1 is quite unnecessary: we need only require that the chain has a greatest element, and require this element to be the image of any tautology. The resulting logic is the same: we get exactly the same consequence relations $\mathrel{\vert\!\sim}_\pi$.

Once we have shed the numerical trappings, we can also see that the approach is the same, in content, as one that we have seen in a qualitative context, namely comparative expectation inference, a variant of default-assumption consequence which we described in section 2.3.

Suppose we take a possibility function π on the Boolean language into a chain and 'upend' it. That is, suppose we define a function σ also on the same language by putting $\sigma(a) = \pi(\neg a)$ and at the same time inverting the chain order. Then the homomorphism of disjunction with respect to *max* becomes homomorphism of conjunction with respect to *min*. In other words, $\sigma(x \wedge y) = \pi(\neg(x \wedge y)) = \pi(\neg x \vee \neg y) = \max(\pi(\neg x), \pi(\neg y)) = \min(\sigma(x), \sigma(y))$, where maximality is understood with respect to the initial chain $<$ and minimality with respect to its inverse, which we write here as $<'$.

This is already beginning to look familiar. To complete the picture, define a relation $<''$ between Boolean formulae by putting $x <'' y$ iff $\sigma(x) <' \sigma(y)$. Then $<''$ satisfies the condition that whenever $x <'' y$ and $x <'' z$ then $x <'' y \wedge z$, which is a salient property of comparative expectation, as outlined in section 2.3. For if $x <'' y$ and $x <'' z$ then by definition $\sigma(x) <' \sigma(y)$ and $\sigma(x) <' \sigma(z)$ so that $\sigma(x) <' \min(\sigma(y), \sigma(z)) = \sigma(y \wedge z)$ and thus by definition again, $x <'' y \wedge z$. Indeed, all the properties required of comparative expectation relations emerge from this transformation, and we can also go in the reverse direction, transforming an arbitrary expectation relation into a qualitative possibility function.

The definition of the possibilistic inference relation $\mathrel{\vert\!\sim}_\pi$ by the rule $a \mathrel{\vert\!\sim}_\pi x$ iff $\pi(a \wedge \neg x) < \pi(a)$ or $\neg a \in Cn(\emptyset)$ becomes, under this transformation, equivalent to the one for comparative expectation inference in section 2.3. For in the principal case, $a \mathrel{\vert\!\sim}_\pi x$ iff $\pi(a \wedge \neg x) < \pi(a)$, iff $\sigma(\neg a \vee x) < \sigma(\neg a)$, iff $\sigma(\neg a) <' \sigma(\neg a \vee x)$, iff $\neg a <'' \neg a \vee x$. We thus have $a \mathrel{\vert\!\sim}_\pi x$ iff $\neg a <'' \neg a \vee x$ or $\neg a \in Cn(\emptyset)$. As remarked *en passant* in section 2.3, it is not difficult to verify, using the conditions imposed on comparative expectation relations, that this last holds iff $x \in Cn(\{a\} \cup \{y : \neg a <'' y\})$, which is the definition of comparative expectation inference.

It is also possible to see how possibility functions relate to ranked preferential models. In effect, given a finite ranked preferential model, we can define a function π on formulae by putting $\pi(a)$ to be the least rank of any state in the preferential model that satisfies a (and to be the top rank if a is not satisfied by any of its states). Then π will be a possibility function, in the abstract sense indicated above, into the chain that is the converse of the ranking order. Conversely, given a possibilistic model, we may build an equivalent ranked preferential one.

It is easy to get lost in the details of these connections. The important point to remember is that when we pass from probability functions to possibility functions by making maximality do the work of addition, the numerical clothing becomes redundant and we are really working with functions into a chain with greatest element. These functions are homomorphic with disjunction, but we may equivalently replace them by functions into the converse chain that are homomorphic with respect to conjunction, giving us the qualitative notion of an expectation ordering and its associated inference relations.

For further reading on the use of possibility functions to generate nonmonotonic consequence relations, see e.g. section 4.2 of Makinson (1994), which is presented in terms of the 'upended' functions σ homomorphic for conjunction with respect to *min*, there called 'plausibility functions'. For a presentation in terms of the functions π, see Benferhat, Dubois and Prade (1997), Dubois, Lang and Prade (1994), or Dubois and Prade (2001).

The border between logic and probability is long, with many crossing-points. We have visited one of them, directly related to our general theme: how can we use the notion of probability to characterize classical and supraclassical consequence relations, both monotonic and nonmonotonic?

Other Issues Concerning Logic and Probability

It should be said that this is not what is most often discussed in examinations of the interconnections between probability and logic. Three main issues currently occupy the centre of the stage.

- The most commonly discussed preoccupation is whether probability may, in some mathematical or philosophical sense, be *reduced* to logic. In particular, whether the Kolmogorov postulates may be given a purely logical justification of some kind, perhaps even providing a logical meaning for the notion of probability. Also, whether purely logical considerations may be used to help us find, in the space of all possible probability distributions, ones that play a special role. We have not discussed these issues and as the reader may guess, we are sceptical about the chances of success for such quest. For an introduction to these matters, see e.g. Williamson (2002) and Howson (2003).

- Conversely, some authors have raised the question of whether the concept of logical consequence may be reduced to that of probability without creating circularity of the kind that was noted at the beginning of section 5.2. We have not discussed the issue, and are even more sceptical of success.

- Finally, there is a group of concepts on the borderline between logic, probability and the philosophy of science, such as confirmation, induction and abduction. For an introduction to some of them, see e.g. Skyrms (1999).

Exercises

1*. Show that for any formula x, either $\pi(x) = 1$ or $\pi(\neg x) = 1$, for any possibility function π.

2*. Show the equivalence of the two definitions of a possibilistic inference relation.

3. Show that every possibilistic inference relation is supraclassical and, for finite languages, also satisfies conjunction in the conclusion, cumulative transitivity, cautious monotony disjunction in the premisses, and also the non-Horn rule of rational monotony.

Problem

Show that every 'limiting probability' consequence relation is supraclassical and, for finite languages, also satisfies conjunction in the conclusion, cumulative transitivity, cautious monotony and disjunction in the premisses.

Projects

1. Study the 'limiting probability' and the 'infinitesimal probability' constructions of nonmonotonic inference relations, using the references of this section, and write a report.
Warning: This project needs background in both epsilon/delta style definitions and nonstandard analysis.

2. Study the 'possibility function' approaches to nonmonotonic logic, using the references of this section, and write a report.

5.5   Review and Explore

Recapitulation

There are deep relations between classical consequence, probability and nonmonotonic consequence. To begin with, classical consequence can be characterized in probabilistic terms in half a dozen ways. We can also define supraclassical consequence relations in the same terms, by instantiating the conditions to individual probability functions rather than quantifying over all of them.

Most of these relations are monotonic, but the most interesting one, defined in terms of conditional probability, is notoriously nonmonotonic. They all fail to validate conjunction of conclusions — a feature that may be regarded as poor behaviour by logicians and as good behaviour by epistemologists.

It is however possible to tamper with the probabilistic approach in various ways to make it behave in a more regular manner, indeed just like certain qualitative approaches. One of these uses limiting probabilities (or infinitesimals). Another of them transforms the very notion of a probability function into another kind of function, often called 'possibility functions', where *max* does the work of addition. Despite their quantitative clothing, and the way in which their definition runs parallel to that of a probability function, possibility functions are essentially qualitative in nature.

Checklist of Concepts and Definitions for Revision

Section 5.1:   Kolmogorov postulates for probability, state-descriptions, unique extension property for Boolean assignments, unique extension property for probability distributions, (Bayesian) conditionalization, Jeffrey conditionalization, PC=CP property, Lewis' impossibility theorem. *Section 5.2*: Five probabilistic conditions for characterizing classical consequence, thresholds, the role of quantifiers. *Section 5.3*: Instantiated probabilistic conditions, monotonic and nonmonotonic relations thus generated, failure of AND and related properties, lottery paradox, paradox of the preface, sufficient probability versus incremental probability. *Section 5.4*: Epsilon-good probability functions, epsilon/delta consequence relations, possibility functions, possibilistic consequence relations, connection with comparative expectation inference.

Further Reading

- S. Benferhat, D. Dubois and H. Prade. Nonmonotonic reasoning, conditional objects and possibility theory, *Artificial Intelligence*, **92**, 259–276, 1997.

- D. Makinson. General Patterns in Nonmonotonic Reasoning. In *Handbook of Logic in Artificial Intelligence and Logic Programming, Vol. 3*, Gabbay, Hogger and Robinson, eds., pp. 35–110. Oxford University Press, 1994. (See sections 3.5 and 4.2).

- J. Pearl. Probabilistic semantics for nonmonotonic reasoning: a survey. In *Proceedings of the First International Conference on Principles of Knowledge Representation and Reasoning, KR'89*. Brachman *et al.*, eds., pp. 505–515. Morgan Kaufmann, San Mateo, CA, 1989.

Chapter 6

Some Brief Comparisons

While working through previous chapters, some readers may have sensed parallels between nonmonotonic reasoning and certain other areas of logic that they have studied. Indeed, there are close similarities with the logics of belief change, update, counterfactual conditionals, and conditional directives — domains that have also emerged over the last quarter-century, in some cases before and in other cases after nonmonotonic logic.

The similarities appear on two levels. Syntactically, they manifest themselves as resemblances between properties of the logical operations that are generated. Semantically, they are apparent as parallels between the various modes of generation.

At the same time, there are a number of residual differences. Some are merely notational, or in other ways trivial. Some are 'circumstantial' in the sense that they reflect options that could be reproduced within each domain but which historically happen to have been proposed in one arena rather than another.

In the first two sections of this chapter we sketch some of these parallels and residual differences. Our emphasis will be on the modes of generation, although we will also mention some of the syntactic conditions that they lead to. In the third section, we review some representation theorems, both for paraclassical logics (gathering together material from earlier chapters) and for their nonmonotonic counterparts.

6.1 Relations with Belief Revision

Perhaps the closest parallel is with the logic of *belief (or theory) change*. This branch of logic studies the ways in which existing beliefs may be modified when new things are learned. It focuses on three main operations: expansion, contraction, and revision.

Expansion is very simple. Let K be any set of Boolean formulae, serving as a set of beliefs, and let a be any formula. By the expansion of K by a, often written as $K + a$, we mean the set of all consequences of K and a taken together, i.e. $Cn(K \cup \{a\})$, where Cn is classical consequence. This is a fully defined operation, in the sense that given K and a, the set $K + a$ is uniquely determined. In particular, using a notorious property of classical consequence, when K is inconsistent with a, $K + a = L$, where L is the set of all formulae of the language.

Contraction, conversely, is the process of removing a proposition a from a belief set K in such a way that the resulting set $K - a$ no longer implies a — unless, of course, a is a tautology, in which case it remains classically implied even by the empty set of beliefs. It is understood as part of the concept of contraction that while K will generally need to be diminished to get rid of a, it should not be gratuitously impoverished or distorted. This is often known as the principle of *minimal mutilation*. Downsizing systematically to the empty set or to the set of all tautologies will thus usually not be considered reasonable.

Revision is the process of adding a proposition to a belief set K in such a way that the resulting set $K * a$ contains a, yet is consistent — unless, of course, a is itself inconsistent, in which case introducing it necessarily creates inconsistency even if everything from K is jettisoned. Again, it is part of the concept that this is done in a way that does not create wildly unnecessary swings by bringing in too much along with a, or throwing out too much in the effort to maintain consistency. This is again a notion of minimal mutilation.

Unlike expansion, these two processes are not fully defined by the components that we have mentioned. Given only K and a, together with the background operation of classical consequence, the operations of contraction and revision are not uniquely determined. There can be many reasonable ways of paring off material so that a proposition is no longer implied; and many ways of adjusting K so that a proposition may be brought in consistently.

The logic of belief change is thus faced with three main questions, echoing those for the logic of nonmonotonic inference raised in Chapter 1:

- Given the indeterminacy of the notions of contraction and revision, are there any syntactic conditions which they should always satisfy or which, at least, are of interest to entertain as valuable properties?

- Are there any interesting ways of generating belief change operations, i.e. of providing semantics for them?

- Among the many contraction and revision operations that can be generated, satisfying conditions that we may wish to deem as reasonable, can we identify a pair that can be described as 'the correct' ones?

The answers run along similar lines. There is no single operation of contraction, or of revision, that is 'correct' or even appropriate in all situations. Specific operations may perhaps be singled out for particular purposes; but they will depend very much on the kind of situation in hand and will not in general be identified in purely formal terms. On the other hand, there are a number of very interesting conditions that may be entertained for belief change operations, and even regarded as candidates for rationality constraints so long as we do not become doctrinaire about them. There are also just a few salient modes of generation.

The processes of contraction and revision are not independent of each other. It is plausible to see revision as a compound process of contraction then expansion: given a belief set K and a proposition a that we wish to integrate into it, first eliminate from K all the material that is inconsistent with a, and then add a in. In other words, put $K * a = (K - \neg a) + a$, i.e. $Cn((K - \neg a) \cup \{a\})$. This definition is known as the Levi identity, after the philosopher Isaac Levi who first formulated it. It was taken as conceptually basic by Alchourrón, Gärdenfors and Makinson (1985), who developed a theory of contraction and then examined the kind of revision that it determines under the Levi identity. Conversely but less obviously, when dealing with a classically closed belief set K, it is plausible to define contraction by the rule $(K - a) = K \cap (K * \neg a)$. In other words, a proposition remains after contracting K by a iff it was in K and is also in the result of revising K by $\neg a$. This definition is known as the Harper identity, again after the philosopher William Harper who proposed it.

Of the two operations, the one that is most directly related to nonmonotonic consequence is revision, and so we will focus on it in this section. Now revision is a two-place operation $K * a$, while consequence, seen likewise as an operation, has only one argument. Evidently, from any two-place operation we can form unary ones by projection onto either the left or the right argument. Thus we can consider the family of operations $*_a(K)$ of revision-of-K, modulo a, and also the family of operations $*_K(a)$ of revision-with-a, modulo K, defined by putting $*_a(K) = *_K(a) = K * a$.

Now the operations $*_a(K)$ fail monotony when interpreted on the so-called AGM paradigm of Alchourrón, Gärdenfors and Makinson (see below), although when reread as Katsuno/Mendelzon update they are monotonic (see next section). But they have a much more striking failure: they do not satisfy inclusion. In other words, we do not always have $K \subseteq *_a(K)$, since $K \subseteq K * a$ can fail. In fact, for revision operation along the general lines we have described, this inclusion *must* fail whenever a is consistent but inconsistent with K, for something will have to be discarded from K to restore consistency. In view of this failure, the left projection of a revision operation can hardly be called a form of inference.

On the other hand, as first noticed by Makinson and Gärdenfors (1991), the right projections $*_K(a)$ of a belief revision operation $K * a$ satisfying suitable postulates for revision may indeed be read as consequence operations; conversely, consequence operations satisfying appropriate conditions can be seen as revision functions. To bring this out, we consider one by one the AGM postulates for revision, formulated by Alchourrón, Gärdenfors and Makinson (1985). First, the so-called 'basic postulates':

($K * 1$) $K * a = Cn(K * a)$

($K * 2$) $a \in K * a$

($K * 3$) $K * a \subseteq Cn(K \cup \{a\})$

($K * 4$)   Whenever $\neg a \notin Cn(K)$ then $Cn(K \cup \{a\}) \subseteq K * a$

($K * 5$)   Whenever $Cn(a) \neq L$ then $K * a \neq L$

($K * 6$)   Whenever $Cn(a) = Cn(b)$ then $K * a = K * b$.

Then, the so-called 'supplementary postulates':

($K * 7$) $K * (a \wedge b) \subseteq Cn((K * a) \cup \{b\})$

($K * 8$)   Whenever $\neg b \notin K * a$ then $Cn((K * a) \cup \{b\}) \subseteq K * (a \wedge b)$.

Now express these postulates using the right projections $*_K(a)$ in place of the two-place functions $K * a$. As the index K in $*_K$ is not allowed to vary in any of the postulates, we might as well simplify the notation by dropping it. Finally, to facilitate visual comparison with nonmonotonic inference, write the $*$ as C. Then the above postulates for belief revision become the following conditions on the operations C:

($C1$) $C(a) = CnC(a)$

($C2$) $a \in C(a)$

($C3$) $C(a) \subseteq Cn(K \cup \{a\})$

(C4)   Whenever $\neg a \notin Cn(K)$ then $Cn(K \cup \{a\}) \subseteq C(a)$

(C5)   Whenever $Cn(K) \neq L$ then $C(a) \neq L$

(C6)   Whenever $Cn(a) = Cn(b)$ then $C(a) = C(b)$.

In addition, for the 'supplementary postulates':

(C7) $C(a \wedge b) \subseteq Cn(C(a) \cup \{b\})$

(C8)   Whenever $\neg b \notin C(a)$ then $Cn(C(a) \cup \{b\}) \subseteq C(a \wedge b)$.

These are all familiar properties for nonmonotonic consequence operations. In some cases, indeed, they have been formulated explicitly in earlier chapters, in relational or operational notation. For example, (C2) is just inclusion (reflexivity) for singleton premiss sets, and (C6) is left classical equivalence. In other cases, they are easy consequences of conditions that were formulated explicitly. For example, (C1) is an immediate consequence (using compactness of classical consequence) of conjunction in the conclusion (AND) and right weakening.

On the semantic level, the correspondence is just as close. The literature contains various different ways of generating revision operations satisfying the AGM postulates, and each of them resembles closely (although not always in every detail) one that we have considered for nonmonotonic consequence relations. Most of them mirror default-assumption procedures described in Chapter 2. This is partly because that kind of procedure also lends itself naturally to the construction of contractions, which play a primordial role in the AGM account of belief change. Some presentations in the literature on belief revision relate directly to the default-valuation procedures that we described in Chapter 3. However, as far as the author is aware, none of them correspond to default-rules procedure. On the mathematical level there is nothing to stop one working in that way, but it has not been explored.

We describe just one of the constructions for belief revision, and compare it with its consequence counterpart. It is the *partial meet revision* of Alchourrón, Gärdenfors and Makinson (1985).

Let K be any set of Boolean formulae serving as a belief set (closed or not under classical consequence). For each formula a, let K_a be the family of all subsets $K' \subseteq K$ maxiconsistent with a. Let δ be any selection function that associates with each family K_a a subfamily $\delta(K_a) \subseteq K_a$. We require that $\delta(K_a)$ is nonempty whenever K_a is nonempty. For each such structure, define the revision operation $*$ that has K as left argument by the rule:

- $K * a = Cn(\cap \delta(K_a) \cup \{a\})$.

In other words:

- $K * a = Cn(\cap \{K' : K' \in \delta(K_a)\} \cup \{a\})$.

This is very close to the notion of *consequence via a selection function*, which we mentioned briefly in section 2.3. There, for singleton premiss sets $A = \{a\}$, we put:

- $C_K(A) = \cap \{Cn(K' \cup \{a\}) : K' \in \delta(K_a)\}$.

The right hand side is almost the same in the two definitions. Almost, but not quite! For revision, we first intersected the maximum a-consistent subsets, then expanded by a. For the consequence relation we did things in the reverse order: we first took each maximum a-consistent subset, expanded it by a, and then intersected the resulting sets. It is easy to check that the former is always a subset of the latter, i.e. we have:

$$Cn(\cap \delta(K_a) \cup \{a\}) \subseteq \cap \{Cn(K' \cup \{a\}) : K' \in \delta(K_a)\}.$$

Moreover, it is not difficult to show that the converse inclusion holds whenever $K = Cn(K)$. But for a belief set K that is not closed under classical consequence, the converse inclusion can fail.

Why the difference? It stems from the conceptual background of the two subjects. In the case of belief revision, the AGM trio took contraction as the basic notion, with revision defined from it. Partial meet contraction was defined by the rule:

- $K - x = \cap \delta(K_{\neg x}) = \cap \{K' : K' \in \delta(K_{\neg x})\}$

so that revision may be expressed in terms of contraction as:

- $K * a = Cn((K - \neg a) \cup \{a\}) = Cn(\cap \{K' : K' \in \delta(K_a)\} \cup \{a\})$.

In the case of nonmonotonic inference, on the other hand, no preliminary concept of contraction is involved, and so it is just as natural to use the other definition. As attention tended to concentrate on belief (alias background assumption) sets that are closed under Cn, where the two definitions are equivalent, the difference was not often emphasized, although well known to those working in the area.

A salient feature of the AGM postulates for revision, already noted in passing, is that none of them involve more than one belief set K. In other words, although they tell us quite a bit about the relations between $K * a$ and $K * b$ when a, b are distinct propositions, none of them tell us anything about the relationship between $K * a$ and $J * a$ when K, J are distinct belief sets. In particular, they do not say anything explicitly about *iterated belief revision*, i.e. revisions of revisions. The AGM account may therefore be called a *one-shot* theory of revisions. A few points about iterated revision are already implicit in even this meagre starting point; for example, the basic postulates imply that $(K * a) * a = K * a$. But very little is forthcoming in this way. It is thus natural to look for a theory that tells us something more interesting about repeated revision of our beliefs. For this reason, the theory of iterated belief change is an active research area, with many proposals in the literature although not yet a very settled consensus.

Exercises

1*. In the text, it was said that revision may be seen as a compound process of contraction then expansion. Why not expansion then contraction?

2. Express the translation of each of the AGM postulates in relational notation.

3. For each of the AGM postulates for belief revision, derive its translation into the language of consequence relations/operations from conditions that have been discussed in earlier chapters.

4. Express the condition of rational monotony as a principle about belief revision, and derive it from the extended set of AGM postulates.

5*. Show that the basic AGM postulates imply that $(K * a) * a = K * a$.

Problems

1. Show that $Cn(\cap \delta(K_a) \cup \{a\}) \subseteq \cap \{Cn(K' \cup \{a\}) : K' \in \delta(K_a)\}$ always holds.

2. Show that the converse also holds whenever $K = Cn(K)$.

3. Give a small finite counterexample to the converse in the case that $K \neq Cn(K)$.

6.2   Links with Update, Counterfactuals and Conditional Directives

The links between nonmonotonic reasoning and other domains do not come to an end with the logic of belief change. There are a number of other areas in which they show themselves, notably in the logics of update, counterfactual conditionals, and conditional directives. In this section we briefly sketch the essential ideas.

In each area, the logics have been conceived with a particular intuitive interpretation in mind, reflecting a kind of reasoning activity that is carried out by humans. On the formal level, they are presented in both semantic and syntactic manner. The semantic apparatus is usually of the same general kind as for the various kinds of default-valuation consequence described in sections 3.2 and 3.3. In other words, in each case the modelling consists of a set of states together with an ordering relation (or family of relations) over that set, possibly with further ingredients (such as auxiliary relations); with the notion in question characterized by some kind of minimality condition on the relation (or relations). For this reason, Makinson (1993) refers to the semantic constructions as exhibiting *five faces of minimality*.

Update

It is customary to distinguish between *revising* a belief set and *updating* it. From an intuitive point of view, revision is seen as a process of changing our stock of beliefs upon changing our mind about a particular point or receiving supplementary information about it. Update, on the other hand, is conceived as a process of changing our beliefs to keep track of changes that have taken place in the world. The difference between the two was already noted in a paper of Keller and Winslett Wilkins (1985), but was neglected until a formal modelling for update was given by Katsuno and Mendelzon (1992), often called the KM account.

Their modelling uses a minimality construction. Let S an arbitrary nonempty set, whose elements we will call *states* (or, in the terminology of some authors, 'worlds'). We consider a family of relations $<_s$ over S, one for each element $s \in S$. Intuitively, each relation $<_s$ in the family is understood as comparing the distances of worlds from s, so that $t <_s u$ means that t is closer to s than u is. With this reading in mind the relations $<_s$ are usually required to be at least irreflexive, transitive and stoppered. They are also usually subjected to a constraint called *weak centering*. This says that no state is closer to s than s itself, i.e. we never have $t <_s s$.

Sometimes a stronger condition of *full centering* is required: no state is as close to s as s itself, i.e. always $s <_s t$ except when $t = s$.

Consider any such set S and family of relations $<_s$ ($s \in S$), together with a labelling function associating a classical truth-value assignment v_s to each $s \in S$ (so that, in effect, we may have copies of valuations and some valuations may be ignored). Such a triple may be called a *KM update model*, and determines an update operation as follows. Let K be any set of Boolean formulae (to serve as the belief set to be to be updated) and let a be a formula (to play the role of update input). For the definitions that follow, it will not make any difference to the output whether these sets are closed under classical consequence.

The result $K \# a$ of *updating* K by a is defined to be the set of all formulae x that are true in every state $s' \in S$ that satisfies a and is as close as possible to some state s satisfying K. More precisely, $K \# a$ is the set of all formulae x such that for every K-state s, x is true in every state s' that is minimal under the relation $<_s$ in the set of all a-states. Note the double quantification in this definition: once over K-states s and again over $<_s$-minimal a-states s'. Using a notation introduced in Chapter 3, we may express the definition more compactly: $K \# a = \{x : \min_{<_s}(|a|) \subseteq |x|$ for every $s \in |K|\}$.

In its use of the belief set K, update resembles revision. But whereas AGM revision takes K as an undivided unit, KM update distributes the operation over all the states s satisfying K. This difference in semantic structure modifies the behaviour of the engendered logical operation. It gives rise to some new properties, brings about the loss of some, and leaves the status of yet others untouched.

- For example, when $K \subseteq K'$ then clearly every K'-state is a K-state. So it is immediate from the distributional structure of the definition that when $K \subseteq K'$ then $K \# a \subseteq K' \# a$. This is monotony for the left (belief-set) argument K, which we saw fails for AGM revision. We note however that for KM update just as for AGM revision, monotony still fails for the right (update input) argument a. In other words, the inclusion $K \# a \subseteq K \#(a \wedge b)$ can fail.

- An example of something lost is the AGM principle that whenever K is consistent with a then $K * a = Cn(K \cup \{a\})$ where Cn is classical consequence. More to the point, it can fail even when Cn is strengthened to the pivotal-valuation consequence operation Cn_W, where W is the set of all valuations v_s labelling states $s \in S$ of the update model. We do then have $K \# a \subseteq Cn_W(K \cup \{a\})$, but the converse need not hold even when the update model satisfies full centering. This is essentially because there may be a K-state s with $v_s(a) = 0$, for which one of the closest a-states s' lies outside $|K|$. There may be a formula x that is false in some such s', even though it is true in every state that satisfies both K and a.

- A basic property shared by both revision and update is $a \in K\#a$. Again, the inclusion $(K\#a) \cap (K\#b) \subseteq K\#(a \lor b)$ holds for KM update and for relational AGM partial meet revisions satisfying the extended postulates.

Of course, it remains quite debatable how far the formal contrast between a holistic and a distributional treatment of the belief set K, used respectively in the AGM and KM semantics, really corresponds to the intuitive distinction between revising and updating. But that is another question, which we will not attempt to answer here.

Just as with revision, update may be reconceptualized as a consequence relation modulo K. In other words, each choice of a set K of formulae determines the relation $\|\approx_K$ defined by putting $A\|\approx_K x$ iff $x \in K\#A$, i.e. iff for every K-state s, x is true in every state t that is minimal under the relation $<_s$ in the set of all A-states. The properties of update as initially conceived then translate into properties of such relations. This kind of consequence relation has not been the focus of much attention in the literature. But it turns out to be closely related to what is known as the logic of counterfactual conditionals, which has been the object of intensive study and which we now briefly describe.

Counterfactual Conditionals

In ordinary discourse, a counterfactual conditional is one that tells us what *would* be the case if its antecedent *were* true, and is typically stated in a situation in which it is common knowledge that the antecedent is in fact false. A famous example is sometimes attributed to Lady Astor and Winston Churchill. She scolded him: 'If you were my husband, I would put poison in your cup'; he replied 'If you were my wife, I would drink it'.

Philosophical logicians have been discussing these conditionals ever since Chisholm (1946) and Goodman (1947) first noticed their distinctive character. Formal studies of counterfactual conditionals with axiom systems and semantic characterizations date from Stalnaker (1968), with Lewis (1973) generally regarded as a *locus classicus*.

In one respect, the logic of counterfactual conditionals is more complex than any of nonmonotonic inference, AGM belief revision, or KM update. It treats the conditional as a connective of the object language, allowing unlimited iteration. But in another respect, its flat part, i.e. the part consisting of conditionals between purely Boolean formulae, can be seen as a special case of KM update.

Consider any nonempty set S (whose elements we again call *states*), together with a family of relations $<_s$ ($s \in S$) over S, and also a labelling function λ associating a classical truth-value assignment v_s to each $s \in S$. Fix a specific state $s \in S$. We may define a consequence relation $\|\approx_s$ by the rule: $a\|\approx_s x$ iff x is true in every state s' that is minimal under the relation $<_s$ in the set of all a-states. This is essentially the construction used in the Stalnaker/Lewis semantics of counterfactual conditionals. We can think of it as expressing the notion that when we are in the state s, the proposition x *would* be true if a *were* true, while other things vary as little as possible. It can also be seen as a special case of Katsuno-Mendelzon update — the case where the belief set K is satisfied by exactly one state $s \in S$.

However, as already remarked, in its standard presentations the logic of counterfactuals goes one step further. It *internalizes* the relation $\|\approx_s$ to become a connective of the object language, with iteration allowed. Writing say $\rightsquigarrow$ for this connective, we thus allow formulae such as $p \rightsquigarrow (q \rightsquigarrow r), (p \rightsquigarrow q) \rightsquigarrow r, (p \rightsquigarrow q) \rightsquigarrow (r \rightsquigarrow s)$, their Boolean compounds, and deeper iterations. And in any given model we extend Boolean valuations to to give truth values to formulae containing the new connective by the rule: $v_s(a \rightsquigarrow x) = 1$ iff $v_t(x) = 1$ for every state $t \in \min_{<s}(a)$.

With this presentation, we are no longer defining a *family of consequence relations*. We are defining a *distinguished set of formulae*, the set of theorems or theses of the logic. This is the set of all those formulae a such that for *every* counterfactual model structure $(S, \{ <_s \}_{s \in S})$ satisfying suitable conditions on the relations $<_s$ (such as irreflexivity, transitivity, weak centering and, if desired, stoppering *alias* the limit assumption and full centering), and every labelling function λ, i.e. every family $\{v_s\}_{s \in S}$ of Boolean valuations into that structure, we have $v_s(a) = 1$ for all $s \in S$. Whereas the individual consequence relations $\|\approx_s$ between Boolean formulae are not in general closed under substitution (cf. section 1.3), the set of formulae serving as theorems of the counterfactual logic *is* closed under substitution.

So generated, what does a logic of counterfactuals look like? For purely Boolean formulae, it will coincide with classical logic. That is, the theses of the counterfactual logic that are purely Boolean formulae will be just the set of all classical tautologies. For first-degree formulae, the logic will contain theses corresponding to the Horn and non-Horn formulae that we have considered as conditions for nonmonotonic consequence relations. For example, corresponding to the conditions of reflexivity and cumulative transitivity we have the theses $a \rightsquigarrow a$ and $((a \rightsquigarrow x) \wedge ((a \wedge x) \rightsquigarrow y)) \rightsquigarrow (a \rightsquigarrow y)$. When the modelling satisfies the limit assumption then we get a formula internalising the rule of cautious monotony, $((a \rightsquigarrow x) \wedge (a \rightsquigarrow y)) \rightsquigarrow ((a \wedge x) \rightsquigarrow y)$; when the relations $<_s$ of the model are ranked we get a formula expressing the non-Horn condition of rational monotony: $((a \rightsquigarrow x) \wedge \neg(a \rightsquigarrow \neg y)) \rightsquigarrow ((a \wedge x) \rightsquigarrow y)$.

The weak and strong centering conditions also give rise to theses that have no direct counterpart for consequence relations. Weak centering gives us a formula expressing modus ponens for the counterfactual connective: $(a \wedge (a \rightsquigarrow x)) \rightarrow x$. This lacks an exact counterpart because of its 'lopsided' form: while the second conjunct of the antecedent is a counterfactual conditional, the first conjunct and the consequent are purely Boolean. The closest we can get to it on the relational level is the rule: whenever $t \not\hspace{-2pt}\sim \neg a$ and $a \hspace{1pt}\sim\hspace{-7pt}\mid\hspace{2pt} x$ then $t \not\hspace{-2pt}\sim \neg x$, where t is an arbitrary tautology. In Horn form: whenever $t \hspace{1pt}\sim\hspace{-7pt}\mid\hspace{2pt} \neg x$ and $a \hspace{1pt}\sim\hspace{-7pt}\mid\hspace{2pt} x$ then $t \hspace{1pt}\sim\hspace{-7pt}\mid\hspace{2pt} \neg a$. In terms of preferential models, this means that if there is some minimal state s of the entire model that satisfies a, and every minimal a-state satisfies x, then x is satisfied by some minimal state (in fact by the same s, although the syntactic rule is incapable of expressing that). It is also close to a rule that we may call limiting case transitivity: whenever $t \hspace{1pt}\sim\hspace{-7pt}\mid\hspace{2pt} a$ and $a \hspace{1pt}\sim\hspace{-7pt}\mid\hspace{2pt} x$ then $t \hspace{1pt}\sim\hspace{-7pt}\mid\hspace{2pt} x$. In preferential models: if every minimal state of the entire model satisfies a, and every minimal a-state satisfies x, then every minimal state satisfies x.

Full centering in the modelling gives rise to another well-known thesis of the logic of counterfactuals, called conjunctive sufficiency: $(a \wedge x) \rightarrow (a \rightsquigarrow x)$. Again there is no exact counterpart for consequence relations. The closest is: whenever $t \not\hspace{-2pt}\sim \neg(a \wedge x)$ then $a \not\hspace{-2pt}\sim \neg x$. In Horn form: whenever $a \hspace{1pt}\sim\hspace{-7pt}\mid\hspace{2pt} \neg x$ then $t \hspace{1pt}\sim\hspace{-7pt}\mid\hspace{2pt} \neg(a \wedge x)$; equivalently: whenever $a \hspace{1pt}\sim\hspace{-7pt}\mid\hspace{2pt} y$ then $t \hspace{1pt}\sim\hspace{-7pt}\mid\hspace{2pt} \neg a \vee y$. Semantically, in preferential models: if some minimal state s of the entire model satisfies $a \wedge x$ then some minimal a-state (namely the same s) satisfies x. Also close is the rule: whenever $t \hspace{1pt}\sim\hspace{-7pt}\mid\hspace{2pt} (a \wedge x)$ then $a \hspace{1pt}\sim\hspace{-7pt}\mid\hspace{2pt} x$. This holds whenever the preferential model is *bottom-stoppered* (every non-minimal state of the entire model has a minimal state below it).

In passing, we remark that in the logic of counterfactuals, conjunctive sufficiency has some odd consequences. For example, it implies $(a \rightsquigarrow b) \vee (a \rightsquigarrow \neg b) \vee (\neg a \rightsquigarrow b) \vee (\neg a \rightsquigarrow \neg b)$.

All of the above formulae are of modal depth 1: there are no nested occurrences of $\rightsquigarrow$. Are there any interesting theses of the logic of counterfactuals of modal depth 2 or more? There do not appear to be any, other than ones derivable from those of depth 0 or 1.

The literature also contains accounts of counterfactual conditions similar to the default-assumption constructions of section 2.2 and 2.3: see for example Veltman (1976; 1985) and Kratzer (1981). Lewis (1981) compares the two approaches in the counterfactual context.

Conditional Directives

Default-valuation constructions based on minimality have also been used in the area known as deontic logic — the logic of obligation, permission, interdiction, commitment, etc. Specifically, they are used in the study of conditional obligations. The seminal paper in this connection was by Bengt Hansson (1969). It introduced an apparatus that is mathematically indistinguishable from the preferential semantics for nonmonotonic reasoning described in section 3.2, but with a different interpretation of the relation $<$ between valuations or states. Whereas for preferential consequence this relation was read as relative normality, in the deontic context it is read as relative (moral, legal etc.) acceptability. Under Hansson's semantics, to say that x is obligatory given a is to say that x is true in all of the best a-worlds. 'Best' is understood as minimality under the relation $<$ over the set W of valuations (or states) of the modelling, so that the requirement is: $min_<|a|_W \subseteq |x|_W$. This is the same condition as for preferential consequence, but with $<$ reinterpreted.

Since Hansson's classic paper of 1969, the preferential semantics for conditional obligation has been extended to treat conditional obligation as a connective of the object-language, usually written $O(x/a)$, thus allowing nesting in the same manner as does the logic of counterfactuals. It has also been refined and elaborated by indexing the relation of comparative goodness so that it depends on the world or state in which one is currently evaluating, and introducing auxiliary relations, sets and functions into the semantic apparatus to represent such ingredients as levels of normality, the passage of time, and the possibility of transition from one state to another with (or without) deliberate action on the part of the agents concerned. For further discussion of some of these questions see e.g. Makinson (1993). For a general overview of deontic logic, see Åqvist (2002).

As one would expect, the literature also contains some alternative accounts of conditional directives using background assumption sets, in both pivotal and default versions. One example of the latter is Sven Ove Hansson and Makinson (1997).

An account of conditional directives in terms of additional background rules is given by Makinson and van der Torre (2000). Their 'input/output logics' are like the pivotal-rule systems of section 4.1, but with the output determined in a different manner so that when the antecedent of a conditional directive is satisfied (becoming an 'input'), it is not automatically included among the ensuing outputs. The motivation behind this modification comes from the intuitive reading of conditional directives. While, in the context of nonmonotonic reasoning, it is perfectly natural to say that every proposition is a consequence of itself, in the context of conditional directives it is extremely odd to say that every proposition is obligatory when it is true! Rule-based input/output logics avoid this oddity in a natural manner. But constructions based on a relative goodness relations between valuations or states, or on background assumption sets, almost inevitably incur it unless *ad hoc* restrictions are imposed. The rule-based approach also opens the way to interesting treatments of the unsettled areas of contrary-to-duty obligations and conditional permissions — see Makinson and van der Torre (2001; 2003).

Exercises

1*. Verify, in more detail than in the text, the left-argument monotony principle for Katsuno/Mendelzon update.

2. Give a counterexample to right-argument monotony for Katsuno/Mendelzon update.

3. Verify that $K\#a \subseteq Cn_W(K \cup \{a\})$ where W is the set of all valuations v_s labelling states $s \in S$ of the update model.

4. Fill out in full detail the sketch of a counterexample to $Cn_W(K \cup \{a\}) \subseteq K\#a$ in an update model satisfying full centering.

5. Verify the inclusion $(K\#a) \cap (K\#b) \subseteq K\#(a \vee b)$ for both KM update and relational AGM partial meet revision.

6*. Show that the set of theses of any logic of counterfactuals, as defined in the text, is closed under substitution (of arbitrary formulae for elementary letters).

7. Show by an example that logics of counterfactuals do not in general contain as a thesis the formula internalising the principle of monotony (alias strengthening the antecedent): $(a \rightsquigarrow x) \rightsquigarrow ((a \wedge b) \rightsquigarrow x)$.

8. Verify each of the theses of logics of counterfactuals mentioned in the text.
Hint: In each case consider the class of models satisfying the conditions specified, and show that the logic that it generates contains the thesis in question.

9*. Express in words, using the notion of conditional obligation, the rules of cumulative transitivity, cautious monotony, conjunction in the consequent, and disjunction in the antecedent. Comment on their intuitive plausibility.

6.3 Some Representation Theorems for Consequence Relations

As indicated in our general discussion of representation and completeness theorems in section 2.1, a *representation theorem* for consequence relations tells us that *every* relation satisfying certain syntactic conditions (Horn rules, or more general conditions with e.g. negative premisses or disjunctive conclusions) may be defined or generated (in a specified way) from some structure of a certain kind.

Such theorems are interesting when the converse is also true, i.e. when the syntactic conditions in question all hold in every consequence relation generated by a structure of the specified kind. Such results are known as *soundness theorems*, and the individual syntactic conditions are said to be *sound* with respect to the specified semantics. Evidently, this concept is relative: a syntactic condition may be sound with respect to one semantic structure but not another.

Generally speaking, soundness theorems tend to be easy to prove. We take each syntactic condition in turn and verify that it holds in any structure of the specified kind. Representation (and completeness) theorems tend to be much more difficult to prove. To show the corresponding representation theorem, we have to consider an arbitrary logical operation satisfying the syntactic conditions, and make an imaginative effort to find a structure in the class that generates exactly that operation.

Historically, in many systems of logic the first investigations were syntactic in nature. Certain formulae were deemed desirable, or certain conditions regarded as plausible, and these were grouped together and studied. Later investigations sought ways of generating objects satisfying these conditions. Sometimes, however, the order of discovery is reversed: a class of semantic structures is defined, and investigations are carried out to determine the syntactic properties of the consequence relations or other logical objects that the structures in the class determine.

In so far as one is able to prove both soundness and representation one has confirmation of a certain degree of stability. We then know that a consequence relation satisfies certain listed syntactic conditions if and only if it may be defined from some structure of a certain kind. The class of those consequence relations may thus be seen in either of two quite different ways. It appears at the intersection of two different paths of thought, and so appears to occupy a strategic or interesting position.

But this sense of satisfaction and security should not be exaggerated. Being able to prove a soundness-plus-completeness theorem is no guarantee that we have found a 'correct' or even a strategically significant concept. Even a quite unmotivated set of syntactic conditions can often, with sufficient effort, be given an *ad hoc* semantic representation. Even for a weird class of semantic structures, we may be able to find syntactic conditions for which we can prove soundness and completeness. Judgement and discrimination is as important in these matters as elsewhere, and this implies the possibility of different appreciations and assessments. Not everything in logic is cut and dried.

In the course of earlier chapters, we mentioned in passing some specific representation theorems. Now we bring them together and give some more. It is convenient to consider them in two groups. First: representation theorems for the monotonic bridge systems which, as we saw, are all paraclassical (i.e. supraclassical closure operations in the sense of Chapter 1). Second: for selected nonmonotonic systems, i.e. for default systems whose construction allows certain parameters of the semantics to vary with the premiss set under consideration.

Representation Theorems for Pivotal Systems

In section 2.1 we saw that for any set K of formulae, the consequence operation Cn_K is paraclassical, compact, and satisfies disjunction in the premisses. This is a soundness observation. We also proved the converse representation theorem:

Theorem 2.2. *Let Cn^+ be any paraclassical consequence operation that is compact and satisfies disjunction in the premisses. Then there is a set K of formulae such that $Cn^+ = Cn_K$.*

This is a very satisfying result, in so far as it connects certain very natural conditions (compactness, disjunction in the premisses, the conditions defining a closure operation, and supraclassicality) with generation from some set K of formulae by the simple definition $Cn^+(A) = Cn(K \cup A)$.

For pivotal-rule consequence, another representation theorem was stated and proven in section 4.1. Expressing it in slightly different words to bring out the parallel with the one above, it says:

Theorem 4.5. *Let Cn^+ be any paraclassical consequence operation that is compact. Then there is a rule-set R such $Cn^+ = Cn_R$.*

Despite the parallel, this seems to be a much less interesting result. As remarked in section 4.1, the proof works only because the definition of a pivotal-rule consequence relation places no constraints on the rule set, i.e. relation, R. This permits us to 'cheat' by taking R to be the very consequence relation that we are seeking to represent, restricted to singletons. It would be more interesting if we could impose some kind of regularity constraints on R.

For pivotal-valuation consequence, we had no infinitary representation theorem. Indeed, we saw in section 3.1 that the conjecture that comes naturally to mind is demonstrably false. It is not the case that for every paraclassical consequence operation Cn^+ satisfying the condition of disjunction in the premises there is a set W of valuations such that $Cn^+ = Cn_W$. However, as shown in the same section, this does hold in a finitary form, which we reword slightly to facilitate comparisons:

Theorem 3.6.   *Let Cn^+ be any paraclassical consequence operation satisfying disjunction in the premises. Then there is a set W of valuations such that $Cn^+(A) = Cn_W(A)$ for all finite A.*

This holds because the finite part of such an operation Cn^+ is equal to the finite part of a suitably chosen pivotal-assumption operation (cf. section 3.1). For a logician or mathematician, the really interesting aspect of the concept of pivotal-valuation consequence is its infinitary part, and there the question of a good representation theorem appears to remain open.

Representation Theorems for Default Systems

Most of the nonmonotonic systems in the literature defined using default-assumption and default-valuation constructions have been provided with soundness plus representation theorems, at least for their finite parts (i.e. for finite sets of premises; equivalently for individual formulae as premises). But, as far as the author is aware, none of those defined using default-rule constructions have been so certified. The question of representation in that area thus appears to remain open.

In this section, we single out just two representation results, one for a default-assumption construction and the other for a default-valuation one.

For default assumptions, we give a basic theorem, easy compared to some others in the literature, but still quite challenging. It concerns one of the notions of consequence via an arbitrary selection function, discussed in section 2.3, and was first proven in Gärdenfors and Makinson (1994). It holds in a finitary form, i.e. for individual formulae as premisses.

On the one hand, we consider structures (K, δ) of the following kind:

- K is a set of Boolean formulae. We require that it is consistent and is closed under classical consequence, i.e. $K = Cn(K)$.

- δ is any selection function that associates with each family K_a a subfamily $\delta(K_a) \subseteq K_a$. Here, as in section 6.1, K_a is the family of all subsets $K' \subseteq K$ maxiconsistent with a. We require that $\delta(K_a)$ is nonempty whenever K_a is nonempty.

For each such structure, we define the consequence relation $\mathbin{\mid\!\sim}_\delta$ between individual formulae by putting:

- $a \mathbin{\mid\!\sim}_\delta x$ iff $K' \cup \{a\} \vdash x$ for all $K' \in \delta(K_a)\}$.

On the other hand, we consider the following finitary syntactic conditions on a consequence relation $\mathbin{\mid\!\sim}$ between individual formulae. As usual, t is an arbitrary tautology and f is an arbitrary contradiction.

- Supraclassicality: whenever $a \vdash x$ then $a \mathbin{\mid\!\sim} x$

- Left classical equivalence: whenever $a \vdash b$ and $b \vdash a$ then $a \mathbin{\mid\!\sim} x$ iff $b \mathbin{\mid\!\sim} x$

- Right weakening: whenever $a \mathbin{\mid\!\sim} b$ and $b \vdash x$ then $a \mathbin{\mid\!\sim} x$

- Conjunction in the conclusion (AND): whenever $a \mathbin{\mid\!\sim} x$ and $a \mathbin{\mid\!\sim} y$ then $a \mathbin{\mid\!\sim} x \wedge y$

- Consistency preservation: whenever $a \not\vdash f$ then $a \mathbin{\mid\!\not\sim} f$

- Limiting case conditionalization: whenever $a \mathbin{\mid\!\sim} x$ then $t \mathbin{\mid\!\sim} a \to x$

- Limiting case rational monotony: whenever $t \mathbin{\mid\!\not\sim} \neg a$ and $t \mathbin{\mid\!\sim} a \to x$ then $a \mathbin{\mid\!\sim} x$.

Theorem 6.1 (Soundness) *Let $\mathbin{\mid\!\sim}_\delta$ be any consequence relation defined from a structure as described. Then it satisfies the conditions enumerated.*

Representation: Conversely, any consequence relation between individual formulae that satisfies the enumerated conditions may be defined in the way described.

We leave the soundness part for the exercises, and focus on the representation part. We will need a lemma.

Lemma 6.2 (for Theorem 6.1)

1. K_a *is empty iff* a *is inconsistent.*

2. *Suppose* $K = Cn(K)$ *and let* $K' \in K_a$. *Then* $K' = Cn(K')$.

3. *Suppose* $K = Cn(K)$ *and let* $K' \in K_a$. *Then* $K' \in K_b$ *for all* b *such that* $\neg b \in K$ *and* $\neg b \notin K'$.

4. *Suppose that* K, δ *satisfy the requirements for the theorem. Then* $\delta(K_t) = K_t = \{K\}$.

Verification of the Lemma. For (1): Suppose first that a is inconsistent. Then a is inconsistent with every subset of K, so that K_a is empty. Conversely, suppose that a is consistent. Then it is consistent with $\emptyset$, so using compactness of classical logic and Zorn's Lemma there is a maximal subset $K' \subseteq K$ with which a is consistent. By the definition of K_a, $K' \in K_a$ so that K_a is not empty.

For (2): Remembering that K_a is the collection of all maximal a-consistent subsets of K, this fact was already noted in section 2.2, with a proof in the answer to exercise 7 of that section.

Point (3) follows easily from Observation 2.8, whose proof is given in the answer to problem 2 of section 2.2.

For (4): Suppose K and δ satisfy the requirements for the theorem. Then K is consistent, so it is consistent with t, so $K_t = \{K\}$. But $\delta(K_t)$ is required to be a nonempty subset of K_t so also $\delta(K_t) = \{K\}$. ∎

Proof. [of Theorem 6.1 (representation part)] Let $\vdash$ be a consequence relation between individual formulae that satisfies the enumerated conditions. Put $K = \{x : t \vdash x\}$. Let δ be the selection function defined by putting $\delta(K_a) = \{K' \in K_a : C(a) \subseteq Cn(K' \cup \{a\})\}$.

Heuristically, these are the natural definitions to try. We are in effect putting our background assumptions to be the conclusions that the consequence relation $\vdash$ permits us to draw in the absence of any specific information; and we are selecting those elements of K_a that are strong enough, when combined with a, to imply classically all of the propositions that $\vdash$ permits us to draw from a. We need to show that K and δ satisfy requirements, and that $\vdash = \vdash_\delta$.

To show $K = Cn(K)$: Suppose $x \in Cn(K)$. Then by compactness for classical logic there are $x_1, \ldots, x_n \in K$ with $x_1 \wedge \ldots \wedge x_n \vdash x$. But by the definition of K, $t \vdash x_i$ for each $i \leq n$, so by conjunction in the conclusion and right weakening we have $t \vdash x$, so $x \in K$ as desired.

To show the consistency of K: Suppose K is inconsistent. Then $K \vdash f$, so since $K = Cn(K)$ we have $f \in K$. Thus $t \mathrel{\vdash\mkern-10mu\sim} f$ by the definition of K, so by consistency preservation $t \vdash f$ giving us a contradiction.

For $\delta(K_a) \subseteq K_a$: This is immediate from the definition of $\delta(K_a)$. We postpone verification of the non-emptiness of $\delta(K_a)$ whenever K_a is non-empty, until the end of our proof.

We now show that $\mathrel{\vdash\mkern-10mu\sim} = \mathrel{\vdash\mkern-10mu\sim}_\delta$. The left-to-right direction is easy. Suppose $a \mathrel{\vdash\mkern-10mu\sim} x$. Take any $K' \in \delta(K_a)$. By the definition of $\mathrel{\vdash\mkern-10mu\sim}_\delta$ we need to show that $K' \cup \{a\} \vdash x$. But by the definition of $\delta(K_a)$ we have $C(a) \subseteq Cn(K' \cup \{a\})$, and so we are done.

For the right-to-left direction, suppose $a \not\mathrel{\vdash\mkern-10mu\sim} x$. We need to find a $K' \in K_a$ with $C(a) \subseteq Cn(K' \cup \{a\})$ and $K' \cup \{a\} \nvdash x$. This is the tough part of the proof.

First we note that $C(a)$ is consistent with $a \wedge \neg x$. For suppose otherwise. Then, using compactness of classical logic there are $x_1, \ldots, x_n$ with $a \mathrel{\vdash\mkern-10mu\sim} x_i$ for each $i \leq n$ and $x_1 \wedge \ldots \wedge x_n \vdash \neg(a \wedge \neg x) \vdash a \to x$. By conjunction in the conclusion and right weakening this gives $a \mathrel{\vdash\mkern-10mu\sim} a \to x$. But $a \mathrel{\vdash\mkern-10mu\sim} a$ by supraclassicality, so by conjunction in the conclusion and right weakening again, $a \mathrel{\vdash\mkern-10mu\sim} x$ contrary to hypothesis.

Since $C(a)$ is consistent with $a \wedge \neg x$, its subset $C(a) \cap K$ is also consistent with $a \wedge \neg x$, and clearly it is also a subset of K. Hence by Zorn's Lemma there is a set $K' \in K_{a \wedge \neg x}$ with $C(a) \cap K \subseteq K'$. It remains to check that $K' \in K_a, C(a) \subseteq Cn(K' \cup \{a\})$ and $K' \cup \{a\} \nvdash x$.

First, we check that $K' \cup \{a\} \nvdash x$. It suffices to show that $K' \nvdash (a \to x)$, i.e. that K' is consistent with $a \wedge \neg x$. But this is immediate from the construction of K'.

Next we check that $C(a) \subseteq Cn(K' \cup \{a\})$. Suppose $a \mathrel{\vdash\mkern-10mu\sim} y$. Then by right weakening $a \mathrel{\vdash\mkern-10mu\sim} a \to y$, and also by limiting case conditionalization $t \mathrel{\vdash\mkern-10mu\sim} a \to y$, so using the definition of K we have $a \to y \in C(a) \cap K \subseteq K'$ and so by classical logic, $y \in Cn(K' \cup \{a\})$ as desired.

Finally, we check that $K' \in K_a$. Since K' is consistent with $a \wedge \neg x$, it is consistent with a. Now suppose $K' \subset K'' \subseteq K$; we need to show that $K'' \vdash \neg a$. By construction of K' we have $K'' \vdash (a \to x)$, so $k_1 \wedge \ldots \wedge k_n \vdash (a \to x)$ for some $k_1, \ldots, k_n \in K''$. Since $K'' \subseteq K$ we know by the definition of K that $t \mathrel{\vdash\mkern-10mu\sim} k_i$ for each $i \leq n$ so by conjunction in the conclusion and right weakening $t \mathrel{\vdash\mkern-10mu\sim} (a \to x)$. From this, it follows that $t \mathrel{\vdash\mkern-10mu\sim} \neg a$. For if $t \not\mathrel{\vdash\mkern-10mu\sim} \neg a$ then since $t \mathrel{\vdash\mkern-10mu\sim} (a \to x)$ we would have $a \mathrel{\vdash\mkern-10mu\sim} x$ by limiting case rational monotony, contradicting the hypothesis of the right-to-left argument. Since $t \mathrel{\vdash\mkern-10mu\sim} \neg a$, the definition of K tells us that $\neg a \in K$. We already know that $K' \in K_{a \wedge \neg x}$. We also know that K' is consistent with a, so $\neg a \notin K'$. Putting these three facts together and applying part (iii) of the Lemma, we have $K' \in K_a$ as desired.

To complete the proof, we make the promised check on the remaining requirement on δ. Suppose K_a is nonempty; we need to show that $\delta(K_a)$ is nonempty. Since K_a is nonempty we know by part (i) of the Lemma that a is consistent, i.e. $a \not\vdash f$. So by consistency preservation, $a \not\hspace{-0.3em}\sim f$. Since we have already shown that $\hspace{-0.3em}\sim \; = \; \hspace{-0.3em}\sim_\delta$ we may conclude that $a \not\hspace{-0.3em}\sim_\delta f$. By the definition of $\hspace{-0.3em}\sim_\delta$ this means that there is a $K' \in \delta(K_a)$ with $K' \cup \{a\} \not\vdash x$. Since $K' \in \delta(K_a)$, we conclude that $\delta(K_a)$ is not empty. ∎

We now state a representation theorem for default valuations. We choose the best-known one, due to Kraus, Lehmann and Magidor (1990), often known as the KLM representation theorem. It concerns the notion of preferential consequence as studied in section 3.2, broadened so as to admit multiple copies of valuations in the manner described in section 3.3, and with the stoppering condition imposed. We recall from section 3.3 that *preferential models* (admitting copies) are structures $(S, <, \lambda)$ where:

- S is an arbitrary set. Its elements are called states.

- $<$ is a relation over S. We assume that it is transitive and irreflexive.

- λ is a function associating a Boolean valuation on formulae with each $s \in S$. It is called a labelling function, and for convenience we write $\lambda(s)$ as v_s.

We assume moreover that:

- $(S, <, \lambda)$ is finitarily stoppered.

This notion was defined in section 3.2 for the special case of preferential models without copies, i.e. where the elements of S are valuations and the labelling function λ is the identity function. In the broadened context where copies are admitted, *finitary stoppering* (alias finitary smoothness) means the following: for all $s \in S$, if v_s satisfies a formula a, then either s is minimal under $<$ among the states t such that v_t satisfies a, or else there is an $s' \in S$ with $s' < s$ that is thus minimal. In compact notation, write $|a|$ for $\{s \in S : v_s(a) = 1\}$. Then $(S, <, \lambda)$ is stoppered iff whenever $s \in S$ and $v_s \in |a|$ then either $s \in min_<|a|$ or there is a $s' < s$ with $s' \in min_<|a|$.

For each such structure, define the consequence relation $\hspace{-0.3em}\sim_<$ between individual formulae by putting:

- $a \hspace{-0.3em}\sim_< x$ iff $v_s(x) = 1$ for every state s that is minimal under $<$ among those making a true.

In other words, using the compact notation introduced above:

- $a \mathrel{\vmid\sim}_< x$ iff $\min_< |a| \subseteq |x|$.

On the other hand, consider the following finitary syntactic conditions on a consequence relation $\mathrel{\vmid\sim}$ between individual formulae.

- Supraclassicality: whenever $a \vdash x$ then $a \mathrel{\vmid\sim} x$

- Left classical equivalence: whenever $a \vdash b$ and $b \vdash a$ then $a \mathrel{\vmid\sim} x$ iff $b \mathrel{\vmid\sim} x$

- Right weakening: whenever $a \mathrel{\vmid\sim} b$ and $b \vdash x$ then $a \mathrel{\vmid\sim} x$

- Conjunction in the conclusion (AND): whenever $a \mathrel{\vmid\sim} x$ and $a \mathrel{\vmid\sim} y$ then $a \mathrel{\vmid\sim} x \wedge y$

- Cumulative transitivity: whenever $a \mathrel{\vmid\sim} x$ and $a \wedge x \mathrel{\vmid\sim} y$ then $a \mathrel{\vmid\sim} y$

- Cautious monotony: whenever $a \mathrel{\vmid\sim} x$ and $a \mathrel{\vmid\sim} y$ then $a \wedge x \mathrel{\vmid\sim} y$

- Disjunction in the premisses (OR): whenever $a \mathrel{\vmid\sim} x$ and $b \mathrel{\vmid\sim} x$ then $a \vee b \mathrel{\vmid\sim} x$.

There is a certain amount of redundancy in these conditions. Given right weakening, supraclassicality can be weakened to simple reflexivity: $a \mathrel{\vmid\sim} a$. Less obviously, AND is redundant given cautious monotony and cumulative transitivity. But these are axiom-chopping details.

Theorem 6.3 *Soundness: Let $\mathrel{\vmid\sim}_<$ be any consequence relation defined from a stoppered preferential structure as described above. Then it satisfies the conditions enumerated.*

Representation: Conversely, any consequence relation between individual formulae that satisfies the enumerated conditions may be defined from a stoppered preferential structure in the way described.

The soundness part can be verified in a straightforward manner. On the other hand, the proof of the representation part is quite deep and difficult — much more so than that for Theorem 6.1 above. Even the construction of a suitable preferential model $(S, <, \lambda)$ is rather intricate. Given a consequence relation $\mathrel{\vmid\sim}$ satisfying the specified syntactic conditions, to ensure an adequate supply of copies of valuations the set S of states is defined as follows:

- $S = \{(v, a) : v$ is a Boolean valuation with $v(C(a)) = 1\}$.

Here, of course, $C(a)$ means $\{x : a \mathrel{|\!\sim} x\}$. Once S is defined, the labelling function λ is specified in the simplest way possible: for every $(v, a) \in S$:

- $\lambda((v, a)) = v$.

The most delicate part of the construction is the definition of the relation $<$:

- $(v, a) < (w, b)$ iff $v(b) = 0$ and $a \vee b \mathrel{|\!\sim} a$.

To help motivate the definition of $<$, we do some reverse engineering. Observe that for any stoppered preferential model $(S, <, \lambda)$, $a \vee b \mathrel{|\!\sim_<} a$ iff for every state $s \in S$ satisfying b (i.e. with $v_s(b) = 1$) there is a state $s' \in S$ satisfying a, such that either $s' = s$ or $s' < s$. If in addition $v_{s'}(b) = 0$ then $s' \neq s$ so $s' < s$.

The verification that the construction above actually does the desired job proceeds via a series of subtle lemmas, for which we refer the reader to Kraus, Lehmann and Magidor (1990).

Exercises

1. State and check the soundness theorem converse to the representation Theorem 4.5 for pivotal-rule consequence.

2. Although the infinitary form of Theorem 3.6 fails, its converse soundness theorem holds. Check it.

3*. Fill in the details of the proof of point (3) of the Lemma for Theorem 6.1. That is, show that it follows easily from Observation 2.8.

4*. Verify the soundness part of Theorem 6.1.

5. Show that the syntactic conditions for Theorem 6.1 imply 'limiting case transitivity' mentioned in section 6.2: whenever $t \mathrel{|\!\sim} a$ and $a \mathrel{|\!\sim} x$ then $t \mathrel{|\!\sim} x$.

6. Verify the 'axiom-chopping details' mentioned in the preliminaries to formulating Theorem 6.3.

7. Verify the soundness part of Theorem 6.3.

8. Verify the 'reverse engineering' claim made to motivate the construction of the relation $<$ between states in the KLM proof of Theorem 6.3.

Problem

Do the syntactic conditions for Theorem 6.1 imply cumulative transitivity?

Project

Study in detail Kraus, Lehmann and Magidor (1990).

Advanced Project

Study the problems arising for representation theorems for default-valuation operations with infinite premiss sets, using Freund and Lehmann (1994) and Schlechta (2004).

Remark: This project should be undertaken only by students who are mathematically well equipped.

6.4   Review and Explore

Recapitulation

The logics of belief revision, update, counterfactual conditionals and conditional obligation bear a family resemblance to each other and to the logic of nonmonotonic inference. This resemblance shows itself on the syntactic level, that is, with respect to the logical principles entertained in each kind of logic, and we can construct partial translations between them. It also manifests itself in the generating semantics, which is usually akin to that of default-assumption consequence (in the cases of belief revision and update) and/or preferential consequence (update again, counterfactual conditionals and conditional obligation).

In the monotonic case, representation theorems can be proven for both pivotal-assumption and pivotal-rule consequence operations. No infinitary representation theorem appears to be known for pivotal-valuation consequence, although a finitary one follows from its pivotal-assumption cousin. In the default arena, there are many representation theorems (usually finitary) for various forms of default-assumption and especially default-valuation consequence; two sample ones are given in the text. However, there do not appear to be any analogous results for default-rule consequence.

Checklist of Concepts and Definitions for Revision

Section 6.1: Belief change, revision, contraction, principle of minimal mutilation, Levi identity, Harper identity, AGM basic and extended postulates for revision, partial meet revision, one-shot versus iterated revision. *Section 6.2*: Intuitive concept of update, the Katsuno/Mendelzon modelling for updates, weak centering, full centering; intuitive concept of counterfactual conditional, internalization of a consequence relation as a conditional connective, Stalnaker/Lewis modelling for counterfactuals, modus ponens for counterfactuals, conjunctive sufficiency; intuitive concept of conditional directives, preferential modelling for conditional obligation. *Section 6.3:* Representation theorems, soundness theorems, significance of such results, main representation results for pivotal systems, sample results for default systems.

Further Reading

Belief change

- D. Makinson and P. Gärdenfors. Relations between the logic of theory change and nonmonotonic logic. In *The Logic of Theory Change*, Fuhrmann & Morreau eds., pp. 185–205. Springer, Berlin, 1991.

- P. Gärdenfors and H. Rott. Belief revision. In *Handbook of Logic in Artificial Intelligence and Logic Programming. Volume 4: Epistemic and Temporal Logics*, D. M. Gabbay, C. Hogger and J. A. Robinson, eds., pp. 35–132. Clarendon Press, Oxford, 1995.

Update, counterfactuals, conditional directives

- H. Katsuno and A. O. Mendelzon. On the difference between updating a knowledge base and revising it. In *Belief Revision*, P. Gärdenfors, ed., pp. 183–203. Cambridge University Press, 1992.

- D. Lewis. *Counterfactuals*. Blackwell: Oxford, 1973.

- D. Makinson. Five faces of minimality, *Studia Logica*, **52**, 339–379, 1993. (sections 5–7)

Representation theorems

- S. Kraus, D. Lehmann and M. Magidor. Nonmonotonic reasoning, preferential models and cumulative logics, *Artificial Intelligence*, **44**, 167–207, 1990.

Appendices

A Proof of Theorem 4.12

Theorem 4.12. *Let R be any set of (normal or non-normal) default rules, and A any premiss set. Then the Reiter extensions of A under R are precisely the sets $C_{\langle R \rangle}(A)$ for well-orderings $\langle R \rangle$ of R of order-type at most ω. That is:*

$(\Rightarrow)$ *For every well-ordering $\langle R \rangle$ of R of order-type $\leq \omega$, if the set $C_{\langle R \rangle}(A)$ is well-defined then it is a Reiter extension of A under R.*

$(\Leftarrow)$ *Every Reiter extension of A under R is a well-defined set $C_{\langle R \rangle}(A)$ for some well-ordering $\langle R \rangle$ of R of order-type $\leq \omega$.*

Proof. We begin by proving $(\Rightarrow)$. The argument follows a natural, indeed 'inevitable' pattern given the definitions involved, although care is needed to set it out rigorously.

The definition of an extension in Reiter (1980) tells us that a set E of formulae is an extension of the premiss set A under the default rules in R iff E is the least set X satisfying the following three conditions: (1) $A \subseteq X$, (2) $X = Cn(X)$, (3) whenever $(a, P, x) \in R$ and $a \in X$ and $\neg p \notin E$ for all $p \in P$, then $x \in X$.

Let $\langle R \rangle$ be a well-ordering of R, of order-type $\leq \omega$, and suppose that $C_{\langle R \rangle}(A)$ is well-defined, i.e. that its inductive construction does not abort at any stage. It will suffice to show that $C_{\langle R \rangle}(A)$ is the least set X satisfying conditions (1)–(3) with $C_{\langle R \rangle}(A)$ substituted for E. In other words, we need to show: (a) $C_{\langle R \rangle}(A)$ satisfies conditions (1)–(3), and (b) whenever X satisfies conditions (1)–(3), then $C_{\langle R \rangle}(A) \subseteq X$.

To prove (a), we need to show (ai) $A \subseteq C_{\langle R \rangle}(A)$, (aii) $C_{\langle R \rangle}(A) = Cn(C_{\langle R \rangle}(A))$, $(aiii)$ whenever $(a, P, x) \in R$ and $a \in C_{\langle R \rangle}(A)$ and $\neg p \notin C_{\langle R \rangle}(A)$ for all $p \in P$, then $x \in C_{\langle R \rangle}(A)$. Now (ai) is immediate from the definition of $C_{\langle R \rangle}(A)$, and (aii) is verified easily using the compactness of classical Cn. The key verification is for $(aiii)$.

167

Suppose $r = (a, P, x) \in R$ and $a \in C_{\langle R \rangle}(A)$ and $\neg p \notin C_{\langle R \rangle}(A)$ for all $p \in P$. We want to show $x \in C_{\langle R \rangle}(A)$. Since $a \in C_{\langle R \rangle}(A)$ we have $a \in A_n$ for some $n < \omega$. Since $\neg p \notin C_{\langle R \rangle}(A)$ for each $p \in P$ we know by (aii) that p is consistent with $C_{\langle R \rangle}(A)$ and so by the monotony of classical consequence, is consistent with A_n. If already $x \in A_n \subseteq C_{\langle R \rangle}(A)$ then we are done, so suppose $x \notin A_n$. Then, as can be shown by an easy induction, $r \notin R_n$ so r satisfies the condition for entry into Case 1 of the definition of A_{n+1}. Indeed, we may assume without loss of generality that r is the first such rule. Since by hypothesis $C_{\langle R \rangle}(A)$ is well-defined, we cannot be in Sub-case 1.2, so we must be in Sub-case 1.1 and thus $A_{n+1} = Cn(A_n \cup \{x\})$, so that $x \in A_{n+1} \subseteq C_{\langle R \rangle}(A)$, completing the proof of $(aiii)$ and thus of (a) as a whole.

To prove (b), suppose X satisfies conditions (1)–(3). We want to show that $C_{\langle R \rangle}(A) \subseteq X$. Clearly it suffices to show that $A_n \subseteq X$ for every $n < \omega$, which we do by induction. The basis is immediate since $A_0 = A \subseteq X$ by condition (1). For the induction step suppose $A_n \subseteq X$; we need to show that $A_{n+1} \subseteq X$. If there is no rule satisfying the test for entry into Case 1 of the definition of A_{n+1}, then we are in Case 2 and $A_{n+1} = A_n \subseteq X$ using the induction hypothesis. So suppose there is some rule satisfying the test for entry into Case 1 of the definition of A_{n+1}. Let $r = (a, P, x)$ be the first such rule.

Since by hypothesis $C_{\langle R \rangle}(A)$ is well-defined, A_{n+1} must be well-defined, so we must be in Sub-case 1.1. It follows that $A_{n+1} = Cn(A_n \cup \{x\})$ and $R_{n+1} = R_n \cup \{r\}$, and each element of $\text{just}(R_n \cup P)$ is consistent with $A_n \cup \{x\}$. Since by the induction hypothesis we have $A_n \subseteq X$ it remains only to show that $x \in X$. Since X satisfies condition (3), it suffices to show $a \in X$ and $\neg p \notin C_{\langle R \rangle}(A)$ for all $p \in P$.

We have $a \in X$ since by supposition r satisfies the condition for entry into Case 1 of the definition of A_{n+1} so $a \in A_n \subseteq X$ again by supposition.

Let $p \in P$. We need to show that $\neg p \notin C_{\langle R \rangle}(A)$. By the entry condition to Sub-case 1.1, $\neg p \notin Cn(A_n \cup \{x\}) = A_{n+1}$ by the definition of A_{n+1} in that case. Also, by the definition of R_{n+1} in that case, we have $r \in R_{n+1}$ so $p \in \text{just}(r) \subseteq \text{just}(R_{n+1})$. From this, an easy induction shows that $\neg p \notin A_m$ for all $m > n + 1$. Hence $\neg p \notin C_{\langle R \rangle}(A)$ as desired and the proof of (b), and thus of part $(\Rightarrow)$ of the theorem, is complete.

We now prove part $(\Leftarrow)$. Let E be any Reiter extension of A under R. We want to show that $E = C_{\langle R \rangle}(A)$ for some well-ordering $\langle R \rangle$ of R of order-type $\leq \omega$. We partition R into three subsets, which we call $R1$, $R2$, $R3$, with the indices 1,2,3 written on the same level as R so as not to confuse them with the first three elements of a sequence $R_0, R_1, \ldots$ defined inductively.

R1: the set of all rules $r = (a, P, x) \in R$ such that $a \in E$ and p is consistent with E for all $p \in P$;

R2: the set of all rules $r = (a, P, x) \in R$ such that $a \notin E$;

R3: the set of all rules $r = (a, P, x) \in R$ with $a \in E$ but p inconsistent with E for some $p \in P$.

Clearly these are disjoint, and their union is R. We begin by taking the set $R1$ and putting its elements in any order $\langle R1 \rangle$ of type ω (or finite if R is finite). Our strategy will be to show first that $C_{\langle R1 \rangle}(A)$ is well-defined and is equal to E, and then to show that the elements of $R2$ and $R3$ may be inserted into the ordering $\langle R1 \rangle$ to give an ordering of R which is still of type at most ω without altering the value of the induced output.

To show that $C_{\langle R1 \rangle}(A)$ is well-defined and is included in E we first note from the definition of fixpoint extensions that the conclusion of every rule in $R1$ is in E. A straightforward induction then shows that for every n, the conditions for entry into Case 1 and Sub-case 1.1 are satisfied, so that A_{n+1} is well-defined and is a subset of E. Thus $C_{\langle R1 \rangle}(A)$ is well-defined and $C_{\langle R1 \rangle}(A) \subseteq E$. For the converse inclusion $E \subseteq C_{\langle R1 \rangle}(A)$ we recall that by definition, E is the least set X satisfying conditions (1)–(3) enunciated at the beginning of the entire proof. So we need only check that $C_{\langle R1 \rangle}(A)$ satisfies those same three conditions, i.e. that they hold with $C_{\langle R1 \rangle}(A)$ substituted for X. The first two are immediate, i.e. we have $A \subseteq C_{\langle R1 \rangle}(A)$ and $C_{\langle R1 \rangle}(A) = \text{Cn}\,(C_{\langle R1 \rangle}(A))$. For the third, suppose $(a,P,x) \in R$ and $a \in C_{\langle R1 \rangle}(A)$ and $\neg p \notin E$ for all $p \in P$. We need to show that $x \in C_{\langle R1 \rangle}(A)$. Since $C_{\langle R1 \rangle}(A) \subseteq E$ as already noted we have $a \in E$. By the definition of $R1$ and the fact that $E = Cn(E)$, this means that $(a, P, x) \in R1$. Again, since $C_{\langle R1 \rangle}(A) \subseteq E$ as already noted and $\neg p \notin E$ by supposition, we have $\neg p \notin C_{\langle R1 \rangle}(A)$ for all $p \in P$. Putting this together we have: $(a, P, x) \in R1$, $a \in E$, and $\neg p \notin C_{\langle R1 \rangle}(A)$ for all $p \in P$. We are thus in a position to re-run exactly the same argument as for item $(aiii)$ in part $(\Rightarrow)$ of the proof, with $R1$ substituted for R throughout, giving us $x \in C_{\langle R1 \rangle}(A)$ as desired.

We now need to show that the elements of $R2$ and $R3$ may be sandwiched into the ordering $\langle R1 \rangle$ to give an ordering of R which is still of type at most ω without altering the value of the induced output. We do it in two steps, first with the elements of $R2$ and then with the elements of $R3$.

To insert the elements of $R2$, write the ordering $\langle R1 \rangle$ as $r_0, r_1, \ldots$ and give $R2$ any ordering $r_{20}, r_{21}, \ldots$ of type at most ω. Insert each r_{2i} in the ordering $\langle R1 \rangle$ in any manner that keeps the sequence of order-type at most

ω, e.g. insert r_{2i} just after r_i. By the definition of $R2$, the prerequisite of each rule r_{2i} is outside E and thus outside $C_{\langle R1 \rangle}(A)$ and so outside each A_n used in constructing $C_{\langle R1 \rangle}(A)$, so it is clear that none of the rules r_{2i} satisfies the entry condition of Case 1 in the induction determined by the new ordering, so that the rule is not applied. Hence the old ordering $\langle R1 \rangle$ determines the same induction output as the new ordering, which we will write as $\langle R1 \cup R2 \rangle$. That is, $C_{\langle R1 \rangle}(A) = C_{\langle R1 \cup R2 \rangle}(A)$.

To insert the elements of $R3$, write the ordering $\langle R1 \cup R2 \rangle$ as $r_0, r_1, \ldots$ and give $R3$ any ordering $r_{30}, r_{31}, \ldots$ of type at most ω. Consider any rule $r_{3i} = (a, P, x) \in R3$. Then $a \in E$ and p is inconsistent with E for some $p \in P$. We already know that $E = C_{\langle R1 \rangle}(A) = C_{\langle R1 \cup R2 \rangle}(A)$. Hence p is inconsistent with $C_{\langle R1 \cup R2 \rangle}(A)$ and so $\neg p \in A_n$ for some A_n in the inductive definition of $C_{\langle R1 \cup R2 \rangle}(A)$, with the value of n depending on that of i. Let f be the function putting $f(i)$ to be the first such n.

Insert all the r_{3i} in the ordering $\langle R1 \cup R2 \rangle$ in any manner that puts them somewhere after their counterparts $r_{f(i)}$ and keeps the sequence of length at most ω. For example, insert r_{3i} just after $r_{f(i) \cdot i}$. Write the new ordering as $\langle R1 \cup R2 \cup R3 \rangle$. Now each inserted rule has a justification p that is inconsistent with some earlier A_n in the inductive definition of $C_{\langle R1 \cup R2 \cup R3 \rangle}(A)$, so the rule fails the entry condition of Case 1, and the rule is not applied. Thus the construction of $C_{\langle R1 \cup R2 \cup R3 \rangle}(A)$ never aborts, and moreover $C_{\langle R1 \cup R2 \cup R3 \rangle}(A) = C_{\langle R1 \cup R2 \rangle}(A)$, so that $E = C_{\langle R1 \rangle}(A) = C_{\langle R1 \cup R2 \rangle}(A) = C_{\langle R1 \cup R2 \cup R3 \rangle}(A)$. Since $R1 \cup R2 \cup R3 = R$ we may order R by putting $\langle R \rangle = \langle R1 \cup R2 \cup R3 \rangle$ and we have $C_{\langle R \rangle}(A) = E$ completing the proof of part ($\Leftarrow$) and thus of the entire theorem.   ∎

B   Glossary of Special Symbols

We presume that the reader is already familiar with the classical truth-functional connectives $\neg, \wedge, \vee, \rightarrow, \leftrightarrow$, as well as the classical quantifiers $\forall, \exists$, and do not give them special explanation. The numerals $1, 0$ are used for the two truth-values, and the letters t, f are used to stand for an arbitrary tautology or contradiction, respectively. Sometimes t is used along with s for states of a model, but this should not cause any confusion. Elementary letters of a propositional language are written $p, q, r, \ldots$, except in Chapter 5 where the letter p is reserved for probability functions.

We also presume familiarity with the set-theoretical signs $\in, \subseteq, \subset$, $\supseteq, \emptyset, -, \cap, \cup, \times, 2^X$, as well as curly parentheses for set construction. We use plain (round) parentheses for ordered pairs, although angular parentheses are occasionally used for longer sequences.

The usual signs are used for elementary arithmetic operations such as addition $+$, subtraction $-$, multiplication $\cdot$, division $/$, power a^n etc.

The following table lists, in the order of their introduction, the specialized symbols used, with their names in English and the section where they are introduced and defined. In general, we have tried to keep them to a minimum. We also use Latin letters wherever possible, with few Greek letters and never Gothic.

Symbol	Name/Description	Section Introduced
$\vdash$ Cn	Classical consequence as a relation (gate, turnstile) and as an operation	1.2
Cl	Closure operations over arbitrary sets	1.2
σ, τ	Substitution functions	1.3
$\sigma(A)$	Image of A under a substitution σ	1.3
$\sigma[A]$	Closure of A under a substitution σ	1.3
$\vdash^+$ Cn^+	Supraclassical closure relations and operations	1.3
$\vdash\!\!\!\sim$ C	Supraclassical consequence relations and operations (closure not presupposed)	1.3
$\vdash_K$ Cn_K	Pivotal-assumption consequence relations and operations	2.1
$\vdash\!\!\!\sim_K$ C_K	Default-assumption consequence relations and operations	2.2
C_{KK0}	Screened consequence operations	2.3
δ	Selection functions	2.3
$\mathcal{K}_A$	Family of all subsets $K' \subseteq K$ maxiconsistent with A	2.3

C_δ	Default-assumption consequence operations defined using a selection function	2.3
$\mathrel{\vert\!\sim}_{KJ}$ C_{KJ}	Default-assumption consequence relations and operations with constraints	2.3
S_A	The set of all safe elements of K with respect to A	2.3
$\vdash_W$ Cn_W	Pivotal-valuation consequence relations and operations	3.1
$\mathrel{\vert\!\sim}_W$ C_W	Default-valuation consequence relations and operations	3.2
(a, x)	Ordered pair of formulae, called a rule	4.1
R	Set of rules, i.e. subset of L^2	4.1
$\vdash_R$ Cn_R	Pivotal-rule consequence relations and operations	4.1
$\langle R \rangle$	Well-ordered set of rules	4.1
$\mathrel{\vert\!\sim}_R$ C_R	Default-rule consequence relations and operations	4.2
(a, P, x)	Non-normal default rule	4.3
$C_{\underline{R}}$	Maxfamily consequence operations	4.3
p	Probability functions	5.1
p_a	Conditionalisation of probability function p on proposition a	5.1
$\mathrel{\vert\!\sim}_{tp}$	Supraclassical nonmonotonic consequence, defined probabilistically by the condition $(4pt)$	5.3
$\mathrel{\vert\!\sim}_{tp}^{+}$	Incremental version of the above	5.3
$\mathrel{\vert\!\sim}^R$	Limiting probability consequence	5.4
$P_{R\varepsilon}$	Set of all probability functions that are epsilon-good for R	5.4
π	Possibility functions	5.4
$\mathrel{\vert\!\sim}_\pi$	Consequence relation determined by the possibility function π	5.4

+	Belief expansion	6.1
−	Belief contraction	6.1
∗	Belief revision	6.1
#	Belief update (as an operation of two arguments)	6.2
$\|\approx_K$	Update (as a consequence relation)	6.2
$\|\approx_s$	Counterfactual consequence relations	6.2
$\rightsquigarrow$	Counterfactual conditional (in the object language)	6.2
$O(x/a)$	Conditional obligation (in the object language)	6.2
λ	Labelling functions	6.3
$\vdash_\delta$	Default-assumption consequence relations defined using a selection function δ	6.3

Answers to Selected Exercises

Chapter 1.2

Exercise 2a. Writing $\emptyset$ for the empty set of formulae, what according to our definition of classical consequence does it mean to say that $\emptyset \vdash x$?

Answer: $\emptyset \vdash x$ iff x is a tautology.
Reason: $\emptyset \vdash x$ iff there is no Boolean valuation v with $v(a) = 1$ for all $a \in \emptyset$ and $v(x) = 0$. But there is no $a \in \emptyset$, so vacuously $v(a) = 1$ for all $a \in \emptyset$. Thus $\emptyset \vdash x$ iff there is no Boolean valuation v with $v(x) = 0$, i.e. iff x is a tautology.

Exercise 3a. Establish each of the three closure properties of reflexivity, cumulative transitivity, and monotony for classical consequence, in either their relational or their operational formulations.

Answer (in part): We check monotony; the others are similar in style. Suppose $A \subseteq B$ and $x \notin Cn(B)$; we need to show that $x \notin Cn(A)$. Since $x \notin Cn(B)$ there is a Boolean valuation v with $v(B) = 1$ and $v(x) = 0$. Since $v(B) = 1$, i.e. $v(b) = 1$ for all $b \in B$, and since $A \subseteq B$ we have $v(b) = 1$ for all $b \in A$, i.e. $v(A) = 1$. Thus $v(A) = 1$ and $v(x) = 0$ so that $x \notin Cn(A)$ as desired.

Exercise 3b. Check the equivalence of the closure properties for Cn with those for $\vdash$, via the definition of $Cn(A)$ as $\{x : A \vdash x\}$. Pinpoint where assistance from inclusion is needed to get from $CT(Cn)$ to $CT(\vdash)$.

Answer (in part): To avoid a proliferation of primes, in this exercise and the next two we let $\vdash$ stand for *any* relation between sets of formulae and individual formulae. We define Cn by putting $Cn(A) = \{x : A \vdash x\}$ for every set A of formulae. We check for cumulative transitivity; the others are easier.

First, suppose that $\vdash$ satisfies condition $CT(\vdash)$. We want to show that Cn satisfies condition $CT(Cn)$. Suppose $A \subseteq B \subseteq Cn(A)$. We need to

175

show $Cn(B) \subseteq Cn(A)$. Let $x \in Cn(B)$; we need to show $x \in Cn(A)$. Since $B \subseteq Cn(A)$, by definition $A \vdash b$ for all $b \in B$. Since $x \in Cn(B)$ we have by definition $B \vdash x$. But since $A \subseteq B$ we have $B = A \cup B$ and thus $A \cup B \vdash x$. Hence by $CT(\vdash), A \vdash x$, i.e. by definition $x \in Cn(A)$.

Conversely, suppose that Cn satisfies condition $CT(Cn)$ and inclusion. We want to show that $\vdash$ satisfies condition $CT(\vdash)$. Suppose $A \vdash b$ for all $b \in B$ and $A \cup B \vdash x$. We want to show that $A \vdash x$. Clearly $A \subseteq A \cup B$ and by the supposition together with inclusion we have $A \vdash b$ for all $b \in A \cup B$, i.e. $A \cup B \subseteq Cn(A \cup B)$. Thus $A \subseteq A \cup B \subseteq Cn(A)$ and so by $CT(Cn)$ we get $Cn(A \cup B) \subseteq Cn(A)$. Since $A \cup B \vdash x$ this implies $A \vdash x$ as desired.

Exercise 4b. In the text it was claimed that when we are given reflexivity and monotony, then cumulative transitivity is equivalent to the general version of plain transitivity. Show it.

Answer: Suppose that $\vdash$ satisfies reflexivity and monotony. For one direction, suppose first that it is cumulatively transitive; we want to show that it is transitive. Suppose that $A \vdash b$ for all $b \in B$ and $B \vdash x$. We want to show $A \vdash x$. But by monotony $A \cup B \vdash x$, so by cumulative transitivity $A \vdash x$ as desired. For the converse direction, suppose that $\vdash$ is transitive; we want to show that it is cumulatively transitive. Suppose that $A \vdash b$ for all $b \in B$ and $A \cup B \vdash x$. We want to show $A \vdash x$. Now by reflexivity, $A \vdash a$ for all $a \in A$. Hence $A \vdash b$ for all $b \in A \cup B$. Hence since $A \cup B \vdash x$ plain transitivity gives us $A \vdash x$ as desired.

Exercise 4c. Likewise, in the text it was claimed that in the definition of a closure operation, we can replace cumulative transitivity by idempotence if we are given inclusion and monotony. Show it.

Answer (in part): Let Cn be an operation satisfying inclusion and monotony. Suppose it satisfies cumulative transitivity. We want to show that it satisfies idempotence, i.e. that $Cn(A) = CnCn(A)$. The inclusion LHS $\subseteq$ RHS holds by inclusion. For the converse, inclusion again tells us that $A \subseteq Cn(A) \subseteq Cn(A)$, so by cumulative transitivity $CnCn(A) \subseteq Cn(A)$ as desired.

Exercise 5a. Show that classical consequence satisfies the rule of disjunction in the premises (OR).

Answer: We need to show that whenever $A \cup \{a\} \vdash x$ and $A \cup \{b\} \vdash x$ then $A \cup \{a \vee b\} \vdash x$. Suppose $A \cup \{a \vee b\} \nvdash x$. Then there is a valuation v with $v(A) = 1, v(a \vee b) = 1$ and $v(x) = 0$. But since $v(a \vee b) = 1$ we have either $v(a) = 1$ or $v(b) = 1$. Thus either $A \cup \{a\} \nvdash x$ or $A \cup \{b\} \nvdash x$.

Exercise 5b. Consider the following rule: whenever $A \cup \{a \vee b\} \vdash x$ then either $A \cup \{a\} \vdash x$ or $A \cup \{b\} \vdash x$. Is it a Horn rule? Does it hold for *classical consequence?*

Answer: This is not a Horn rule, as it has a disjunctive conclusion. It holds for classical logic: indeed, the stronger (Horn) rule where 'or' is replaced by 'and' holds for classical consequence.

Exercise 6. *Consider the following rule, known as conjunction in the conclusion, alias AND, alias $\wedge$+(right): whenever $A \vdash x$ and $A \vdash y$ then $A \vdash x \wedge y$. Is it a Horn rule? Does it hold for classical consequence?*

Answer: Yes, it is a Horn rule. It holds for classical consequence. Verification: Suppose $A \nvdash x \wedge y$. Then there is a Boolean valuation v with $v(A) = 1$ and $v(x \wedge y) = 0$. From the latter, either $v(x) = 0$ or $v(y) = 0$, so that either $A \nvdash x$ or $A \nvdash y$ as desired.

Problem 4. Let X be an arbitrary set. To fix ideas you can think of X as the set of all propositional formulae, but the ideas are completely general. Let F be any non-empty family of subsets of X. Define the operation $Cl : 2^X \to 2^X$ by the equality $Cl(A) = \cap\{B \in F : A \subseteq B\}$. Show that Cl is a closure operation.

Answer: We need to show that Cl satisfies inclusion, monotony, and idempotence. For inclusion, we need only observe that by construction $A \subseteq \cap\{B \in F : A \subseteq B\} = Cl(A)$. For monotony, suppose $A \subseteq A'$. Then whenever $A' \subseteq B$ we have $A \subseteq B$ and thus $\{B \in F : A' \subseteq B\} \subseteq \{B \in F : A \subseteq B\}$ and so $Cl(A) = \cap\{B \in F : A \subseteq B\} \subseteq \cap\{B \in F : A' \subseteq B\} = Cl(A')$ as desired.

For idempotence, note that $Cl(Cl(A)) = \cap\{B \in F : Cl(A) \subseteq B\}$ so to show $Cl(Cl(A)) \subseteq Cl(A)$ it suffices to show that $\cap\{B \in F : Cl(A) \subseteq B\} \subseteq \cap\{B \in F : A \subseteq B\}$. So it suffices to show that $\{B \in F : A \subseteq B\} \subseteq \{B \in F : Cl(A) \subseteq B\}$, and so it suffices to show that whenever $B \in F$ and $A \subseteq B$ then $Cl(A) = \cap\{B \in F : A \subseteq B\} \subseteq B$, which is immediate.

Chapter 1.3

Exercise 1a. Suppose that the primitive connectives are just $\neg, \to$. What would be the appropriate definition of a substitution?

Answer: In this context, a substitution is a function $\sigma : L \to L$ such that for all formulae a, b we have: $\sigma(\neg a) = \neg\sigma(a)$ and $\sigma(a \to b) = \sigma(a) \to \sigma(b)$.

Exercise 1e. Recalling the definition of a valuation in section 1.2, show that the composition $v\sigma$ of a substitution σ followed by a valuation v is well-defined and is itself a valuation.

Answer (in part): When a is a formula, $v\sigma(a) = v(\sigma(a))$, and so is a function on L into $\{1, 0\}$. We need to show that it is well behaved with respect to the connectives. For $\neg : v\sigma(\neg a) = v(\neg\sigma(a))$ by the definition of a substitution. Also since v is a valuation, $v(\neg\sigma(a)) = 1$ iff $v(\sigma(a)) = 0$. Thus $v(\sigma(\neg a)) = 1$ iff $v(\sigma(a)) = 0$ and we are done. Similarly for $\wedge, \vee$.

Exercise 2a. Verify that always $\sigma(A) \subseteq \sigma[A]$ and give an example where $A \not\subseteq \sigma(A)$.

Answer: For the first part, suppose $x \in \sigma(A)$. Then there is $a \in A$ with $x = \sigma(a)$. Hence x is in the least set that includes A and is closed under σ, i.e. $x \in \sigma[A]$. For the second part, let σ be (say) the substitution that puts the single elementary letter p in place of all elementary letters, and let A be, say, $\{q\}$.

Chapter 1.4

Exercise 1a. Show that any supraclassical relation $\hspace{0.5mm}\vdash\hspace{-2mm}\sim\hspace{0.5mm}$ that satisfies plain transitivity satisfies singleton conjunctive monotony.

Answer: Suppose $a \hspace{0.5mm}\vdash\hspace{-2mm}\sim\hspace{0.5mm} x$; we want to show $a \wedge b \hspace{0.5mm}\vdash\hspace{-2mm}\sim\hspace{0.5mm} x$. We know that $a \wedge b \vdash a$ so by supraclassicality $a \wedge b \hspace{0.5mm}\vdash\hspace{-2mm}\sim\hspace{0.5mm} a$, so by transitivity $a \wedge b \hspace{0.5mm}\vdash\hspace{-2mm}\sim\hspace{0.5mm} x$ as required.

Exercise 1b. Show that any supraclassical relation $\hspace{0.5mm}\vdash\hspace{-2mm}\sim\hspace{0.5mm}$ that satisfies cumulative transitivity satisfies conjunction in the conclusion.

Answer: Let $\hspace{0.5mm}\vdash\hspace{-2mm}\sim\hspace{0.5mm}$ be any supraclassical consequence relation that satisfies cumulative transitivity. Suppose $A \hspace{0.5mm}\vdash\hspace{-2mm}\sim\hspace{0.5mm} x, A \hspace{0.5mm}\vdash\hspace{-2mm}\sim\hspace{0.5mm} y$. We want to show $A \hspace{0.5mm}\vdash\hspace{-2mm}\sim\hspace{0.5mm} x \wedge y$. But we have the classical consequence $A \cup \{x, y\} \vdash x \wedge y$ so by supraclassicality $A \cup \{x, y\} \hspace{0.5mm}\vdash\hspace{-2mm}\sim\hspace{0.5mm} x \wedge y$ and combining this with the first two suppositions we have $A \hspace{0.5mm}\vdash\hspace{-2mm}\sim\hspace{0.5mm} x \wedge y$ by cumulative transitivity.

Chapter 2.1

Exercise 1. Check the claim made in the text that pivotal-assumption consequence operations satisfy inclusion, cumulative transitivity and monotony, and thus are closure operations.
Hint: Recall the fact, established in Chapter 1, that classical consequence itself has all these three properties, and show that they are inherited by pivotal-assumption operations

Answer: All three follow similar patterns. To give the feel of verifying with both relational and operational concepts, we verify inclusion in the language of operations, monotony in the language of relations, and cumulative transitivity in the language of operations again (for further exercise, do the reverse). We give full details.

For inclusion: let Cn_K be a pivotal-assumption consequence operation and let A be any set of formulae, x an individual formula. We want to show $Cn(A) \subseteq Cn_K(A)$. Suppose $x \in Cn(A)$; we need to show $x \in Cn_K(A)$, i.e. by the definition of Cn_K, that $x \in Cn(K \cup A)$. But this is immediate from the hypothesis by monotony of classical consequence, so we are done.

For monotony: let $\vdash_K$ be any pivotal-assumption consequence relation, and let A be any set of formulae, x an individual formula. Suppose that $A \vdash_K x$ and $A \subseteq B$; we want to show $B \vdash_K x$. Since $A \vdash_K x$ we have by the definition of $\vdash_K$ that $A \cup K \vdash x$, so by monotony for classical consequence and the hypothesis $A \subseteq B$ we have $B \cup K \vdash x$, i.e. $B \vdash_K x$ as desired.

For cumulative transitivity: let Cn_K be a pivotal-assumption consequence operation. Suppose $A \subseteq B \subseteq Cn_K(A)$. We need to show $Cn_K(B) \subseteq Cn_K(A)$. Since $A \subseteq B \subseteq Cn_K(A) = Cn(K \cup A)$ we have, using inclusion for Cn, that $K \cup A \subseteq K \cup B \subseteq Cn(K \cup A)$ and so by cumulative transitivity for Cn, $Cn(K \cup B) \subseteq Cn(K \cup A)$, i.e. $Cn_K(B) \subseteq Cn_K(A)$ as desired.

Exercise 3. *Verify that pivotal-assumption consequence operations are compact.*

Hint: As for the first exercise.

Answer: We verify in the language of relations. For further exercise, transcribe to the language of operations. Let $\vdash_K$ be any pivotal-assumption consequence relation, and let A be any set of formulae, x an individual formula. Suppose that $A \vdash_K x$; we want to find a finite $F \subseteq A$ with $F \vdash_K x$. Since $A \vdash_K x$ we have by the definition of $\vdash_K$ that $A \cup K \vdash x$, so by compactness for classical consequence there is a finite $G \subseteq A \cup K$ with $G \vdash x$. But since $G \subseteq A \cup K$ there area sets $F \subseteq A, H \subseteq K$ with $G = F \cup H$. Since G is finite, so are both F, H. Since $G = F \cup H$ we have $F \cup H \vdash x$, so since $H \subseteq K$ monotony of classical consequence gives us $F \cup K \vdash x$ and thus $F \vdash_K x$ as desired.

Exercise 5. Verify the Lemma for Theorem 2.2.

Answer (in part): We verify left classical equivalence. Let Cn' be any paraclassical consequence operation. Let A, B be sets of formulae with $Cn(A) = Cn(B)$. We want to show that $Cn'(A) = Cn'(B)$. We show that $Cn'(A) \subseteq Cn'(B)$; the verification of the converse is similar. By the hypothesis, $B \subseteq Cn(A) = Cn(B) \subseteq Cn'(B)$ using supraclassicality for Cn'. Hence by cumulative transitivity for Cn' we have $Cn'(Cn(A)) \subseteq Cn'(B)$. To complete the argument, it thus suffices to show $Cn'(A) \subseteq Cn'(Cn(A))$.

But $A \subseteq Cn(A)$ so by monotony for Cn' we have $Cn'(A) \subseteq Cn'(Cn(A))$ as desired.

Chapter 2.2

Exercise 1. Let $K = \{p \to q, q \to p, p \vee q\}$ and let $A = \{\neg p \vee \neg q\}$ where p, q are elementary letters. What are the maximal subsets of K consistent with A? Now let $K = \{p \leftrightarrow q, p \vee q\}$, let A be as before, and answer the same question.

Answer: When $K = \{p \to q, q \to p, p \vee q\}$, its maximal subsets consistent with A are its three two-element subsets. When $K = \{p \leftrightarrow q, p \vee q\}$, its maximal subsets consistent with A are its two singleton subsets.

Exercise 3. Consider the Boolean language generated by just two elementary letters p, q. Let $K = Cn(p, q)$ and let $A = \{\neg p\}$. What are the maximal subsets of K consistent with A?
Hint: First enumerate all the elements (up to classical equivalence) of $Cn(p, q)$.

Answer: One way of finding the elements (up to classical equivalence) of $Cn(p, q)$ is to write down in a fixed order the four possible state-descriptions in just the letters p, q, then consider the 2^3 disjunctions of them that contain $p \wedge q$, and then simplify. This gives the 8 formulae: $p \wedge q$, p, q, $p \leftrightarrow q$, $p \vee q, p \vee \neg q$, $\neg p \vee q$, $p \vee \neg p$. So we need to find the maximal subsets of this eight-element set that are consistent with $\neg p$. Evidently, none of them can contain $p \wedge q$ or p. There are two of them: (1) $\{q, p \vee q, \neg p \vee q, p \vee \neg p\}$ — which is equivalent to q, (2) $\{p \leftrightarrow q, p \vee \neg q, \neg p \vee q, p \vee \neg p\}$ — which is equivalent to $p \leftrightarrow q$.
Remark: Students often miss out on the second one.

Exercise 6. When a consequence operation satisfies both cumulative transitivity and cautious monotony it is said to be cumulative. Write out a single Horn principle, in both relational and operational notation, to express this condition.

Answer: In relational notation: Whenever $A \vdash b$ for all $b \in B$ then $A \cup B \vdash x$ iff $A \vdash x$. In operational notation: $A \subseteq B \subseteq Cn(A)$ implies $Cn(B) = Cn(A)$

Exercise 7. Verify the claim made in the text, that when $K = Cn(K)$ and A is inconsistent with K, then $K' = Cn(K')$ for every maximal A-consistent subset of K.

Answer: Suppose $K = Cn(K)$ and A is inconsistent with K. Let K'

be any maximal A-consistent subset of K. Suppose $x \in Cn(K')$. We need to show that $x \in K'$. Since $K' \subseteq K$ we have by monotony of classical consequence that $Cn(K') \subseteq Cn(K)$, and so $x \in K = K$ using the supposition that $K = Cn(K)$. Now suppose for reductio ad absurdum that $x \notin K'$. Then by the maximality of K' and the fact that $x \in K$ we know that $K' \cup \{x\}$ is inconsistent with A. But since $x \in Cn(K')$ we have $Cn(K') = Cn(K' \cup \{x\})$ so that K' is inconsistent with A, contrary to hypothesis.

Problem 2. Prove Observation 2.8. That is: Suppose $K = Cn(K)$ and let A be a set of formulae that is inconsistent with K. Then the following three conditions are equivalent, for any $K' \subseteq K$:

  a. K' is maximal among the subsets of K that are consistent with A

  b. K' is maximal among the classically closed proper subsets of K that are consistent with A

  c. K' is maximal among the classically closed proper subsets of K, and also K' is consistent with A.

Answer: We cycle around the three conditions. The implications (a) $\Rightarrow$ (b) and (c) $\Rightarrow$ (a) are both straightforward, so we begin with them. For the implication (b) $\Rightarrow$ (c) we will need to apply compactness, and we leave it to last. It is essential to be clear, at each step, what we are assuming and what we are trying to show.

First, suppose (a); we want to show (b). Clearly it suffices to show that K' is a classically closed proper subset of K. It must be a proper subset of K because by (a) it is a subset of K and is consistent with A, whereas by initial supposition K is not consistent with A. And it is classically closed, i.e. $K' = Cn(K')$, as already shown in exercise 7.

Next, suppose (c); we want to show (a). By (c), K' is a subset of K and is consistent with A. To show that it is maximally so, suppose $K' \subset K'' \subseteq K$; we need to show that K'' is inconsistent with A. But by (c), $Cn(K') = K'$, so $Cn(K') \subset K''$ so $Cn(K') \subset Cn(K'') \subseteq K$ so by (c) again $Cn(K'') = K$, so by the initial hypothesis $Cn(K'')$ is inconsistent with A, and thus K'' is inconsistent with A as desired.

Finally, suppose (b); we want to show (c). By (b), K' is consistent with A. Also by (b), K' is a classically closed proper subset of K. It remains to show that it is maximal among the classically closed proper subsets of K. Suppose $K' \subset K'' \subseteq K$ and $K'' = Cn(K'')$; we need to show that $K'' = K$. Let k be any element of K; we need to show that $k \in K''$. Now by (b), K'' is inconsistent with A. Hence by compactness of classical logic,

K'' is inconsistent with a, where a is the conjunction of all the formulae in some finite subset of A. Thus $\neg a \in Cn(K'')$. To complete the proof, it will suffice to show that $a \vee k \in K' \subseteq K''$, for then $k \in Cn(K'') = K''$ as desired.

Suppose $a \vee k \notin K'$; we derive a contradiction. By (b), $Cn(K' \cup \{a \vee k\})$ is inconsistent with A, so by classical logic $Cn(K' \cup \{a\})$ is inconsistent with A. But a is the conjunction of some finite subset of A, so by classical logic again, $Cn(K')$ is inconsistent with A, i.e. K' is inconsistent with A, giving a contradiction and completing the proof.

Chapter 2.3

Exercise 1. Closed world assumption. Suppose the language is based on the elementary letters p, q, r, s, t, u. Put $A = \{p, q, (p \wedge q) \rightarrow r, (p \wedge r) \rightarrow s, (s \wedge t) \rightarrow u\}$. Which literals may be inferred from A using the closed world assumption – i.e. which are in $C_K(A)$ when K is the set of all negative literals?

Answer: p, q, r, s, $\neg t$, $\neg u$.

Exercise 2(a). Screened consequence. Put $K = \{p \rightarrow q, q \rightarrow r, r \rightarrow s, s \rightarrow \neg p\}$ and let $A = \{p\}$ be a premiss set. Put $K_0 = \{p \rightarrow q\}$. Determine the maximal subsets K' with $K_0 \subseteq K' \subseteq K$ that are consistent with A. Identify in the most specific way that you can the screened consequences of A given K_0, K.

Answer: The maximal subsets K' with $K_0 \subseteq K' \subseteq K$ that are consistent with p are the three two-element subsets of K that contain $p \rightarrow q$, i.e. $K_1 = \{p \rightarrow q, q \rightarrow r, r \rightarrow s\}, K_2 = \{p \rightarrow q, q \rightarrow r, s \rightarrow \neg p\}$ and $K_3 = \{p \rightarrow q, r \rightarrow s, s \rightarrow \neg p\}$. Now $Cn(A \cup K_1) = Cn(\{p, q, r, s\})$ while $Cn(A \cup K_2) = Cn(\{p, q, r, \neg s\})$ and $Cn(A \cup K_3) = Cn(\{p, q, \neg r, \neg s\})$. So the screened consequences of A given K_0, K are just the classical consequences of the formula in disjunctive normal form $(p \wedge q \wedge r \wedge s) \vee (p \wedge q \wedge r \wedge \neg s) \vee (p \wedge q \wedge \neg r \wedge \neg s)$. This formula simplifies to $(p \wedge q \wedge r) \vee (p \wedge q \wedge \neg s)$, and so to $(p \wedge q \wedge (r \vee \neg s))$. So the screened consequences of A given K_0, K are just the classical consequences of $(p \wedge q \wedge (r \vee \neg s))$.

Problem 1. Prove the uniqueness property for inference under the closed world assumption, assuming that the background assumption set K is the set of all the negative literals of the language, and the premiss set A consists only of Horn formulae.
Hint: Exploit the two assumptions to the hilt, for they are both indispensable for the proof.

Answer: In this answer as elsewhere, we reserve the letters $p, q, \ldots$ for elementary letters, using the letters $a, b, \ldots x, y, \ldots$ for arbitrary formulae. Let K, A be as specified. We need to show that there is a unique maximal A-consistent subset of K.

Let $K_1 = \{\neg p : \neg p$ is consistent with $A\}$. In other words, $K_1 = \{\neg p : A \nvdash p\}$. Thus every element of K_1 is a negative literal, i.e. $K_1 \subseteq K$. We will show that K_1 is the unique A-maxiconsistent subset of K. That is, we will show:

1. K_1 is consistent with A;

2. Whenever $K_1 \subset J \subseteq K$ then J is inconsistent with A;

3. There is no A-maxiconsistent subset J of K distinct from K_1.

For (1), define the assignment v by $v(p) = 1$ iff $A \vdash p$. We want to show that $v(K_1 \cup A) = 1$. Now for all $\neg p$ in K_1, since $A \nvdash p$ we have $v(p) = 0$ so $v(\neg p) = 1$. Thus $v(K_1) = 1$. It remains to show $v(A) = 1$. Let $a \in A$. (Note that since a is not necessarily an elementary letter, we can't conclude $v(a) = 1$ directly from the definition of v, so we need a more careful argument using the hypothesis that A contains only Horn formulae.) Since $a \in A, a = (p_1 \wedge \ldots \wedge p_n) \to q$ for some elementary letters $p_1, \ldots, p_n, q$. Suppose $v(p_1 \wedge \ldots \wedge p_n) = 1$; it will suffice to show that $v(q) = 1$. Since $v(p_1 \wedge \ldots \wedge p_n) = 1$ we have each $v(p_i) = 1$ $(i \leq n)$, so by the definition of $v, A \vdash p_i$ $(i \leq n)$, so $A \vdash p_1 \wedge \ldots \wedge p_n$. But since $a = (p_1 \wedge \ldots \wedge p_n) \to q \in A$ we thus have $A \vdash q$ and so $v(q) = 1$ by the definition of v, as desired.

For (2), suppose $K_1 \subset J \subseteq K$. We want to show that J is inconsistent with A. By the supposition, there is a negative literal $\neg p \in J$ but $\neg p \notin K_1$. By the definition of K_1 this means that $\neg p$ is inconsistent with A, so J is inconsistent with A and we are done.

For (3), the argument is almost the same. Suppose that J is an A-maxiconsistent subset of K distinct from K_1. Since K_1 is itself an A-maxiconsistent subset of K, as shown by (1) and (2) above, we cannot have $J \subseteq K_1$. So there is an element of J, i.e. a negative literal $\neg p$, with $\neg p \in J$ but $\neg p \notin K_1$. By the definition of K_1 this means that $\neg p$ is inconsistent with A, so J is inconsistent with A and we are done.

Chapter 3.1

Exercise 1. Let the elementary letters of our language be $p_1, p_2, p_3, \ldots$ Let W be the set consisting of just the four valuations v_1, v_0, v_e, v_{10}, where:

v_1 *makes every elementary letter true*

v_0 *makes every elementary letter false*

v_e *makes exactly the even elementary letters true*

v_{10} *makes exactly the elementary letters* $p_1 \ldots p_{10}$ *true.*

Put $A = \{\neg p_1 \wedge p_2\}$. *Which of the following hold?*

$A \vdash p_2$	$A \vdash_W p_2$
$A \vdash p_3 \vee \neg p_4$	$A \vdash_W (p_3 \vee \neg p_4)$
$A \vdash p_{11} \vee p_{12}$	$A \vdash_W (p_{11} \vee p_{12})$

Answer:

$A \vdash p_2$	$A \vdash_W p_2$
$A \nvdash p_3 \vee \neg p_4$	$A \nvdash_W (p_3 \vee \neg p_4)$
$A \nvdash p_{11} \vee p_{12}$	$A \vdash_W (p_{11} \vee p_{12})$

Exercise 2. Why is it immediate from the definition that pivotal-valuation consequence operations are supraclassical, i.e. that $Cn \leq Cn_W$ *for any choice of* W?

Answer: We need to show that always $Cn(A) \subseteq Cn_W(A)$. Suppose $x \in Cn(A)$. Then $v(x) = 1$ for every valuation v with $v(A) = 1$. So $v(x) = 1$ for every valuation $v \in W$ with $v(A) = 1$. So $x \in Cn_W(A)$.

Exercise 4. Show that pivotal-valuation consequence relations satisfy disjunction in the premisses.

Answer guide: The verification is the same as that given for exercise 5a of Chapter 1.2, with W written in the appropriate places.

Chapter 3.2

Exercise 1. Explain why every irreflexive transitive relation is asymmetric (i.e. never both $v < v'$ *and* $v' < v$) *and more generally acyclic (never* $v_1 < v_2 < \ldots < v_n < v_1$ *for* $n \geq 1$).

Answer: Asymmetry is acyclicity for $n = 2$, so we need only check for acyclicity. Suppose $<$ is transitive and fails acyclicity; we want to show that it fails irreflexivity. Since acyclicity fails, there is an n and $v_1, v_2, \ldots v_n$ with $v_1 < v_2 < \ldots < v_n < v_1$. By transitivity applied $n - 2$ times, $v_1 < v_1$ so irreflexivity fails as desired.

Exercise 2. *Draw a diagram for a preferential model consisting of an infinite descending chain, labelling the nodes with valuations in such a way that the model is not stoppered and cautious monotony and consistency preservation both fail.*

Sample answer: The simplest one is an infinite descending chain with elementary letter p true at all nodes. Put the elementary letter q true at (say) the top node only, and the elementary letter r true nowhere. Since there is no minimal p-node, we have $p \mathrel{|\!\sim} f$ where f is a contradiction; but clearly $p \not\vdash f$ where $\vdash$ is classical consequence. This shows the failure of consistency preservation. Again, since there is no minimal p-node we have $p \mathrel{|\!\sim} q$ and also $p \mathrel{|\!\sim} r$. But there is just one $(p \wedge q)$-node, namely the top one, and it is thus the unique minimal $(p \wedge q)$-node, and it is not an r-node, so $p \wedge q \mathrel{|\!\!\!\not\sim} r$.

Exercise 4. *Show that every preferential consequence operation is supraclassical and satisfies cumulative transitivity.*

Answer: Let $\mathrel{|\!\sim}$ be the consequence relation determined by the preferential model $(W, <)$. For supraclassicality: suppose $A \mathrel{|\!\!\!\not\sim} x$; we want to show that $A \not\vdash x$. Since $A \mathrel{|\!\!\!\not\sim} x$ there is a minimal A-valuation v with $v(x) = 0$. Since v is a minimal A-valuation, $v(A) = 1$. Hence $A \not\vdash x$. For cumulative transitivity: suppose $A \mathrel{|\!\sim} b$ for all $b \in B$ and that $A \mathrel{|\!\!\!\not\sim} x$. We show that $A \cup B \mathrel{|\!\!\!\not\sim} x$. By the second hypothesis there is a minimal A-valuation v with $v(x) = 0$. By the first hypothesis $v(b) = 1$ for all $b \in B$. Hence v is a $A \cup B$-valuation. Moreover, it must be a minimal $A \cup B$-valuation, because if $v' < v$ and $v'(A \cup B) = 1$ then $v'(A) = 1$ contradicting the fact that v is a minimal A-valuation. Thus v is a minimal $A \cup B$-valuation with $v(x) = 0$ and so $A \cup B \mathrel{|\!\!\!\not\sim} x$ as desired.

Exercise 12. *Show that for ranked preferential models, whenever $|A|_{min(W)} \neq \emptyset$ then $C_<(A) = Cn_{min(W)}(A)$.*

Answer: Suppose that a preferential model $(W, <)$ is ranked and $|A|_{min(W)} \neq \emptyset$, i.e. $v(A) = 1$ for some valuation $v \in min(W)$. Suppose further that $x \notin C_<(A)$; we want to show that $x \notin Cn_{min(W)}(A)$. Since $x \notin C_<(A)$ there is a $u \in min|A|_W$ with $u(x) = 0$. Since $u \in min|A|_W$ and $v(A) = 1$ we cannot have $v < u$. Hence since $v \in min(W)$ and the relation $<$ is ranked it follows that also $u \in min(W)$. Since $u(A) = 1$ and $u(x) = 0$, it follows that $x \notin Cn_{min(W)}(A)$.

Chapter 3.3

Exercise 1.   Take the preferential model (with copies) in Example 3.9 (the Kraus, Lehmann and Magidor example) and consider the following orderings:

(a) Like that of 3.9 but with also $s_1 < s_4$

(b) Like that of 3.9 but with also $s_1 < s_4$ and also $s_2 < s_3$

(c) Like that of 3.9 but upside-down

(d) The transitive ordering $s_1 < s_2 < s_3 < s_4$

(e) The transitive but cyclic ordering $s_1 < s_2 < s_3 < s_4 < s_1$

> *(i) Which of these are ranked? Which contain infinite descending chains?*
>
> *(ii) For each of these five preferential models (with copies), determine the status of the following consequences (whose status we checked in the text for Example 3.9 itself): $p \wedge q \mathrel{\vert\!\sim} f$ (where f is any self-contradiction), $t \mathrel{\vert\!\sim} \neg q$ (where t is any tautology), $p \mathrel{\vert\!\sim} \neg q$ and $p \leftrightarrow q \mathrel{\vert\!\sim} \neg p \wedge \neg q$.*

Answer to part (i): The only ones that are ranked are (b), (d). In particular, (e) is not ranked, because it is part of the definition of a ranked preferential model that its relation is irreflexive. The only one that contains an infinite descending chain is (e).

Answer to part (ii):

	$p \wedge q \mathrel{\vert\!\sim} f$	$t \mathrel{\vert\!\sim} \neg q$	$p \mathrel{\vert\!\sim} \neg q$	$p \leftrightarrow q \mathrel{\vert\!\sim} \neg p \wedge \neg q$
(a)	0	1	1	0
(b)	0	1	1	1
(c)	0	0	0	0
(d)	0	1	1	1
(e)	1	1	1	1

Chapter 4.1

Exercise 1. Let R be the set of the following rules: $(p,r),(p \wedge q,s),(r,u),(w,v)$. Let $A = \{p,q,\neg v\}$. Determine each of $R(A), R(R(A))$, $R(A \cup R(A)), R(Cn(A \cup R(A)))$ and note the differences.

Answer: $R(A) = \{r\}, R(R(A)) = \{u\}, R(A \cup R(A)) = \{r,u\}, R(Cn(A \cup R(A))) = \{r,u,s\}$. They are all distinct; the inclusion of the first two in the last two is a manifestation of the monotony of both operations.

Exercise 2. Let R be any set of rules, in the sense defined in the text. Explain why $R(\emptyset) = \emptyset$. Explain why, for any set, whenever $x \in R(A)$ then there is an $a \in A$ with $x \in R(\{a\})$.

Answer: By the definition, $x \in R(\emptyset)$ iff there is an $a \in \emptyset$ with $(a,x) \in R$. But there is no $a \in \emptyset$. Hence there is no $x \in R(\emptyset)$. Also, when $x \in R(A)$ then there is an $a \in A$ with $(a,x) \in R$. Since $a \in \{a\}$ we thus have $x \in R(\{a\})$.

Exercise 4. Let R be the set of the following rules: $(p,u),(p \wedge q,v),(s,w),(\neg y,w),(r \wedge q,\neg w)$. Let A consist of the three formulae $p \wedge q, r \wedge q, s \vee \neg y$. Calculate the sequences $A_0, A_1, A_2,\ldots$ and their union for the first of the inductive definitions given in this section. Then, taking R in the order written, calculate $A_0, A_1, A_2,\ldots$ and their union under the second of the inductive definitions given. Comment on the differences.

Answer: For the first inductive definition, $A_0 = Cn(A) = Cn(\{p,q,r,s \vee \neg y\})$. So $R(A_0) = \{u,v,\neg w\}$, so $A_1 = Cn(A \cup R(A_0)) = Cn(\{p,q,r,s \vee \neg y, u, v, \neg w\})$. Thus $R(A_1) = \{u,v,\neg w\} = R(A_0)$ so $A_2 = Cn(A \cup R(A_1)) = Cn(A \cup R(A_0)) = A_1$ and likewise for all following terms in the sequence. Thus $\cup\{A_i : i < \omega\} = A_1$.

For the second inductive definition, $A_0 = Cn(A) = Cn(\{p,q,r,s \vee \neg y\})$. So $A_1 = Cn(A_0 \cup \{u\}) = Cn(\{p,q,r,s \vee \neg y, u\})$. So $A_2 = Cn(A_1 \cup \{v\}) = Cn(\{p,q,r,s \vee \neg y, u, v\})$. So $A_3 = Cn(A_2 \cup \{\neg w\}) = Cn(\{p,q,r,s \vee \neg y, u, v, \neg w\})$. Succeeding elements of the sequence give nothing new, so each of them and thus also their union equals A_3.

Whereas the first sequence adds u, v, $\neg w$ to A_0 in one step, and then has nothing more to add, the second sequence needs three steps to get them in. The end result is the same.

Problem 4. Show, as claimed in the text, that pivotal-rule consequence is compact.

Hint: Make use of the characterization of pivotal-rule consequence given by Observation 4.6.

Answer: Suppose $x \in Cn_R(A)$. We need to show that $x \in Cn_R(B)$ for some finite subset $B \subseteq A$. By the definition of $Cn_R(A)$ as $\cup\{A_n : n < \omega\}$, since $x \in Cn_R(A)$ we have $x \in A_n$ for some $n < \omega$. So it suffices to show that for all $n < \omega$, if $x \in A_n$ then there is a finite subset $B \subseteq A$ (depending on n) such that $x \in B_n$. We do this by induction on n.

For the basis, suppose $x \in A_0$. We need to show that there is a finite $B \subseteq A$ such that $x \in B_0$. But since $x \in A_0 = Cn(A)$ we have by the compactness of classical consequence that there is a finite $B \subseteq A$ with $x \in Cn(B) = B_0$ as desired.

For the induction step, suppose that the property holds for n; we need to show that it holds for $n+1$. Suppose $x \in A_{n+1} = Cn(A_n \cup R(A_n))$. We will complete the proof by showing that there is a finite $B \subseteq A$ such that $x \in B_{n+1} = Cn(B_n \cup R(B_n))$. Applying classical compactness to the supposition we have $x \in Cn(\{c_1, \ldots, c_j\} \cup \{x_1, \ldots, x_k\})$ where each $c_i \in A_n$ and for each x_i there is a $d_i \in A_n$ with $(d_i, x_i) \in R$. By the induction hypothesis there are finite subsets $C_1, \ldots, C_j, D_1, \ldots, D_k$ of A with each $c_i \in (C_i)_n$ and each $d_i \in (D_i)_n$. Put $B = C_1 \cup \ldots \cup C_j \cup D_1 \cup \ldots \cup D_k$. Then B is a finite subset of A, and clearly by the monotony of the construction of the sequences we have each $c_i \in B_n$ and each $d_i \in B_n$ so also each $x_i \in R(B_n)$ so $x \in Cn(B_n \cup R(B_n)) = B_{n+1}$ and we are done.

Chapter 4.2

Exercise 1. Assume that p, q, r are the only elementary letters in the language. Consider the rule set $R = \{(p, q), (q, r), (q, \neg r)\}$, and the premiss set $A = \{p\}$. List all possible orderings $\langle R \rangle$ of R. For each ordering, determine the extension $C_{\langle R \rangle}(A)$. Finally, determine $C_R(A)$.

Answer: There are $3 \cdot 2 \cdot 1 = 6$ possible orderings. They are:

$$(p, q), (q, r), (q, \neg r) \quad C_{\langle R \rangle}(A) = Cn(\{p, q, r\})$$

$$(p, q), (q, \neg r), (q, r) \quad C_{\langle R \rangle}(A) = Cn(\{p, q, \neg r\})$$

$$(q, r), (p, q), (q, \neg r) \quad C_{\langle R \rangle}(A) = Cn(\{p, q, r\})$$

$$(q, r), (q, \neg r), (p, q) \quad C_{\langle R \rangle}(A) = Cn(\{p, q, r\})$$

$$(q, \neg r), (p, q), (q, r) \quad C_{\langle R \rangle}(A) = Cn(\{p, q, \neg r\})$$

$$(q, \neg r), (q, r), (p, q) \quad C_{\langle R \rangle}(A) = Cn(\{p, q, \neg r\})$$

Finally, we have $C_R(A) = Cn(p, q)$.

Exercise 2. Consider the rule-set $R = \{(p,q),(q,r),(r,s),(s,\neg p)\}$ and the premiss set $A = \{p\}$. Show that $C_{\langle R \rangle}(A) = Cn(\{p,q,r,s\})$ irrespective of the ordering $\langle R \rangle$ of R, so that also $C_R(A) = \cap\{C_{\langle R \rangle}(A)\} = Cn(\{p,q,r,s\})$. This example is a rule-based form of the Möbius strip (with four elements), already considered in a propositional form (with three elements) in chapter 2.2.

Answer: There are $4 \cdot 3 \cdot 2 = 24$ orderings of R. No matter which we take, the rules can only be applied in the order as written in the statement of the exercise, with the exception of the last rule, which cannot be applied under any of the orderings. Thus in each case we get $C_{\langle R \rangle}(A) = Cn(\{p,q,r,s\})$. Thus immediately by the definition of $C_R(A)$ as $\cap\{C_{\langle R \rangle}(A)\}$, we have also $C_R(A) = Cn(\{p,q,r,s\})$.

Exercise 3. (a) Explain why the set $C_{\langle R \rangle}(A)$ is well-defined for every set A of formulae, i.e. why the definition guarantees that it exists. (b) Show that the operations $C_{\langle R \rangle}$ are consistency-preserving, in other words, that $C_{\langle R \rangle}(A)$ is consistent whenever A is consistent. (c) Explain why it follows that the sceptical operation C_R is also consistency-preserving.

Answer: (a) To show that $C_{\langle R \rangle}(A)$ is well defined it suffices to show by induction that each A_n is well defined. Clearly, $A_0 = Cn(A)$ is well defined. And equally clearly, the induction step of the definition defines a unique A_{n+1} given any A_n. (b) Suppose that A is consistent. To show that $C_{\langle R \rangle}(A)$ is consistent it suffices to show by induction that each A_n is consistent. By the hypothesis, $A_0 = Cn(A)$ is consistent. And it is immediate from the induction step of the definition that whenever A_n is consistent, so too is A_{n+1}. (c) This follows from (b) and the fact that by definition, $C_R(A) \subseteq C_{\langle R \rangle}(A)$.

Chapter 4.3

Exercise 1. Let $A = \{a\}$. In the examples below, for each possible ordering of the rules in R, determine whether $C_{\langle R \rangle}(A)$ exists. If $C_{\langle R \rangle}(A)$ does not exist, identify the exact point in its construction where it aborts, and why. If it does exist, say what it is.

(a) $R = \{(a, t, \neg a)\}$

(b) $R = \{(a, x, x), (x, t, \neg a)\}$

(c) $R = \{(a, x, x), (x \vee y, t, y), (y, t, \neg x)\}$

(d) $R = \{(t, x \wedge y, \neg x)\}$

(e) $R = \{(a, x, y), (y, t, \neg x)\}$

Answer:

(a) One rule, one order. $A_0 = Cn(a)$, but A_1 does not exist. This is because the constraint (justification) t is consistent with A_0, so we enter case 1, but the head (conclusion) $\neg a$ is not consistent with the body (prerequisite) a, so the entry condition to subcase 1.1 fails and the construction aborts. In general terms, there is a conflict between the head (conclusion) of the rule and its own body (prerequisite).

(b) Two rules, two orders. Both orders give the same result. $A_0 = Cn(a)$ and $A_1 = Cn(a, x)$, but A_2 does not exist. This is because the constraint (justification) t is consistent with A_1, so we enter case 1, but the head (conclusion) $\neg a$ is not consistent with A_1 already constructed, so the entry condition to subcase 1.1 fails and the construction aborts. In general terms, there is a conflict between the head of the rule and the part of the extension that is already constructed.

(c) Three rules, six orders. All orders give the same result. $A_0 = Cn(a)$ and $A_1 = Cn(a, x)$ and $A_2 = Cn(a, x, y)$, but A_3 does not exist. This is because the constraint (justification) t is consistent with A_2, so we enter case 1, but the head (conclusion) $\neg x$ is not consistent with A_2 already constructed, so the entry condition to subcase 1.1 fails and the construction aborts. In general terms, there is a conflict between the head of the rule and the part of the extension that is already constructed.

(d) One rule, one order. $A_0 = Cn(t)$, but A_1 does not exist. This is because the constraint (justification) $x \wedge y$ is consistent with A_0, so we enter case 1, but the head (conclusion) $\neg x$ is not consistent with the constraint $x \wedge y$, so the entry condition to subcase 1.1 fails and the construction aborts. In general terms, there is a conflict between the head of the rule and its constraint.

(e) Two rules, two orders. Both orders give the same result. $A_0 = Cn(a)$ and $A_1 = Cn(a, y)$, but A_2 does not exist. This is because the constraint (justification) t is consistent with A_1, so we enter case 1, but the head (conclusion) $\neg x$ is not consistent with the justification of a rule already used (specifically, in R_1), so the entry condition to subcase 1.1 fails and the construction aborts. In general terms, there is a conflict between the head (conclusion) of the rule and a constraint used at an earlier stage of the construction.

Exercise 2. When the initial premiss set A is inconsistent and every rule has a non-empty set of justifications, what is $C_{\langle R \rangle}(A)$? Illustrate with a simple example.

Answer: In this case $C_{\langle R \rangle}(A) = A_0 = Cn(A) = L$. For example, put $A = \{f\}$ and $R = \{(t, t, t)\}$ then the constraint (justification) of the rule is inconsistent with $A_0 = Cn(f) = L$ and so when constructing A_1 we are in Case 2, so $A_1 = A_0$.

Exercise 3. When every rule has an inconsistent justification, what is $C_{\langle R \rangle}(A)$? Illustrate with a simple example.

Answer: Again, $C_{\langle R \rangle}(A) = A_0 = Cn(A)$, although typically in this case $Cn(A) \neq L$. For example, put $A = \{t\}$ and $R = \{(t, f, t)\}$ then the constraint (justification) of the rule is inconsistent with $A_0 = Cn(t)$, and so when constructing A_1 we are in Case 2, so $A_1 = A_0$.

Chapter 5.1

Exercise 1. Show, as claimed in the text, that the Boolean valuations of classical logic satisfy all four of the Kolmogorov axioms for probability functions.

Answer: For K1, it suffices to observe that for any formula $a, v(a) \in \{0, 1\} \subseteq [0, 1]$. For K2, it suffices to note that $v(t) = 1$ whenever t is a tautology. For K3, suppose $x \vdash y$; we want to show that $v(x) \leq v(y)$. But if $v(x) \not\leq v(y)$ then $v(x) = 1$ and $v(y) = 0$, contradicting $x \vdash y$. For K4, suppose $x \vdash \neg y$; we want to show that $v(x \vee y) = v(x) + v(y)$. In the case that $v(x) = 1$ then by the rules for Boolean valuations, $v(x \vee y) = 1$ and also the hypothesis tells us that $v(y) = 0$ so that $v(x) + v(y) = 1$ as desired. In the case that $v(x) = 0$ then by the rules for Boolean valuations, $v(x \vee y) = v(y)$ and by the rules of arithmetic also $v(x) + v(y) = v(y)$ as desired.

Exercise 2. Verify the claim made in the text that from (K1), (K2), (K3) we may infer that $p(x) = 1$ whenever $x \in Cn(\emptyset)$.

Answer: By K2, $p(y) = 1$ for some formula y. Suppose $x \in Cn(\emptyset)$. Then $y \vdash x$ so by K3, $p(y) \leq p(x)$, i.e. $1 \leq p(x)$, so by K1, $p(x) = 1$.

Exercise 3 (in part). Show each of the following, which will be used in the next section, from the Kolmogorov axioms.
Hint: Make use of the result of exercise 2 whenever appropriate.

(a) $p(a) = p(b)$ whenever a and b are classically equivalent

(b) $p(\neg a) = 1 - p(a)$

Answer: For (a), simply apply K3 in both directions. For (b) note that $a \vdash \neg\neg a$ so by K4 and the result of exercise 2, $1 = p(a \vee \neg a) = p(a) + p(\neg a)$ so by arithmetic $p(\neg a) = 1 - p(a)$.

Problem 3. In the text we gave an example of a function f on elementary letters into $[0,1]$ that can be extended in at least two ways to a probability function $p : L \to [0,1]$, i.e. uniqueness of extensions from elementary letters can fail. Show that nevertheless the existence of such extensions never fails for finite languages. That is, show that every function f on the finitely many elementary letters of the language into $[0,1]$ has at least one extension to a probability function $p : L \to [0,1]$.
Hint: By the unique extension property for probability with respect to state-descriptions, it will suffice to find a function g on state descriptions into $[0,1]$, summing to unity, such that for each elementary letter q_i, $f(q_i) = \Sigma(g(s) : s$ a state description with $s \vdash q_i)$.

Answer: Without loss of generality, write the elementary letters $q_1, \ldots, q_n$ in increasing order of their values under f. Now consider the state-descriptions $s_1, \ldots, s_n$ defined by putting $s_j = (\neg q_1 \wedge \ldots \wedge \neg q_{j-1}) \wedge (q_j \wedge \ldots \wedge q_n)$. Thus $s_1 = (q_1 \wedge \ldots \wedge q_n), s_2 = (\neg q_1 \wedge q_2 \wedge \ldots \wedge q_n)$ etc. Note that $s_j \vdash q_i$ for all $j \leq i$ but $s_j \nvdash q_i$ for all $j > i$. Define $g(s_1) = f(q_1)$ and $g(s_{j+1}) = f(q_{j+1}) - f(q_j)$. An easy induction shows that for all $i \leq n$, $f(q_i) = \Sigma(g(s_j) : j \leq i)$. To complete the definition of g on all state-descriptions, put $g(\neg q_1 \wedge \ldots \wedge \neg q_n) = 1 - f(q_n)$ and $g(s) = 0$ for all remaining state descriptions. Then the function g on state-descriptions sums to unity, and also each $f(q_i) = \Sigma(g(s) : s$ a state-description with $s \vdash q_i)$. So the unique probability function that extends g also extends f and we are done.

Problem 6. Verify the claim made in the text that if p is a probability function and a is a formula with $p(a) \neq 0$, then p_a is the unique probability function satisfying the following two conditions: (1) $p_a(a) = 1$, (2) for all b, b', if both $b \vdash a$ and $b' \vdash a$ then $p(b)/p(b') = p_a(b)/p_a(b')$.

Answer (in part): We show that under the left-hand conditions, p_a has property (2). Suppose $x \vdash a$, $y \vdash a$. We want to show that $p(x)/p(y) = p_a(x)/p_a(y)$. But $p_a(x) = p(a \wedge x)/p(a)$ and $p_a(y) = p(a \wedge y)/p(a)$ so that $p_a(x)/p_a(y) = [p(a \wedge x)/p(a)]/[p(a \wedge y)/p(a)] = p(a \wedge x)/p(a \wedge y) = p(x)/p(y)$ using the hypothesis.

Chapter 5.2

Exercise 1. Show that the implication $\forall p(2t \Rightarrow 1)$ can fail.

Sample answer: Consider a language with just two elementary letters q, r. Let p be the unique probability function on this language function that assigns 0.25 to each of the four state-descriptions. Choose $t = 0.6$. Put $a = q$ and $x = q \wedge r$. Then $p(a) = p(q) = 0.5 < 0.6 = t$ so condition (2t) holds vacuously. On the other hand, $p(x) = p(q \wedge r) = 0.25 < 0.5 = p(a)$ so condition (1) fails.

Exercise 2. Show that the implication $\forall p(1 \Rightarrow 5)$ holds but that its converse $\forall p(5 \Rightarrow 1)$ can fail.

Answer: To show that the implication $\forall p(1 \Rightarrow 5)$ holds, let p be any probability function, let $a = a_1 \wedge \ldots \wedge a_n$ and suppose (1) holds, i.e. $p(a) \leq p(x)$. Then $p(\neg x) \leq p(\neg a) = p(\neg(a_1 \wedge \ldots \wedge a_n)) = p(\neg a_1 \vee \ldots \vee \neg a_n)) \leq \Sigma(p(\neg a_i) : i \leq n)$ by an exercise of the previous section. To show that the implication $\forall p(5 \Rightarrow 1)$ can fail, take the same language and probability function as in the answer to exercise 1. Put $a_1 = a_2 = q$ and $x = q \wedge r$. Then $p(\neg x) = 0.75 \leq 1 = p(\neg a_1) + p(\neg a_2)$ but $p(a) = 0.5 \not\leq 0.25 = p(x)$.

Chapter 5.3

Exercise 1. Show that each of the conditions $(2tp), (3tp), (5p)$ is monotonic in the premiss formula a.

Answer: For $(2tp)$, suppose that if $p(a) \geq t$ then $p(x) \geq t$. Then since $p(a \wedge b) \leq p(a)$ we can say that if $p(a \wedge b) \geq t$ then $p(x) \geq t$. For $(3tp)$, if $p(a \rightarrow x) \geq t$ then since $a \rightarrow x \vdash a \wedge b \rightarrow x$ we have $p(a \rightarrow x) \leq p((a \wedge b) \rightarrow x)$ so $p((a \wedge b) \rightarrow x) \geq t$. For $(5p)$, $\Sigma(p(\neg a_i) : i \leq n) \leq \Sigma(p(\neg a_i) : i \leq n+1)$ so that if $p(\neg x) \leq \Sigma(p(\neg a_i) : i \leq n)$ then $p(\neg x) \leq \Sigma(p(\neg a_i) : i \leq n+1)$.

Exercise 2. Show that none of the conditions $(1p), (2tp), (3tp), (5p)$ satisfies AND.

Sample Answer: Take again language with just two elementary letters q, r, and again let p be the probability function that gives each of the four atoms $q \wedge r, \ldots, \neg q \wedge \neg r$ equal values 0.25. For $(1p)$, put (say) $a = q, x = r, y = \neg r$. Then $a \mid\!\sim x, a \mid\!\sim y$, but $a \not\mid\!\sim x \wedge y$. For $(2t)$, use the same example with the threshold value $t = 0.5$. For $(3t)$, the same example with the threshold value $t = 0.75$. For $(5t)$, put $n = 1$ and use the same example as for $(1p)$.

Chapter 5.4

Exercise 1. Show that for any formula x, either $\pi(x) = 1$ or $\pi(\neg x) = 1$, for any possibility function π.

Answer: By $(\pi 1), (\pi 2)$ and $(\pi 3)$, we know that $\pi(a) = 1$ for any tautology. In particular $\pi(x \vee \neg x) = 1$, so by $(\pi 4)$ either $\pi(x) = 1$ or $\pi(\neg x) = 1$.

Exercise 2. Show the equivalence of the two definitions of a possibilistic inference relation.

Answer: As the limiting case is the same for the two definitions, we need only consider the principal case. Suppose first that $\pi(a \wedge \neg x) < \pi(a \wedge x)$. By $(\pi 3), \pi(a \wedge x) \leq \pi(a)$, so $\pi(a \wedge \neg x) < \pi(a)$. For the converse, suppose that $\pi(a \wedge \neg x) < \pi(a)$. Now a is classically equivalent to $(a \wedge x) \vee (a \wedge \neg x)$, so by $(\pi 3)$ we have $\pi(a) = \pi((a \wedge x) \vee (a \wedge \neg x)) = \max(\pi(a \wedge x), \pi(a \wedge \neg x))$ using $(\pi 4)$, so $\pi(a \wedge \neg x) < \max(\pi(a \wedge x), \pi(a \wedge \neg x))$. Thus either $\pi(a \wedge \neg x) < \pi(a \wedge x)$ or $\pi(a \wedge \neg x) < \pi(a \wedge \neg x)$. The latter is impossible, so we have the former, which completes the verification.

Chapter 6.1

Exercise 1. In the text, it was said that revision may be seen as a compound process of contraction then expansion. Why not expansion then contraction?

Answer: Expansion followed by contraction will trivialize the operation in the principal (i.e. the most interesting) case that the proposition a to be introduced is inconsistent with K. This can be shown as follows. Suppose a is inconsistent with K. If we first expand, we get $K + a = Cn(K \cup \{a\}) = L$. Suppose we now contract f (or any other formula, for that matter). No matter how the contraction operation is defined, so long as it acts on a pair consisting of just a belief set and a proposition, we will get $(K + a) - f = L - f = (K' + a) - f$ for any two belief sets K, K' each inconsistent with a.

In other words, if revision is construed as expansion followed by contraction, then the revision of any two belief sets, no matter how dissimilar, by a proposition inconsistent with each, will always give the same new belief set as output!

We remark that in an attempt to get around this highly undesirable result, some authors have experimented with modified versions of the expansion-then-contraction recipe.

Exercise 5. Show that the basic AGM postulates imply that $(K * a) * a = K * a$.

Answer: In the case that a is inconsistent, $(K * 2)$ and $(K * 1)$ together imply that $(K * a) * a = L = K * a$ and we are done. So suppose that a is consistent. Then by $(K * 5), K * a \neq L$ so by $(K * 1), K * a$ is consistent. But by $(K * 2)$ we have $a \in K * a$ so since $K * a$ is consistent $\neg a \notin K * a$, so by $(K * 4)$ and $(K * 3)$ we have $(K * a) * a = Cn((K * a) \cup \{a\})$. Also, since $a \in K * a$, we have $Cn((K * a) \cup \{a\}) = Cn(K * a) = K * a$ by $(K * 1)$. Putting these together, $(K * a) * a = K * a$ and the verification is complete.

Chapter 6.2

Exercise 1. Verify, in more detail than in the text, the left-argument monotony principle for Katsuno/Mendelzon update.

Answer: Suppose $K \subseteq K'$. Then whenever $v(a) = 1$ for all $a \in K'$ we have $v(a) = 1$ for all $a \in K$, i.e. whenever $v(K') = 1$ then $v(K) = 1$, i.e. $|K'| \subseteq |K|$. Suppose $x \notin K' \# A$; we want to show that $x \notin K \# A$. Since $x \notin K' \# A$ the definition of Katsuno/Mendelzon update tells us that there is an $s \in |K'|$ such that for some $s' \in \min_{<s} |A|, s' \notin |x|$. So since $|K'| \subseteq |K|$, there is an $s \in |K|$ such that for some $s' \in \min_{<s} |A|, s' \notin |x|$. That is, $x \notin K \# A$ as desired.

Exercise 6. Show that the set of theses of any logic of counterfactuals, as defined in the text, is closed under substitution (of arbitrary formulae for elementary letters).

Answer: Let a be a formula of the logic of counterfactuals, with elementary letters $p_1, \ldots, p_n$. Let σ be a substitution function. Suppose that the formula $\sigma(a)$ is not valid in a given logic of counterfactuals. We want to show that a is not valid in the same logic. By the supposition there is a counterfactual model (satisfying the appropriate conditions) with a state s and a valuation v_s such that $v_s(\sigma(a)) = 0$. Define valuations w_t for all $t \in S$ by putting $w_t(p) = v_s(\sigma(p))$ for every elementary letter p. Then an easy induction on the length of formulae shows that $w_t(x) = v_s(\sigma(x))$ for every x of the logic of counterfactuals and every state $t \in S$. In particular, $w_s(a) = v_s(\sigma(a)) = 0$, so a is not valid in the same logic of counterfactuals.

Exercise 9. Express in words, using the notion of conditional obligation, the rules of cumulative transitivity, cautious monotony, conjunction in the consequent, and disjunction in the antecedent. Comment on their intuitive plausibility.

Answer (in part): On this reading, cumulative transitivity says: whenever b is obligatory given a, and x is obligatory given $a \wedge b$, then x is obligatory given a. This principle is fine if the obligations are all understood as requiring their heads to hold simultaneously with their bodies. But if we allow time and agency into the reading, complications arise.

For example, imagine that we read the premisses of the rule as follows: in situation a it is obligatory to bring about b, and in situation $a \wedge b$ it is obligatory to bring about x. Suppose we are in situation a. Then it is obligatory to bring about b. But by the time that we comply and bring b about, a may no longer hold, and indeed may never hold again. So although it is obligatory to bring about x when $a \wedge b$ holds, in fact the conjunction $a \wedge b$ is never true. So the obligation in the second premiss is never activated, and we are never in a situation where x is rendered obligatory.

Evidently, this analysis is sensitive to the particular way in which time and agency are folded into the reading of conditional obligation. Other ways of integrating them can re-validate cumulative transitivity.

Chapter 6.3

Exercise 3. Fill in the details of the proof of point (3) of the Lemma for Theorem 6.1. That is, show that it follows easily from Observation 2.8.

Answer: Suppose $K = Cn(K)$ and let $K' \in K_a$. Let b be a formula with $\neg b \in K$ and $\neg b \notin K'$. We need to show that $K' \in K_b$. Now a must be inconsistent with K, for otherwise $K' = K$ which is contrary to the hypotheses on b. Moreover, since $K' \in K_a$, K' is a maximal a-consistent subset of K. Hence by Observation 2.8 (first and last clauses), K' is maximal among the classically closed proper subsets of K. Since $\neg b \notin K'$, K' is also consistent with b. Hence by Observation 2.8 again (last and first clauses), K' is a maximal b-consistent subset of K, i.e. $K' \in K_b$.

Exercise 4. Verify the soundness part of Theorem 6.1.

Answer (in part): Supraclassicality, left classical equivalence, right weakening, and conjunction in the conclusion, are all straightforward. The delicate ones are consistency preservation, limiting case conditionalization and limiting case rational monotony, which we verify.

For consistency preservation, suppose $a \not\vdash f$. Then a is consistent, so by Zorn's Lemma there is a maximal subset K' of K consistent with a, i.e. $K' \in K_a$. Since K_a is nonempty, $\delta(K_a)$ is also nonempty, containing some element K''. Since K'' is consistent with a we have $K'' \cup \{a\} \not\vdash f$ and so by the definition of $\vdash_\delta$, $a \not\vdash f$.

For limiting case conditionalization, suppose $t \not\vdash_\delta a \to x$; we want to show $a \not\vdash_\delta x$. By the hypothesis, there is a $K' \in \delta(K_t)$ with $K' \cup \{t\} \nvdash a \to x$, i.e. $K' \cup \{a\} \nvdash x$. So it suffices to show that $\delta(K_t) = \delta(K_a)$ and thus suffices to show that $K_t = K_a$. But by the Lemma point (4), $K_t = \{K\}$, so since $\delta(K_t) \subseteq K_t$ we have $K' = K$ so that $K \cup \{a\} \nvdash x$. Hence K is consistent with a, so $K_a = \{K\} = K_t$ and we are done.

For limiting case rational monotony, suppose $t \not\vdash_\delta \neg a$ and $a \not\vdash_\delta x$; we show that $t \not\vdash_\delta a \to x$. By the first hypothesis, there is a $K' \in \delta(K_t) = \{K\}$ by the Lemma point (4), with $K' \cup \{t\} \nvdash \neg a$ so that $K \nvdash \neg a$. Hence a is consistent with K and so $K_a = \{K\}$. So by the second hypothesis we know that $K \cup \{a\} \nvdash x$, i.e. $K \nvdash a \to x$ so that $t \not\vdash_\delta a \to x$ as desired.

Bibliography

This reference list contains only those items actually called in the text, together with some additional overviews, collections, and textbooks. It does not seek to be comprehensive. The literature on nonmonotonic reasoning is already vast, and an exhaustive list would itself take up a volume. The reader can find further references in the following books, each of which has its own focus and preferences: Antoniou (1997), Besnard (1990), Bochman (2001), Brewka, Dix and Konolige (1997), Grégoire (1990), Łukaszewicz (1990), Marek and Truszczyński (1993), Rott (2001), Schlechta (1997) and Schlechta (2004). For bibliographies on special topics see the overview papers of Dubois *et al.*, Horty, Konolige, Lifschitz, Makinson, all in Gabbay *et al.*, eds. (1994). For logic programming, see the bibliography in Baral (2003).

(Adams, 1966) E. W. Adams. Probability and the logic of conditionals. In J. Hintikka and P.Suppes eds., *Aspects of Inductive Logic*. North-Holland: Amsterdam 1966.

(Adams, 1975) E. W. Adams. *The Logic of Conditionals*. Reidel: Dordrecht, 1975.

(Adams, 1998) E. W. Adams. *A Primer of Probability Logic*. CSLI: Stanford, 1998.

(Alchourrón and Makinson, 1982) C. Alchourrón and D. Makinson. On the logic of theory change: contraction functions and their associated revision functions, *Theoria*, **48**, 14-37, 1982.

(Alchourrón and Makinson, 1985) C. Alchourrón and D. Makinson. On the logic of theory change: safe contraction, *Studia Logica*, **44**, 405–422, 1985.

(Alchourrón and Makinson, 1986) C. Alchourrón and D. Makinson. Maps between some different kinds of contraction function: the finite case, *Studia Logica*, **45**, 187–198, 1986.

(Alchourrón et al., 1985) C. Alchourrón, P. Gärdenfors and D. Makinson. On the logic of theory change: partial meet contraction and revision functions, *The Journal of Symbolic Logic*, **50**, 510–530, 1985.

(Antoniou, 1997) G. Antoniou. *Nonmonotonic Reasoning*. MIT Press, Cambridge Mass, 1997.

(Åqvist, 2002) L. Åqvist. Deontic logic. In *Handbook of Philosophical Logic, Second Edition, Volume 3*, D. M. Gabbay and F. Guenthener, eds., pp. 265–344. Kluwer, Dordrecht, 2002.

(Baral, 2003) C. Baral. *Knowledge Representation, Reasoning and Declarative Problem Solving*. Cambridge University Press, Cambridge UK, 2003.

(Ben-David and Ben-Eliyahu-Zohary, 2000) S. Ben-David and R. Ben-Eliyahu-Zohary. A modal logic for subjective default reasoning, *Artificial Intelligence*, **116**, 217–236, 2000.

(Benferhat et al., 1993) S. Benferhat, C. Cayrol, D. Dubois, J. Lang, and H. Prade. Inconsistency management and prioritized syntax-based entailment. In *Proceedings IJCAI-93*, pp. 640–645. Morgan Kaufmann, Los Altos, 1993.

(Benferhat et al., 1997) S. Benferhat, D. Dubois and H. Prade. Nonmonotonic reasoning, conditional objects and possibility theory, *Artificial Intelligence*, **92**, 259–276, 1997.

(Besnard, 1990) P. Besnard. *An Introduction to Default Logic*. Springer, Heidelberg, 1990.

(Bochman, 2001) A. Bochman. *A Logical Theory of Nonmonotonic Inference and Belief Change*. Springer-Verlag, Berlin, 2001.

(Brewka, 1989) G. Brewka. Preferred subtheories: an extended logical framework for default reasoning. In *Proceedings IJCAI-'89*, pp. 1043–1048. Morgan Kaufmann, Los Altos, 1989.

(Brewka, 1991) G. Brewka. Cumulative default logic: in defense of nonmonotonic inference rules, *Artificial Intelligence*, **50**, 183–205, 1991.

(Brewka, 1994) G. Brewka. Adding priorities and specificity to default logic. In *Logics in Artificial Intelligence: Proceedings of the JELIA '94 Workshop*, C. MacNish *et al.*, eds., pp. 247–260. Springer Verlag, Berlin, 1994.

(Brewka *et al.*, 1997) G. Brewka, J. Dix, and K. Konolige. *Nonmonotonic Reasoning – An Overview*. CSLI Publications, Stanford, 1997.

(Brewka *et al.*, 1991) G. Brewka, D. Makinson and K. Schlechta. Cumulative inference relations for JTMS and logic programming. In *Nonmonotonic and Inductive Logic*, Dix, Jantke and Schmitt, eds., pp. 1–12, vol. 543 of *Lecture Notes in Artificial Intelligence*. Springer, Berlin, 1991.

(Brown and Suszko, 1973) D. J. Brown and R. Suszko. Abstract logics, *Dissertationes Mathematicae*, **102**, 9–41, 1973.

(Calabrese, 2003) P. Calabrese. Operating on functions with variable domains. *Journal of Philosophical Logic*, **32**, 1–18, 2003.

(Chisholm, 1946) R. Chisholm. The contrary-to-fact conditional. *Mind*, **55**, 289–307, 1946.

(Cohn, 1965) P. M. Cohn. *Universal Algebra*. Harper and Row, New York, 1965.

(de Finetti, 1936) B. de Finetti. La logique de la probabilité. In *Actes du Congrès International de Philosophie Scientifique*, pp. IV1-IV9. Hermann, Paris, 1936.

(Dubois and Prade, 1994) D. Dubois and H. Prade. Conditional objects as nonmonotonic consequence relationships, *IEEE Transactions on Systems, Man and Cybernetics*, **24**, 1724–1740, 1994.

(Dubois *et al.*, 1994) D. Dubois, J. Lang and H. Prade. Possibilistic logic. In (Gabbay *et al.*, 1994).

(Dubois and Prade, 2001) D. Dubois and H. Prade. Possibility theory, probability theory and multiple-valued logics: a clarification, *Annals of Math. ad Artificial Intelligence*, **32**, 35–66, 2001.

(Edgington, 2001) D. Edgington. Conditionals. In *The Blackwell Guide to Philosophical Logic*, L. Goble, ed., pp. 385–414. Blackwell, Oxford, 2001.

(Freund, 1993) M. Freund. Injective models and disjunctive relations, *Journal of Logic and Computation*, **3**, 231–247, 1993.

(Freund, 1998) M. Freund. On rational preferences, *Journal of Mathematical Economics*, **30**, 210–228, 1998.

(Freund and Lehmann, 1994) M. Freund and D. Lehmann. Nonmonotonic reasoning: from finitary relations to infinitary inference operations. *Studia Logica*, **53**, 161–201, 1994.

(Friedman and Halpern, 2001) N. Friedman and J. Y. Halpern. Plausibility measures and default reasoning, *Journal of the ACM*, **48**, 648–685, 2001.

(Gabbay, 1985) D. Gabbay. Theoretical foundations for nonmonotonic reasoning in expert systems. In *Logics and Models of Concurrent Systems*, K. Apt ed. Springer-Verlag, Berlin, 1985.

(Gabbay *et al.*, 1994) D. Gabbay, C. Hogger and J. Robinson, eds. *Handbook of Logic in Artificial Intelligence and Logic Programming. Volume 3: Nonmonotonic Reasoning and Uncertain Reasoning*. Clarendon Press, Oxford, 1994.

(Gamut, 1991) L. T. F. Gamut. *Language and Meaning: Volume I. Introduction to Logic*. Chicago University Press, 1991.

(García and Simari, to appear) A. García and G. Simari. Defeasible logic programming: an argumentative approach. *Theory and Practice of Logic Programming*, to appear.

(Gärdenfors, 1988) P. Gärdenfors. *Knowledge in Flux: Modeling the Dynamics of Epistemic States*. MIT Press, Cambridge, Mass, 1988.

(Gärdenfors and Makinson, 1988) P. Gärdenfors and D. Makinson. Revisions of knowledge systems and epistemic entrenchment. In *Proceedings of the Second Conference on Theoretical Aspects of Reasoning about Knowledge*, M. Vardi, ed. pp. 83–95. Morgan Kaufmann, Los Altos, 1988.

(Gärdenfors and Makinson, 1994) P. Gärdenfors and D. Makinson. Non-monotonic inference based on expectations, *Artificial Intelligence*, **65**, 197–245, 1994.

(Gärdenfors and Rott, 1995) P. Gärdenfors and H. Rott. Belief revision. In *Handbook of Logic in Artificial Intelligence and Logic Programming. Volume 4: Epistemic and Temporal Logics*, D. M. Gabbay, C. J. Hogger and J. A. Robinson, eds., pp. 35–132. Clarendon Press, Oxford, 1995.

(Gelfond and Leone, 2002) M. Gelfond and N. Leone. Logic programming and knowledge representation — the A-prolog perspective, *Artificial Intelligence*, **138**, 37–38, 2002.

(Ginsberg, 1994) M. Ginsberg. AI and nonmonotonic reasoning. In (Gabbay *et al.*, 1994).

(Ginsberg, 1987) M. Ginsberg, ed. *Readings in Nonmonotonic Logic.* Morgan Kaufmann, Los Altos, 1987.

(Goodman, 1947) N. Goodman. The problem of counterfactual conditionals, *Journal of Philosophy*, **44**, 113–128, 1947.

(Grégoire, 1990) E. Grégoire. Logiques non-monotones et intelligence artificielle. Hermès, Paris, 1990.

(Hájek, 2001) A. Hájek. Probability, logic and probability logic. In *The Blackwell Guide to Philosophical Logic*, L. Goble, ed., pp. 362–384. Blackwell, Oxford, 2001.

(Hansson, 1969) B. Hansson. An analysis of some deontic logics, *Nous*, **3**, 373–398, 1969. Reprinted in *Deontic Logic: Introductory and Systematic Readings*, Hilpinen, ed., pp. 121–147. Reidel, Dorddrecht, 1971.

(Hansson and Makinson, 1997) S. O. Hansson and D. Makinson. Applying normative rules with restraint. In *Logic and Scientific Methods*, M. Dalla Chiara *et al.*, eds. pp. 313–332. Kluwer, Dordrecht, 1997.

(Halmos, 1960) P. Halmos. *Naïve Set Theory.* van Nostrand, New York, 1960.

(Hein, 2002) J. Hein. *Discrete Structures, Logic, and Computability* (second edition). Jones and Bartlett, Boston, 2002.

(Hodges, 2001) W. Hodges. Classical logic I: first-order logic. In *The Blackwell Guide to Philosophical Logic*, L. Goble, ed., pp. 9–32. Blackwell, Oxford, 2001.

(Horty, 1994) J. Horty. Some direct theories of nonmonotonic inheritance. In (Gabbay *et al.*, 1994).

(Horty, 2001) J. Horty. Nonmonotonic Logic. In *The Blackwell Guide to Philosophical Logic*, L. Goble, ed., pp 336–361. Blackwell, Oxford, 2001.

(Howson, 2003) C. Howson. Probability and logic, *Journal of Applied Logic* **1**, 151–165, 2003.

(Jeffrey, 1965) R. C. Jeffrey. *The Logic of Decision.* McGraw-Hill, New York, 1965.

(Katsuno and Mendelzon, 1992) H. Katsuno and A. O. Mendelzon. On the difference between updating a knowledge base and revising it. In *Belief Revision*, P. Gärdenfors ed., pp. 183–203. Cambridge University Press: UK.

(Keller and Winslett Wilkins, 1985) A. Keller and M. Winslett Wilkins. On the use of an extended relational model to handle changing incomplete information, *IEEE Transactions on Software Engineering*, **SE-11:7**, 620–633, 1985.

(Kolmogorov, 1950) N. Kolmogorov. *The Foundations of Probability*. Chelsea Publishing Co, New York, 1950.

(Konolige, 1994) K. Konolige. Autoepistemic logic. In (Gabbay *et al.*, 1994).

(Kratzer, 1981) A. Kratzer. Partition and revision: the semantics of counterfactuals, *Journal of Philosophical Logic*, **10**, 201–216, 1981.

(Kraus *et al.*, 1990) S. Kraus, D. Lehmann and M. Magidor. Nonmonotonic reasoning, preferential models and cumulative logics, *Artificial Intelligence*, **44**, 167–207, 1990.

(Kyburg, 1961) H. E. Kyburg. *Probability and the Logic of Rational Belief*. Wesleyan University Press, Middletown, 1961.

(Kyburg, 1970) H. E. Kyburg. Conjunctivitis. In *Induction, Acceptance and Rational Belief*, M. Swain, ed., pp. 55–82. Reidel, Dordrecht, 1970.

(Lehmann, 2001) D. Lehmann. Nonmonotonic logics and semantics, *Journal of Logic and Computation*, **11**, 229–256, 2001.

(Lehmann, 2002) D. Lehmann. Connectives in quantum and other cumulative logics. Technical Report TR-2002-28 of the Leibniz Center for Research in Computer Science, Hebrew University of Jerusalem, 2002.

(Lehmann and Magidor, 1992) D. Lehmann and M. Magidor. What does a conditional knowledge base entail? *Artificial Intelligence*, **55**, 1–60, 1992.

(Levi, 1996) I. Levi. *For the Sake of the Argument*. Cambridge University Press, Cambridge UK, 1996.

(Lewis, 1973) D. Lewis. *Counterfactuals*. Blackwell, Oxford, 1973.

(Lewis, 1976) D. Lewis. Probabilities of conditionals and conditional probabilities, *Philosophical Review*, **85**, 297–315, 1976. Reprinted with postscripts in D. Lewis, *Philosophical Papers Volume II*, pp. 133–56, Oxford University Press, Oxford.

(Lewis, 1981) D. Lewis. Ordering semantics and premise semantics for counterfactuals. *Journal of Philosophical Logic*, **10**, 217–234, 1981.

(Lifschitz, 1994) V. Lifschitz. Circumscription. In (Gabbay *et al.*, 1994).

(Lindström, 1991) S. Lindström. A semantic approach to nonmonotonic reasoning: inference operations and choice. Uppsala Prints and Reprints in Philosophy n° 6, Department of Philosophy, University of Uppsala, 1991.

(Lipschutz, 1998) S. Lipschutz. *Set Theory and Related Topics* (second edition). McGraw-Hill Education, New York, 1998.

(Łukaszewicz, 1984/8) W. Łukaszewicz. Considerations on default logic: an alternative approach. In *Proceedings of the AAAI Workshop on Non-Monotonic Reasoning*, pp. 165–193. New Palz, New York, 1984. Also *Computational Intelligence*, **4**, 1–16, 1988.

(Łukaszewicz, 1990) W. Łukaszewicz. *Non-Monotonic Reasoning–Formalization of Commonsense Reasoning*. Ellis Horwood, 1990.

(Makinson, 1965) D. Makinson. The paradox of the preface, *Analysis*, **25**, 205–207, 1965.

(Makinson, 1973) D. Makinson. *Topics in Modern Logic*. Methuen, London, 1973.

(Makinson, 1989) D. Makinson. General theory of cumulative inference. In *Nonmonotonic Reasoning*, M. Reinfrank et al., eds., pp. 1–17. Vol 346 of *Lecture Notes on Artificial Intelligence*. Springer-Verlag, Berlin, 1989.

(Makinson, 1993) D. Makinson. Five faces of minimality, *Studia Logica*, **52**, 339–379, 1993.

(Makinson, 1994) D. Makinson. General Patterns in Nonmonotonic Reasoning. In (Gabbay *et al.*, 1994).

(Makinson, 1997) D. Makinson. Screened revision, *Theoria*, **63**, 14–23, 1997.

(Makinson, 2003a) D. Makinson. Bridges between classical and nonmonotonic logic, *Logic Journal of the IGPL*, **11**, 69–96, 2003. http://www3.oup.co.uk/igpl/Volume_11/Issue_01/.

(Makinson, 2003b) D. Makinson. Supraclassical inference without probability. In *Cognitive Economics: An Interdisciplinary Approach*, P. Bourgine and J.P. Nadal eds., pp. 95–112. Springer, Berlin, 2003.

(Makinson, to appear) D. Makinson. How to go nonmonotonic. In *Handbook of Philosophical Logic, Second Edition, Volume 14*, D. Gabbay and F. Guenthner, eds. Kluwer, Dordrecht. To appear.

(Makinson, in preparation) D. Makinson. Logical friendliness and sympathy.

(Makinson and Gärdenfors, 1991) D. Makinson and P. Gärdenfors. Relations between the logic of theory change and nonmonotonic logic. In *The Logic of Theory Change*, Fuhrmann and Morreau, eds., pp. 185–205. Springer, Berlin, 1991.

(Makinson and van der Torre, 2000) D. Makinson and L. van der Torre. Input/output logics, *Journal of Philosophical Logic*, **29**, 383–408, 2000.

(Makinson and van der Torre, 2001) D. Makinson and L. van der Torre. Constraints for input/output logics, *Journal of Philosophical Logic*, **30**, 155–185, 2001.

(Makinson and van der Torre, 2003) D. Makinson and L. van der Torre. Permission from an input/output perspective, *Journal of Philosophical Logic*, **32**, 391–416, 2003.

(Marek and Truszczyński, 1989) V. W. Marek and M. Truszczyński. Relating autoepistemic and default logics. In *Proceedings of the First Conference on Principles of Knowledge Representation and Reasoning*, pp. 276–288. Morgan Kaufmann, Palo Alto, 1989.

(Marek and Truszczyński, 1993) V. W. Marek and M. Truszczyński. *Nonmonotonic Logic: Context Dependent Reasoning*. Springer, Berlin, 1993.

(McCarthy, 1980) J. McCarthy. Circumscription — a form of non-monotonic reasoning, *Artificial Intelligence*, **13**, 27–39, 1980. Reprinted in (Ginsberg, 1987, pp. 145–152).

(Pearl, 1988) J. Pearl. *Probabilistic Reasoning in Intelligent Systems*. Morgan Kaufmann, Los Altos, 1988.

(Pearl, 1989) J. Pearl. Probabilistic semantics for nonmonotonic reasoning: a survey. In *Proceedings of the First International Conference on Principles of Knowledge Representation and Reasoning (KR'89)*, Brachman *et al*, eds., pp. 505–516. Morgan Kaufmann, San Mateo, 1989.

(Pino Pérez and Uzcátegui, 2000) P. Pérez, Ramón and C. Uzcátegui. On representation theorems for nonmonotonic inference relations, *The Journal of Symbolic Logic*, **65**, 1321–1337, 2000.

(Poole, 1988) D. Poole. A logical framework for default reasoning, *Artificial Intelligence*, **36**, 27–47, 1988.

(Poole, 1989) D. Poole. What the lottery paradox tells us about default reasoning. In *Proceedings of the First International Conference on Principles of Knowledge Representation and Reasoning*, pp. 333–340. Morgan Kaufmann, Los Altos, 1989.

(Prakken and Vreeswijk, 2001) H. Prakken and G. Vreeswijk. Logics for defeasible argumentation. In *Handbook of Philosophical Logic: Second Edition, Volume 4*. Kluwer, Dordrecht, 2001.

(Reiter, 1978) R. Reiter. On closed world data bases. In *Logic and Data Bases*, H. Gallaire and J. Minker eds., pp. 55–76. Plenum, New York, 1978. Reprinted in (Ginsberg, 1987, pp. 300–310).

(Reiter, 1980) R. Reiter. A logic for default reasoning, *Artificial Intelligence*, **13**, 81–132, 1980. Reprinted in (Ginsberg, 1987, pp. 68–93).

(Rott, 1991) H. Rott. Two methods of constructing contractions and revisions of knowledge systems, *Journal of Philosophical Logic*, **20**, 149–173, 1991.

(Rott, 1993) H. Rott. Belief contraction in the context of the general theory of rational choice, *Journal of Symbolic Logic*, **58**, 1426–1450, 1993.

(Rott, 2001) H. Rott. Change, Choice and Inference: A Study of Belief Revision and Nonmonotonic Reasoning, Vol 43 of *Oxford Logic Guides*. Clarendon Press, Oxford, 2001.

(Rott, 2003) H. Rott. Basic entrenchment, *Studia Logica*, **73**, 257–280, 2003.

(Rott and Pagnucco, 1999) H. Rott and M. Pagnucco. Severe withdrawal—and recovery, *Journal of Philosophical Logic*, **28**, 501–547, 1999. Reprinted with corrections of corrupted text in ibid, **29**, 121, 2000.

(Sandewall, 1985) E. Sandewall. A functional approach to non-monotonic logic, *Computational Intelligence*, **1**, 80–87, 1985. Also appeared as Research Report LITH-IDA-R-85-07 of the Department of Computer and Information Science, Linköping University, Sweden.

(Schlechta, 1992) K. Schlechta. Some results on classical preferential models, *Journal of Logic and Computation*, **2**, 676–686, 1992.

(Schlechta, 1997) K. Schlechta. *Nonmonotonic Logics: Basic Concepts, Results and Techniques*. Vol 1187 of *Lecture Notes in Artificial Intelligence*, Springer, Berlin, 1997.

(Schlechta, 2004) K. Schlechta. *Coherent Systems*. Elsevier, 2004.

(Shoham, 1988) Y. Shoham. *Reasoning About Change*. MIT Press, Cambridge USA, 1988.

(Skyrms, 1999) B. Skyrms. *Choice and Chance* (fourth edition). Wadsworth, Belmont, CA, 1999.

(Stalnaker, 1968) R. Stalnaker. A theory of conditionals. In *Studies in Logical Theory*, N. Rescher, ed. Blackwell, Oxford, 1968.

(Stalnaker, 1970) R. Stalnaker. Probability and conditionals, *Philosophy of Science*, **37**, 64–80, 1970.

(Tan and Treur, 1992) Y. H. Tan and Jan Treur. Constructive default logic and the control of defeasible reasoning. In *Proceedings of the Tenth European Conference on Artificial Intelligence (ECAI '92)*, B. Neumann ed., pp. 299–303. John Wiley, New York, 1992.

(Tarski, 1930) A. Tarski. Über einige fundamentale Begriffe der Meta-mathematik. Comptes Rendus des Seances de la Société des Sciences et les Lettres de Varsovie, d.III,23: 22–29, 1930. Translated as On some fundamental concepts of metamathematics. In *Logic, Semantics, Metamathematics*. Clarendon Press: Oxford, 1956.

(Veltman, 1976) F. Veltman. Prejudices, presuppositions and the theory of counterfactuals. In *Truth, Interpretation and Information: Selected Papers from the Third Amsterdam Colloquium*, J. Groenendijk and M. Stokhof eds. Foris, Dordrecht, 1976.

(Veltman, 1985) F. Veltman. *Logics for Conditionals*. Doctoral thesis, University of Amsterdam, 1985.

(Williamson, 2002) J. Williamson. Probability logic. In *Handbook of the Logic of Argument and Inference*, D. Gabbay *et al.*, pp. 397–424. Elsevier, Amsterdam, 2002.

(Wójcicki, 1988) R. Wójcicki. *Theory of Logical Calculi: Basic Theory of Consequence Operations*. Kluwer, Dordrecht, 1988.

(Zhu *et al.*, 2002) Z. Zhu, Z. Pan, S. Chen and W. Zhu. Valuation structure, *The Journal of Symbolic Logic*, **67**, 1–23, 2002.

Index

209

Printed in the United Kingdom
by Lightning Source UK Ltd.
109670UKS00001B/68